DEFYING ROME

THE REBELS OF ROMAN BRITAIN

DEFYING ROME

THE REBELS OF ROMAN BRITAIN

GUY DE LA BÉDOYÈRE

TEMPUS

A little rebellion now and then is a good thing
T. Jefferson

First published 2003

Tempus Publishing Limited
The Mill, Brimscombe Port,
Stroud, Gloucestershire, GL5 2QG

British Library Cataloguing in Publication Data.
A catalogue record for this book is available from the British Library.

ISBN 0 7524 2561 7

Typesetting and origination by Tempus Publishing Limited
Printed in Great Britain by Midway Colour Print, Wiltshire

CONTENTS

NOTE ABOUT THE BLACK AND WHITE ILLUSTRATIONS

Frontispiece	From Plutarch's *Life of Corialanus*, J. Tonson 1727
Contents	From *The Parallel of Architecture* (2nd ed.), trans. John Evelyn 1707
Introduction	*Sestertius* of Nero, depicting Roma
Chapter 1	Central motif from the late Iron Age 'Battersea Shield'
Chapter 2	Reverse of a coin of Caratacus
Chapter 3	Chariot wheel from a Yorkshire Iron Age burial
Chapter 4	Roman cavalry horse decoration from Newstead
Chapter 5	*Denarius* of Mark Antony naming the *XIV* legion
Chapter 6	Britannia on a *sestertius* of Antoninus Pius
Chapter 7	*Denarius* of Clodius Albinus
Chapter 8	Christian medallion from the Water Newton Treasure
Chapter 9	Postumus on a radiate from the Normanby hoard
Chapter 10	Carausius radiate
Chapter 11	Magnentius *centenionalis*
Chapter 12	Magnus Maximus
Chapter 13	Constantine III *siliqua*
Chapter 14	The Hinton St Mary villa mosaic 'Christ'
Chapter 15	The Gorgon from the temple pediment at Bath
Principal Dates	*See* Contents
Further Reading	Victory on a *denarius* of Maximinus I (235-8)
Index	Nero and companion on horseback, *sestertius* of 64

INTRODUCTION

⟫⬦⟪

We know from our own lives how much happens because of the dynamic of personalities, flawed individuals and their reaction to the unpredictable natural disasters and events that maintain the ebb and flow of prosperity and disaster. The prehistorian can know this in general but is powerless to reconstruct the people, episodes and phenomena that influenced events in the world he or she seeks to understand. Even Stonehenge is unavoidably relegated to the emotional neutrality of generalisations, detached forever by the illiteracy of its builders from the idiosyncratic minds that thought the building up and organised its execution, and the factors that had motivated them. But the Roman historian Tacitus, who wrote around the beginning of the second century, knew only too well how unpredictable occasions impacted upon human history, and it was what helped provoke his interest in the way his world had been shaped. *Eventusque rerum, qui plerumque fortuiti sunt,* 'events and affairs are generally due to chance', he said, and amongst these were the rise and fall of idiosyncratic emperors, soldiers, rebels, chancers and even imperial impersonators (*Histories* i.4).

The rebels of Roman Britain attracted the attention of ancient historians for precisely the same reasons that we today look back at the personalities who defined the cataclysmic events of, say, the American War of Independence or the Second World War.

Historians also use personalities as vehicles for opposing ideologies, or to present good against evil. The result is always a kind of caricature, and we can see this perfectly in the accounts of the Boudican Revolt of AD 60-1. Boudica, the woman with a man's qualities, is juxtaposed by Tacitus and the third-century historian Dio Cassius against the decadent Roman leadership mainly in the person of Nero, presented as an effeminate pervert acting through his agent, the governor Suetonius Paullinus. It was typical of Roman narcissism that a remote provincial rebellion could be commemorated in history this way. Boudica became a moral lesson for the Roman world; indeed she may even have been created in the form we know as a literary device to that end. Her leadership, valour and determination symbolised the very qualities that had brought Rome the empire men like Nero nearly destroyed.

This book then is really a series of short stories. Most are historical accounts built around one of the more dramatic personalities in Roman Britain's history, loosely drawn together because each of them in his or her own way rebelled against Roman power. They are necessarily short because the material we have is extremely limited. But compared to what normally survives from antiquity, these people are remarkably well recorded and that reflects their importance both at the time and to later historians. Like all historical accounts though they suffer from bias, additions, outright fabrications, contradictions and excisions, but to a historian like myself their overriding appeal is being able to see the effect of individuals on the way things happen and the way they illustrate a pattern.

But every historian has an agenda so not only do we know a good deal less than we would like, but also we have to decide what that agenda was and why Boudica, for instance, was portrayed as she was by Tacitus and Dio. After all, a historian's 'flattery brings the nauseating charge of subservience, and malignity poses as independence' (Tacitus, *Histories* i.1). Tacitus reminded his readers that people listen far too easily to tales of *obtrectatio et livor*, 'disparagement and malice', something the present-day tabloid press makes the most of. But Tacitus, outstanding though he is amongst Roman historians, still had his own perspective. The speeches he placed in the mouths of Rome's enemies in some respects read like an incongruous attack on Rome, especially the one 'attributed' to the northern tribal leader Calgacus in 84, and certainly lean towards a graphic objectivity. Such sentiments broadened the perspective of the stories Tacitus wanted to tell, and prevented them becoming banal, but they also enhanced the contrast he wished to draw between the more enlightened Empire of his own time (including especially his father-in-law Agricola) and the corrupt and decadent early principate. So how much of the historical Caratacus, Boudica and Calgacus is literary invention, and how much is the real thing?

Conversely, Carausius (286-93) exists for us mainly in the form of his own regime's propaganda on coinage, countered by the 'malice' circulated by the Empire's spin machine in which Carausius was slated as a criminal, not even worthy of being named. In the sixth century Gildas produced a pseudo-historical tract called *De Excidio Britanniae*, 'On the Ruin of Britain'. Essentially a moralising rant on the consequences of evil deeds, it is selectively peppered with tantalising glimpses of real events in the latter days of Roman Britain. Yet while the revolt of Magnus Maximus (383-8) is included, that of Constantine III (407-11) passes without mention. Bias is nothing new in history, whether the bias of selection or the bias of malice. Indeed it would be absurd if there were no such thing, since bias is what makes history: one person's spin on his time or another's. As the Boudica we possess in the record clearly is a Roman invention in part, what does that tell us about those who wrote accounts of her rebellion? When we come to Gildas, what can be believed, and what cannot? Sometimes it is impossible to know.

All the individuals covered in this book, from Caratacus to Pelagius, share a common thread. Each took on Rome with an army, or with an ideology, and mostly the trails they blazed began abruptly, as sudden storms, with uprisings, coups, or even religious conversions. They included tribal leaders who wanted to repel the Roman conquest, a Christian martyr, those who wanted to become emperors in their own right, and even a legion with its eye on the main chance.

Every one of them came from Britain, or began their rebellions in Britain, or used Britain for its resources. Britain was not unique in this respect. Plenty of other provinces generated rebellious generals, local usurpers, troublemakers or nationalist uprisings. But Britain was remarkably productive in this way, and each of these stories helps us to understand not only the more general character of Roman Britain, but also the character of rebellion at other times and places.

To the Roman world Britain was a perplexing mass of contradictions. The modern world map or globe shows Britain not only as a peripheral feature to the colossal mass of Europe and Asia but also as a kind of midway point between the Old and New Worlds. The role is reinforced by the Greenwich Meridian that centralises Britain in the concept of the daily cycle: it is forever high noon in the British Isles. The Roman mindset, indeed most ancient mindsets, was entirely different and it is essential to grasp that concept. Looking down on the Earth from some imaginary point in space was scarcely considered, except by those Greek mathematicians and astronomers who had realised the Earth was a globe and even measured it with starling accuracy.

Instead the world simply radiated out and away from Rome and the Mediterranean. In every direction it eventually faded into unfathomable remoteness and dissipated into the oblivion of endless oceans, trackless wastes and deserts, and the terrifying gloom of fog-laden mountainous forests, reflected on maps of the period. Even those who knew the earth to be 'a solid spherical mass gathered into a globe' still perceived the world in a Rome-centric way (Cicero, *On the Nature of the Gods* ii.98).

Occasional stories of the rest of the world flickered in and out of this twilight zone. Britain was considered so extraordinary some people even doubted it really existed. In 54 BC, Cicero received a letter from his brother Quintus, then on campaign in Britain with Caesar. Cicero was transfixed by the tale and excitedly replied that, 'the Ocean terrified me, and I was scared by the coast of the island!' (*Letters* ii.16.4). Around 150 years later Plutarch commented that Caesar's exploits in Britain had gone beyond the limits of the known world, and silenced scholars who had gone about saying Britain was just a figment of popular imagination (*Caesar* 23). Tales of India and China also existed, and Africa's endlessness was hinted at. Under Nero, an expedition of troops from the Praetorian Guard was sent to Ethiopia to see if it was worth conquering (Pliny, *Natural History*, vi.181). It turned out to be only 'desert' so the plan was abandoned. Of America, the poles and the Pacific, of course no one in Europe knew anything, despite the recent theory based on stone axe and DNA evidence that some Europeans might have made their way along the edge of the North Atlantic ice around 16,000 BC to settle in North America.

The basic concept of a two-dimensional world has survived in modern fantasy literature, as readers of C.S. Lewis' *Narnia* stories, and Tolkien's *Lord of the Rings* know well. In each the imagined worlds of Narnia and Middle Earth rest in the centre of maps, surrounded by increasingly remote, frightening and forbidding distant lands and sea. So it was for Rome, which was in every sense the physical, emotional and scientific centre of the world. As late as 396 St Jerome used Britain as one of his four reference points to mark the end of the world. The others were India, the Atlantic and the 'ice-bound north' (*Letters* lx.4). A scattered collection of remote and windswept islands, Britain was little understood as a geographical feature and instead she served more as a living metaphor for the unknown. To traders and chancers Britain was less inscrutable thanks to occasional voyages of exploration and more often of commerce. In any case tribal links existed between Britain and northern Gaul, while older traditions circulated about settlers from Spain and other places. Britain had resources, her peoples could be traded with, and it was known that Britain extended sufficiently far north for the length of day and night to vary by extremes with the seasons and for its coastline to be washed by tides of epic dimensions.

Even once Britain was brought within the Roman orbit, she never evolved into a trusted component of the classical world. She was, as Tacitus called her, *feroci provincia*, 'a warlike province' (*Agricola* 8). This is perfectly illustrated by the figure of Britannia occasionally depicted on Rome's coins. No other province ever appeared exactly this way. Britain as Rome's Britannia is a military personification, forever defined in Roman consciousness as the frontier where reason met resistance, and order met chaos. She sits as Roma does on other coins, with her spear and shield but invariably bareheaded. The figure is not a representation of the Britons in their defeat. The coins of Antoninus Pius of 143 show Britannia with a shield and Roman standard. This is Roman Britain, not British Britain, and she represents the garrison world of an island province that was incontrovertibly defined as the wild North-West. The endless parade of rebels and troublemakers only reinforced the image.

The Romans admired the spirited leadership of Caratacus and Boudica but poured resources into annihilating them. Britain was regarded by Rome in every rational sense as a waste of space, a home to undesirables, crass provincials, and a frustrating source of problems. She was also a source of undisguised fascination. Included in the Empire as a curiosity and trophy, and as an example of Rome's munificent accommodation, she was permanently excluded from full integration with long-lasting consequences. What the Britons thought of Rome is altogether more difficult to assess since as an historical society they largely exist to us only in the Roman record. The only alternatives to that are systems and structures imposed on the artefact record by archaeologists from an intellectual resource of anthropological observations of contemporary societies. Both are subjective for entirely different reasons. There is no doubt that prehistoric artefacts and monuments point to a rich culture that was as complex as any of the time, and indeed existed in numerous variants across Europe throughout the first two millennia BC. But by the first century AD most of the Mediterranean world had mutated into something different. The growth of literacy and more sophisticated concepts of order, recording information, architecture, and a political system that operated outside the idiosyncrasies of leaders in the classical world meant Britain was becoming something of an anachronism. In being almost entirely illiterate, the world of prehistoric Britain was by definition one founded on ignorance. Not empirical ignorance of course, because the farmers, smiths and artisans of Britain had an abundant fund of hand-me-down skills and verbal traditions that allowed them to produce works of art of an exceptional standard. But there is an exponential impact on society when information becomes recorded on paper, and can be read not just then but generations later. This is how new ideas are circulated, and in the end it is the most liberating dynamic in human society.

There is no question of a moral judgement here. It is simply a matter of fact that a prehistoric type of society will eventually evolve into something else, and that process is graphically accelerated when it happens by force. It is paradoxical that, while most people are intensely conservative and become more so as they age, society is galvanised by the tensions brought through change. In other words, most people hate change but are at their best when dealing with it. In fact, Britain was already changing and for two main reasons. Firstly, the successful exploitation of the landscape by prehistoric communities had generated population growth with increasing pressure on primary land. This contributed to the emergence of tribal identities and leaders, which was the natural sociological consequence of human beings living in increasingly concentrated communities. Knowing one's identity becomes more important, and knowing one's enemies even more so. Pressure on resources led to the inevitable friction and disputes that characterise all human societies trying to assert control over limited food and land. Secondly, the world of prehistoric Britain was unavoidably part of greater Europe and had been so ever since people settled there. This meant that part of British society began to adopt symbols, goods and even subtler influences like language, from the continent. By the first century BC, the continent meant the Roman world.

This absorption of influence from Rome created a fundamental tension, not least because the absorption was so unbalanced. It was a choice exercised by the élite in British society in the south-east, and even those who resisted were bound in some way to be affected by Roman culture. When it came to the actual process of military invasion, some of the tribes were disposed to accept the fact. Others resisted, sometimes in dramatic fashion, but within two generations of the conquest of AD 43, southern and central Britain was settled as a Roman province and remained that way. Ultimately, it is compliance that makes conquest work. No one has ever achieved a durable conquest exclusively by force. It is easy enough to present the Roman world as exclusively an oppressive state. That matches our own contemporary revulsion at the fascist dictatorships of the twentieth century. But this overlooks the reality of a very remarkable balance of power, accommodation and compliance, and as such reduces history to a simplistic state of monochrome alternatives. Those who instinctively slate conspicuous imperial power rarely recognise the control or power systems within their organisations or regimes, and also never countenance the possibility that a supremely powerful nation's ruling class might operate with a modicum of moral leadership. The truth as ever is much more opaque. Imperial power structures have both good and bad elements, and the places or peoples they come to control both win and lose from the arrangements.

There is no such thing as absolute power, and no such thing as freedom, though political rhetoric throughout the ages has talked in such terms. Roman coins that depicted 'Libertas' were meaningless in a world where universal suffrage was inconceivable and the machinery that kept the world going was slavery. Boudica was not selling her people 'freedom', but simply an alternative source of power. What she meant by freedom (and even that was put into her mouth by a Roman historian) was her freedom to rule instead of a Roman governor. It is very easy to equate the status of 'freedom' in antiquity, compared to slavery, with modern freedom. It is certainly true that being a slave in the ancient world meant a total lack of self-determination, but 'free' people then enjoyed very few of the privileges modern citizens of liberal democracies take for granted. Most in fact experienced something closer to feudalism, and were tied financially, legally and practically to men of higher status or to their jobs. So being conquered by Rome did not in any sense resemble what it would mean for a citizen of modern Europe being conquered by a violent dictatorship. It is probably impossible for us to make a valid comparison in any case. A Roman or Briton might very well regard his modern counterpart as incomprehensibly incarcerated in a world of unlimited restrictive legislation and burdensome taxation enforced by electronic surveillance, and hag-ridden by fears of pensions disappearing, obscure new diseases and the rising price of oil.

Caratacus was fighting for his position as a tribal leader, which was his birthright; he was not a political or ideological revolutionary. He was also probably having the time of his life, revelling in the electrifying thrill of facing up to the greatest world power in history and giving it a monumental run-around. In the warrior society he led, the war against Rome was a highly prestigious life-or-death struggle. It is as well to remember that for the men who fought alongside him, this was their chance for immortality as legendary heroes. Like General Patton who once said how much he loved war, Caratacus was nothing without it. Had it not been for the Roman record of his exploits in battle we would know nothing about him, and not even his whole name.

However, Roman power was pervasive and decisive and that was why Caratacus had to carry his war into Wales to find tribes prepared to carry on the fight, notwithstanding the possibility that the rapidity of the Roman advance left pockets of resistance behind. In general, human beings make their long-term choice or accept-ance of government based on the prospect of certainty, stability and security. Faced by the stark terrors of the uncontrollable natural world, the permanence of Rome represented a choice that most people easily made. If that represented foregoing the theoretical freedoms, or even self-esteem, of tribal society, it seems to have been a sacrifice many were prepared to make. It is also absurd for the modern commentator to assume that ordinary people automatically shared their leader's beliefs or concerns and even if they did, that they would continue to do so. Coercion and diversion play a role too, and there are plenty of well-recorded historical rebellions that lost momentum when supporters drifted away into the night once the prospect of easy plunder faded, and disaffection grew.

Traditional devices and offices of the Roman Republic were designed to prevent anyone from becoming too powerful. Magistrates, for example, were never appointed as singletons. Instead they were placed in post in pairs, or in larger numbers. This prevented any one man from overstepping the mark; his colleagues could simply veto him. But by the first century BC the system was falling into disarray. Corruption on a grand scale meant certain families increased their power, almost totally uncontrolled. At the same time, generals used their personal wealth and power to conquer territories that increased their power and wealth, and at the same time their own prestige. Their armies thus became their own personal armies and inevitably the result was a massive power struggle that culminated in the war between Octavian and Antony. In 31 BC Octavian won, and 'restored liberty to the Republic' in what was in effect an empire ruled by a monarch, though he posed as simply an office holder in the Republican system. But under the Empire, the emperor held too many of the offices to sustain the balance. He could be, all at once, tribune, consul, censor, general and chief priest. Instead of the old collegiate balance based on the veto, the only check was the personality of the emperor himself. A republic in name, it was an absolute monarchy in practice. So, it is all the more remarkable that Roman power was usually exercised in so subtle a fashion. The truth was that a Roman emperor's real power was very restricted for simple practical reasons of distance and limitations of ancient technology. So the power was moderated by the need to rely on delegation and compliance.

Oppression and exploitation there was, but the deal was never just one-way. Not only that, but some of the most extreme oppression came from individuals abusing their power as governors, generals, or centurions on the ground. Roman historians were equally aware of the impact of abuse. Tacitus recorded that the Britons came to muse on the replacement of their individual tribal leaders by a pair of 'kings': the governor, who exploited them through bloodshed, and a procurator, who ripped off their wealth (*Agricola* 15.2). It was a key component in the unrest that led to the Boudican Revolt. But the Roman system did have sanctions. At the end of the first century AD for example, Marius Priscus, former governor of Africa, was tried at Rome for his crimes of corruption. In Britain, Agricola was said to have instigated a programme of wiping out corrupt tribute-collecting practices. The Roman Empire could never have lasted as long as it did without such controls.

In the first century AD Rome began to experience a crisis of conscience. A succession of decadent rulers like Caligula and Nero made it look as if the acquisition of Empire had been at a terrible price. Paradoxically, Roman historians were inclined to interpret the qualities of a rebel like Boudica as a reflection of Rome's better days. The problems of the first century were rectified by the relatively stable rule of the Flavians (Vespasian, Titus and Domitian), and more definitively in the second century, but as Tacitus observed, the secret was already out: an emperor could be made in places other than Rome. In the third century a succession of opportunist usurpers brought the Empire almost to its knees. In the middle of all this a new class of rebel emerged. So all encompassing had the concept and manner of presentation of Roman government become, that few of its challengers were able to come up with anything more imaginative than arguing that they would make better Roman emperors than the existing incumbents. This is one of the most curious facets of later rebellion against Rome. Rebels like Postumus and Carausius took the Roman world and claimed they could do it better, and in some ways they did. But in the end, it was the fact that they lost that means they have come down to us as rebels.

This book then is about those personalities whose rebellions, revolts and coups, their good luck and their bad luck, provide British history with some of its earliest heroes and villains. By attracting the attention of historians in antiquity these people resulted in written accounts that also provide some of the most detailed evidence for Britain's time as a Roman province.

Be that as it may, anyone who reads these stories could hardly fail to see that Roman Britain is as much a reflection of human nature in our own time as it is for any other time. The duplicity that ended the life of Carausius, and the retribution meted out by Paul 'the Chain' after Magnentius, would be equally at home in the Italian cities of the Renaissance, the court of Elizabeth I, and countless boardrooms in our own time. The tone of the rebellions have reflections in times and places across the world. The time that separates us from Roman Britain is really no time at all. Things have changed for sure, but human beings have not. Ambition, patriotism, power, greed, jealousy, hatred, bravery and steadfastness are all part of the human condition as they always have been. The glory of the history of Roman Britain is that this is the first time the window is thrown open for us to look through and see our own age, and all ages, reflected in the personalities of the time. Of these, the rebels are the most vivid and memorable.

I would like to thank Peter Kemmis Betty for his comments on the text, and especially Richard Reece not just for his observations on and corrections to the text, but also the lucidity he brought to bear on the underlying themes of this book and his help in sorting out the patterns behind the detail. I'd also like to thank Tim Clarke and Emma Parkin at Tempus for their help in seeing the book through the press. The colour illustrations have been chosen to reflect the themes and individuals explored in the text.

Guy de la Bédoyère
Welby 2003

1

The Battle of Britain
CASSIVELLAUNUS

Cassivellaunus is the first major British tribal leader and monarch to appear in history. This makes him an exceptionally significant individual, though we know tragically little about him. Cassivellaunus stands at the end of Britain's prehistory. In him we meet a man whose personal prestige put him into a position where he could take charge of resistance to the first recorded invasion of Britain. Cassivellaunus' anonymous ancestors stretch back remorselessly into an unknown and unknowable fathomless past, while the names and actions of his descendants would echo down the ages to come. The first to face the full weight of an organised, literate and historical foe, he comes down to us through the words of the Roman world, and specifically those of Gaius Julius Caesar, one of the most famous witnesses to the age of Roman conquest that ever lived. Necessarily then, any account of Cassivellaunus is really an account of Caesar's invasions as Caesar wanted to describe them.

By the mid-first century BC, Cassivellaunus ruled territory in what we now know as Hertfordshire, but his influence extended across much of south-east Britain. He controlled peoples whose origins were closely linked with tribes in northern Gaul and, appropriately enough, they had absorbed practices and a lifestyle that reflected their close links with the continent. But at this stage, Cassivellaunus had no inclination to see his or her tribe's future in a Roman idiom. Bent on expanding his own power, he had already killed a neighbouring king. The arrival of Julius Caesar both helped and hindered him. The prospect of a Roman war meant that some tribes scuttled to seek the protection of Cassivellaunus, while others took one look at the opposition and decided that sucking up to Rome was altogether more promising a prospect than subjecting themselves to a tribal leader who did not hesitate to wipe out the opposition. This anticipated problems that people like Caratacus and Boudica would face later.

In the mid-first century BC the Roman Republic was in a precarious state. Power was now in the hands of Roman generals who had capitalised on personal wealth and position to accumulate influence on an unprecedented scale. The old Republican system of magistracies, based on election in colleges and the protective force of veto, was simply impotent in the face of vast private armies whose loyalty was exclusively directed at their generals, not the Roman state. In 60 BC the First Triumvirate was established between the three most powerful men in the Roman world: Gaius Julius Caesar, Marcus Licinius Crassus, and Cnaeus Pompeius Magnus. In essence they had parcelled up Rome's universe between them though in practice each of them watched the others like a hawk and missed no chance to promote their own interests.

Caesar's conquest of Gaul exhibited his own military brilliance, his spectacular ability to harness the loyalty of his troops, and the box-office consciousness of a one-man publicity machine. Not only was he allocated legions by the state, but he also used his own wealth to raise others. This tied them firmly to Caesar the man, and not in his guise as a representative of the Roman people. He even went as far as raising a legion from Gauls and awarded them Roman citizenship himself. This brought him colossal prestige but bringing Gaul under Roman power also exposed the extended dominions to remote frontiers and interference from more distant territory. Gaul was linked by tribe and tradition to Britain. Not only did British warriors fight alongside Gauls, but also Britain provided a refuge for the Bellovaci who escaped across the Channel in 57 BC. The Belgic Veneti tribe took on Caesar's ships because they were worried their trade with Britain would be disrupted if he crossed over there.

Britain thus was easily presented as a 'legitimate' military target. The United States used the same justification for bombing Laos in the Vietnam War. But Caesar was equally mindful that Britain presented a brilliant opportunity to grab headlines. Britain's exotic remoteness was already established in popular lore, and the sheer excitement of taking a military force across the Channel could not have failed to excite interest at home. Of course, in one sense it was a reckless gamble, but Caesar's whole life had been based on gambles and living on the edge. It was what made him different from the lesser, ordinary, mortals of his time, just as it marks out the inspired lunatic brilliance of men like Napoleon or Lawrence of Arabia, driven by an 'ambition which swell'd so much that it did almost stretch the sides o' the world' (*Cymbeline* III.iii). All of course we know in the end is that Caesar did not stay in Britain, so we are none the wiser about whether he had actually planned to conquer the place and had to abandon this. As a people *ignotos antea*, 'unknown before', the Britons would make an excellent publicity tool (Suetonius, *Julius Caesar* xxv.2). Looking back around 150 years later, the historian Plutarch thought the British campaign extraordinarily 'daring' for going into the unknown to establish Britain as 'fact' rather than fantasy, in spite of the fact that the Britons turned out to be so 'wretched' they had not been worth the trouble (*Caesar* xxiii).

Whether or not Caesar had his eye on historians of later centuries, by 55 BC his position as military commander in Gaul was the most important position he held for maintaining prestige at home. In that year Crassus and Pompey were serving as consuls in Rome. It would have been easy for Caesar, with the bulk of the fighting over, to have faded out of the limelight. Without an excuse to continue fighting, in theory Caesar would have had to give up his position. As Suetonius said, Caesar 'did not let slip any excuse for a war' (*ibid.* xxiv.3). In other words, since Caesar needed a war, the only question was where to fight it. Britain was perfect. Going there at all was something to brag about, and it minimised compromising his hold on Gaul though he still had to take chances.

Caesar's first effort to invade Britain was a virtual debacle though he took care to modify his account so that it seemed otherwise. The pretext was that Gaulish resistance had been actively supported from Britain. Of course, Caesar wrote about the event afterwards so he was bound to dress it up appropriately. For this reason he took care to claim that despite it being late summer, even if there was no fighting to be had he could at least reconnoitre the place. This was apparently essential since the only people with any information were traders, and they knew nothing about inland Britain and certainly nothing about how the tribes were organised or how they fought.

To prepare the way, Caesar sent Gaius Volusenus to see what he could find out, though as it turned out the scout was disinclined to land anywhere and spent less than five days off the coast of Britain. In the meantime news of Caesar's plans was getting around, and as a result some of the British tribes sent representatives who reputedly promised advance capitulation and hostages. This was a conventional spoiling tactic to put invaders off their guard and buy time. About 250 years later, Septimius Severus would find a northern confederation of tribes called the Maeatae trying the same trick. Caesar also sent his own puppet king, Commios, of the Gaulish Atrebates across to Britain to try and break down resistance on the spot. It backfired. The quisling Commios was instantly imprisoned in Britain and was not returned until the peace negotiations on the beach a few days later.

The campaign was to be prosecuted with just two legions and cavalry. The legions embarked at one port, probably Boulogne (used the next year for certain), and the latter following from a different port. Caesar initially faced cliffs lined with British warriors, a hopeless place to land and had to wait for the whole fleet to gather before moving on to a level beach seven miles away. This is now thought to have been somewhere near Deal. Just offshore here is The Downs, a place later used as a sheltered mooring thanks to raised areas of seabed. The landing was almost a disaster. The Britons attacked the landing troops, who were confounded by trying to beach heavy ships on too gradual a slope. This made it impossible to sail in fast enough to let the boats ride up onto the shore under their own momentum. The Roman troops were terrified by the thought of wading in through deep water. If it had not been for the famous standard-bearer of the *X* legion leading the way, and the use of warships to bombard the Britons with artillery, it is doubtful if the invasion would have got much further than the shingle.

Caesar painted a fairly promising picture of the initial fighting, but Dio (writing 250 years later) was less convinced and pointed out that since the Britons were either on horseback or in chariots and could make a rapid get-away, few were captured or killed. Nevertheless, the Britons were apparently struck by the fact that the Romans had crossed at all, and they must have heard plenty about Caesar's wars in Gaul. The Britons sued for peace and handed over Commios, but within a few days, the whole campaign nearly went under – literally. The ships already in Britain were wrecked by a high tide, and the cavalry's transports were forced back to Gaul by a storm. The British tribal leaders spotted their advantage and instantly started to melt away from the Roman camp. The *VII* legion was promptly assaulted while foraging by Britons who had waited for them by hiding in woodland. This theme would be played out constantly during the centuries of campaigning ahead. The problem was that although Caesar arrived to take control, the highly mobile enemy was able to escape easily. At the same time, tribal contacts were being used to seek help much more widely across Britain. These were used to publicise the small size of the Roman force, and the prospect of easy pickings for any warriors who could come and join in. Caesar claimed that when the Britons gathered to attack the Roman camp, they quickly gave up and offered peace once more. Both sides were trying to fight two different wars and neither could defeat the other on its own terms. Thus the elusive charioteers confounded Caesar, but the Britons had no strategy to cope with a fortified Roman camp. Caesar was in no mood to argue the toss, fully aware that his fleet was damaged and winter was approaching. He lacked either the forces or the supplies to do any more. Since the weather was now good, he decided to take advantage of it and made for Gaul.

In this first campaign, Caesar provides no detailed evidence about the British tribes or their leaders. He may not even have been party to the information. At this time, Roman influence had had little impact on the way the tribal leaders portrayed themselves, so there is not much we can add to the picture. Celtic tribal coinage was still anonymous, and it would not be for at least another generation that we have any numismatic verification of historically-testified leaders. Coins of Commios are known, but because a few are marked 'COM COMMIOS' (for *Commi Commios*, 'Commios, son of Commios'), it is believed he was a son of the Commios Caesar knew. The following year Caesar decided to revisit Britain and finish off the business. This time he was considerably more prepared, and he provides a great deal more information.

Caesar's plans to invade Britain again were delayed. Some of the Gaulish Treveri were said to be 'inciting the Trans-Rhine Germans' (*Gallic War* v.2). This turned out to be connected with a dispute within the Treveri between two of the chieftains, Indutiomarus and Cingetorix. To prevent the trouble compromising the British campaign, Caesar took hostages from Indutiomarus (the source of the problems) and set off for Boulogne.

It was a mark of the relative insecurity of his hold on Gaul, and a portent for what lay ahead, that Caesar had to take a number of Gaulish chiefs with him to Britain to prevent them starting rebellions while he was away. One of them, Dumnorix of the Aedui, even absconded and the efforts to bring him back delayed sailing even more. This makes the idea of invading Britain all the more curious, since it could only have added similar problems, and suggests Caesar can have had no intention of occupying Britain. He could not possibly have managed to control both Gaul and Britain in the same way at the same time. Five legions and a body of cavalry set off in around 800 ships, only to find themselves becalmed and at the mercy of what we now call the Gulf Stream. The current sent the fleet towards the North Sea, with Britain off to port. When the tide turned, the opportunity was made to land, probably somewhere on Kent's east coast.

The Britons had been waiting for the invasion but vanished when they saw how big it was – or at least that was how Caesar put it. It is perfectly possible that they knew their best defence lay in drawing Caesar inland, away from supplies and help. Caesar took the bait, and although he initially engaged the Britons with some success his fleet was partly wrecked by the force of the tides. Caesar had to sort this out, allowing most of the Britons the opportunity to regroup and making the radical decision to abandon unilateral tribal action and combine instead under one commander. It was something their descendants might have profitably thought about a century or more later.

The Britons threw in their lot with Cassivellaunus. Caesar says he controlled land to the north of the Thames. This ties Cassivellaunus firmly to the area we know later belonged to the Catuvellauni, a name that does not appear again until the mid-second-century *Geography* of Ptolemy, and Dio's early third-century account of the invasion of AD 43. The suffix *-vellaunus*, shared with the tribal name, means 'good' or 'excellent'. The prefix is thought to invoke a magnification of that quality. Thus Cassivellaunus is 'exceptionally good', while his tribe bore a name that meant something like 'very good warriors'.

They lived up to their name, which was just as well under the circumstances. Caesar found that Britons on horseback or in chariots constantly harassed his troops. The charioteers continually engaged the Roman cavalry, which were trying to protect the slower and more cumbersome infantry. Using woodland to their advantage the Britons drew the Roman escorts off and insisted in fighting in small, dispersed, groups. As the fighting progressed, the

Britons simply deployed fresh warriors so that the others could withdraw and rest. Cassivellaunus was justifying his position and Caesar was forced to admit that his foot soldiers were totally unable to fight effectively in that sort of engagement. Equally, we have only Caesar's account and it would not have served his purpose to present the enemy as an ineffectual bunch of incompetents. A pushover was fine, so long as the opponents stood up long enough to be pushed over in a gratuitously dramatic way.

A near miss followed when a foraging party made up of three of the legions was pounced on. Only swift action by the Roman cavalry saw off the Britons who had, presumably, come to regard the Romans as remarkably easy pickings. According to Caesar there was no further attempt by the Britons to take them on in such numbers again. Cassivellaunus withdrew his forces across the natural barrier of the Thames, and fortified the north bank with stakes. The precaution appears to have had little effect on the Romans as they forded, and once more the Britons withdrew. Cassivellaunus was said by now to have given up the idea of confronting the Romans in battle. He demobilised most of his forces but held on to four thousand charioteers to harass the Romans. Although there is no archaeological confirmation of a force like that, the substantial scale of chariot-fitting production found at the late Iron Age settlement of Gussage All Saints in Dorset demonstrates the existence of support and service industries. At 1.2 hectares Gussage was only a small defended enclosure settlement, but enough material was found there to suggest around fifty chariots could have been kitted out from a couple of seasons' worth of output by this site alone.

From now on, although Caesar's campaign continued, the progress was really limited to the line of advance. Every time a unit of cavalry was sent off to seize supplies and destroy settlements, it was set on by bands of Britons in chariots who had kept the Romans under surveillance the whole way. This was not something the Romans were used to. The Gauls might have been closely connected to the Britons, but they had gone over largely to cavalry in preference to chariot-based warfare. The Britons had resorted to the more effective technique of steadily wearing down their enemies by attrition. Eventually, Caesar had to keep his force together and only start devastating land with whole legions, rather than vulnerable small cavalry wings.

The Trinovantes were a large tribe whose lands lay to the east of the Catuvellauni in an area now called Essex. They had an axe to grind and had not joined Cassivellaunus' federation. Cassivellaunus had killed their king as part of his own personal aggrandisement; in this respect, the Roman invasion must have played directly into his hands. Mandubracius, the Trinovantian heir, had already come to Caesar for help in Gaul. Now the Trinovantes asked that Mandubracius be given back to them, and promised to side with Caesar in return. This was a turning point for Caesar, and it must have been a major setback for Cassivellaunus. Several more tribes surrendered to Caesar and provided him with vital intelligence. Although their names are unfamiliar, one of these was called the 'Cenimagni', which is almost certainly an early variant on 'Iceni', with the suffix *magni* or 'great'. If the Iceni were prepared to surrender to Caesar now, their descendants would take a very different approach.

Caesar discovered that the *oppidum* of Cassivellaunus was an area of woodland fortified with a rampart and ditch, as well as woods and marshes. The site has never been verified, but Baldock (Herts) was in use at around this time. Into the settlement the Britons withdrew with their cattle and other valuables. Caesar made an assault on the camp, but Cassivellaunus was still one step ahead. Caesar was now so far from his beachhead that he had exposed himself dangerously in the rear. Using his alliance with Kentish tribes, Cassivellaunus asked that the Roman base on the coast be attacked. The surprise assault was routed and for the first time in the campaign Cassivellaunus was seriously wrong-footed. The outcome was a peace deal by late September. Cassivellaunus handed over hostages, and promised to respect Mandubracius. Caesar, for his part, bought himself time and the prospect of a safer winter in Gaul and the hostages to guarantee Cassivellaunus would not renege. In fact, it was nearly a disaster.

Some of the Roman forces were shipped back in a first wave, but the empty ships returning to Britain to collect Caesar and the rest were largely scattered by the weather. Caesar had to use the ships that did make it, packing his troops in.

Caesar's invasions never resulted in a Roman occupation of Britain, but they did put the island on the popular map, and they also established that ultimately Caesar had controlled events. Cassivellaunus coordinated a remarkable defence, but it was always just that. Caesar chose to leave – he was not made to. Caesar of course never returned and before long he was murdered, his ambitions having saddled him with the fatal accusation that he wanted to become king in Rome. Ironically, it was his own nephew, Octavian, who became Rome's first imperial monarch in all but name as Augustus Caesar. In Britain, Cassivellaunus of course disappears from history, but the invasions left a significant legacy. Communications with the Roman world continued and over the next hundred years the ruling tribal class of the south-east maintained a schizophrenic relationship with the Mediterranean world. Resiliently independent on one hand, on the other they steadily bought into the Roman package, adopting Latin lettering, names and titles and even the imagery. Cassivellaunus might have successfully resisted a military invasion but the tides that had wrecked Caesar's ships thereafter brought an endless succession of traders from the Roman world. It was only a question of time before another imperial fleet embarked from Gaul.

2

The Bitter Bread of Banishment

CARATACUS

Eight years after Aulus Plautius landed his forces in Britain in 43, the tribal chieftain Caratacus was finally captured and taken to Rome. By then his reputation as the pre-eminent British leader had preceded him. His name was known throughout Gaul and Germany and even in Rome herself his protracted and largely successful resistance in Britain had made him notorious. The Emperor Claudius (41-54) took every opportunity to maximise the theatrical spectacle of a defeated barbarian chieftain – after all, the conquest of Britain was the pinnacle of his imperial career and the validation of his succession to the dynasty of Augustus. A parade was arranged in which Caratacus' retainers walked past the emperor, followed by the booty captured in Caratacus' wars. Behind them came the extended family of Caratacus, heads bowed, and finally Caratacus himself who gave no sense of fear or deference. He is said then to have spoken to Claudius, presenting himself as an equal and one whose defeat, and the nature of the defeat, had merely enhanced Claudius' own reputation. Claudius was, of course, entirely aware of this and appreciated that showing mercy would only magnify the achievement further. In this way, the rebel Caratacus earned a pardon and a pension, and disappeared from history.

In 43 Caratacus was a leading member of the Catuvellauni tribe, and one of the sons of its recently dead king Cunobelinus. He might have been a direct descendant of Cassivellaunus. The most successful of all the tribes in the century prior to the Roman conquest, Catuvellaunian power had been waxing for generations. Caesar found himself facing an alliance of tribes that voluntarily placed themselves under Catuvellaunian control. Ruling from what is now Hertfordshire, the Catuvellauni had already made enemies of the Trinovantes to the east. In the longer run they created tensions that made it easier for some tribes to see direct Roman rule as the lesser of two evils.

In the decades before the Roman invasion, the rulers of the Catuvellauni had begun to blur their identity by adopting some of the imagery of Rome, as their power increased. This was neither unusual nor peculiar to the region. Around the Empire, buffer states ruled by client kings insulated the Empire's growing territories from the rival powers like Persia, or barbarian wildernesses, beyond. For example, Juba II ruled Mauretania in north-west Africa from 25 BC to AD 23. In 33 BC the Romans had annexed the territory, but Augustus saw an opportunity to delegate power to a local, but loyal, ruler. Juba posed as a Roman ruler. His coins emulated Roman types, and his portrait resembled that of Augustus. He even styled himself on the coin legends in Roman letters, REX IVBA, 'King Juba'. This was not entirely appreciated by some of his people who resented being effectively ruled by the Romans. There was a rebellion in the year 6, which resulted in the death of many Romans and led to a campaign of sufficient severity for the eventual victory to earn its leader, Cornelius Cossus, a triumph.

The coins of Cunobelinus exhibit on the whole a similar pattern. Thanks to the adoption of Roman lettering it is possible to restore a little of the politics and machinations of the period, though the process is obviously incomplete and more than a little sparse. But

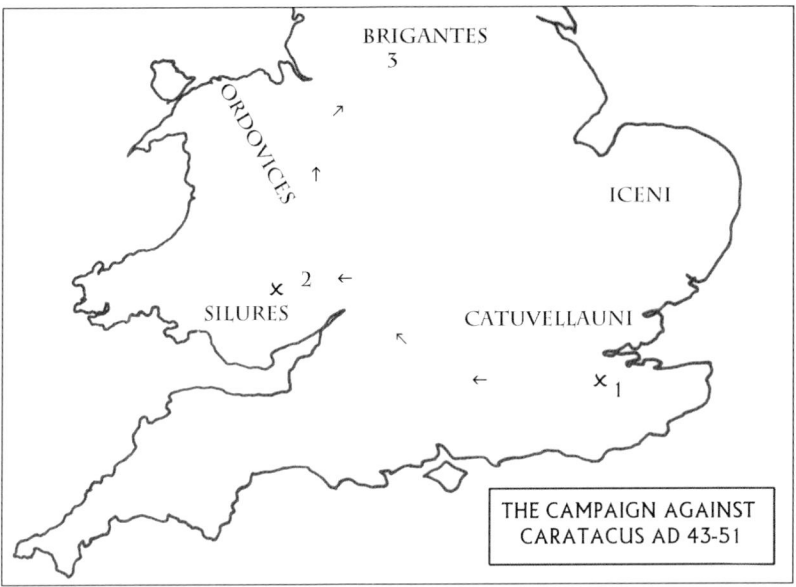

1 The Campaign against Caratacus AD 43-51. After fighting a major battle on a south-east river (X1), Caratacus fled west where he was eventually defeated with his Welsh tribal allies (X2). He fled north to the Brigantes (3) where Cartimandua handed him over to the Romans. Locations are only approximate

Cunobelinus tells us on the coins that he was the son of Tasciovanus though whether that was a literal blood-line or a political statement of fabricated lineage is a moot point. Tasciovanus struck coins at a place called VER or VERL on his coins. The only serious candidate for this is *Verulamium*, or as it was perhaps then spelled in full on one issue, *Verlamio*. Verulamium, or St Albans as we know it, later grew into a substantial Roman city, but it lay beside the remains of a pre-invasion *oppidum* which was presumably the home of Tasciovanus and his retainers.

An *oppidum* is the term used to label British settlements that very loosely resembled towns in the last few decades of British prehistory. Caesar had used it to describe the capital of Cassivellaunus, which was probably Verulamium itself. Generally low-lying, *oppida* were defined by straggling stretches of dyke but lacked any sort of coordinated street plan or building complexes. Instead they were loose coagulations of clustered groups of round houses, pits and enclosures, which also produce evidence for industry, trade and agriculture. Tasciovanus seems to have struck coins at CAM, which must be *Camulodunum* (Colchester), another much larger *oppidum* to the east. The CAM coins are few in number, making it likely that Camulodunum was a place he had only intermittent or limited control over. Exactly how powerful Tasciovanus was we do not know, but the issue of a number of coins with the names of individuals otherwise unknown to us is thought by some to indicate a dilution of power, perhaps amongst some sort of oligarchy. Many of these putative individuals, such as SEGO and ANDOCO, also have the name of Tasciovanus on their coins. However, the names could just be titles or descriptive bragging for Tasciovanus. *Sego-* for example is thought to be mean 'power', and *ande-* 'great'.

By the early first century AD, Cunobelinus had succeeded his father Tasciovanus. It is usually inferred from the coins that Tasciovanus already ruled over the land north of the Thames in an area equivalent to Middlesex and Hertfordshire, with some influence or activity further east into Essex. He may have shared some of his power with Epaticcus, also a son of Tasciovanus, but in terms of the coinage he is nothing like as prominent in the record. Epaticcus' coins tend to turn up to the west and into Berkshire where the Atrebates ruled. This has led to the speculation that the Catuvellauni were expanding east and west. We know nothing about Cunobelinus as an individual but given the Romanised nature of his coinage and contemporary Roman policy it is not only possible, but perhaps even likely, that he was educated in part at Rome and may also have educated some of his sons there.

A few coins associated with the end of this reign name an individual called AGR. This has perplexed scholars but recently it was suggested by the author that the abbreviation is short for Agrippa. During the period a father and son, both called Agrippa, were present in the imperial court and were sponsored as client kings of Judaea throughout the Julio-Claudian period. AGR is entirely unknown as a Celtic form, which makes a Roman expansion the only serious possibility. It is conceivable that we have here evidence for a son of Cunobelinus educated at Rome, and named in a manner to emphasise loyalty and deference. Marcus Agrippa (d.12 BC) had not only been Augustus' most loyal colleague but was also grandfather to Caligula. The name 'Agrippa' was thus in every sense thoroughly appropriate as a gesture of respect. But we can go nowhere with the theory. The putative Catuvellaunian Agrippa evidently did not live long enough to succeed his father or in any other way have an impact on history. There is no other mention of him, and the coins are rare.

If Juba II found himself compromised in Mauretania by being too fond of Roman ways, perhaps the same happened to Cunobelinus. To begin with he seems to have been successful, and relatively long-lived. The bulk of his coins were issued from Camulodunum, which can only mean that Catuvellaunian power had spread east across Trinovantian territory. The stylistic bias to Roman-type coinage became even more obvious. Roman Victories appear, while other coins depict fantastic animals from the canon of classical myth like sphinxes and centaurs, or classical gods like Jupiter and Janus. The implication is clear: Catuvellaunian power must have been subsidised in some way by the Roman Empire. There is evidence from the metallurgical content of some Celtic coins that Roman silver coinage had been melted down to manufacture it. But as Richard Reece has pointed out, 'no coin struck before AD 43 has turned up in an undoubted archaeological context of the same date' in Britain. That doesn't create too much of a problem – if they had been melted down we wouldn't find them. After the conquest, tribal coinage ceased to be issued in areas under Roman control.

Quality coinage, particularly bullion coinage, was synonymous with legitimacy in antiquity. Providing the means to produce it was an easy way of supporting an ally, and so the Roman Empire used its own coinage to do this. That a British tribe could not count on its own supplies of bullion is plain enough from the anonymous coinage issued by the Durotriges in the south-west over the same period. In the decades leading up to the Roman conquest there was a steady debasement of Durotrigan silver, and it degenerated into billon (base silver issues). The reason is that as Roman power extended across Gaul and Spain it exerted a tighter and tighter control on the movement of silver and gold, which was now needed to pay Roman taxes.

Around the year 39 one of the sons of Cunobelinus, Adminius, arrived in Rome after having been sent into exile by his father 'Cynobellinus (sic), king of the Britons' (Suetonius, *Caligula* xliv.2). The latter is a mark of how prominent Cunobelinus had become: from the Roman perspective he was the only significant ruler in Britain. Adminius found Caligula on campaign and planning, in his own mercurial fashion, an invasion of Germany. Receiving Adminius turned out to be the sole achievement of the campaign. Given the experience of other client kings, it is possible Cunobelinus had expelled Adminius in order to appease an anti-Roman faction; or, perhaps, he had decided to sever his connections with the Empire. After two years of Caligula's reign, perhaps that was the only sensible decision to make.

There was, after all, little to be gained by posing to one's people as the associate of a lunatic. Caligula also demonstrated exactly how volatile and unpredictable he could be. In 23 the client king Juba II of Mauretania died and was succeeded by his son Ptolemy. Ptolemy remained in place until Caligula invited him to Rome in 40, only to have him murdered simply because Ptolemy's splendid purple cloak attracted too much admiration. Perhaps the event had repercussions in Britain as men like Cunobelinus began to reconsider their relationships with the Empire. Under the circumstances, Adminius exhibited poorer judgement. Delighted by the chance to pose as the mighty conqueror, Caligula wrote a letter to Rome about the event as if all of Britain had voluntarily submitted to him. Either way, that is the last we hear of Adminius.

The disappearance of Adminius leaves us with the other two sons: Caratacus and Togodumnus. Caratacus is the only one whose existence is verified by coinage marked with the letters CARA and apparently being found in a similar area to those of his uncle(?) Epaticcus. The two men first appear in Dio's account of the invasion campaign of 43. By then Cunobelinus was dead. Given the theoretical length of his reign this was most likely due to old age. Given what followed, he had chosen a good time to leave the stage.

In 43, the Catuvellauni had more to lose than any other British tribe from a Roman invasion. If they fought the Romans off, they would face terrible revenge since the Empire could not sustain a defeat like that. If they lost and the Romans occupied Britain then all their aggrandisement of power and territory was gone. If they lost, but the Romans did not occupy Britain, their prestige would be destroyed. Caratacus and Togodumnus thus led the defence of Britain, but from the outset they were falling back. There is no point in discussing how or where the invasion took place, though plenty of people sweat blood in arguing the toss between a Kentish invasion, a Sussex invasion, or a mixture of both. All that matters is that the Romans were generally in charge from the outset, and regardless of where they landed they were across the south-east in short order. A major battle across a river, either the Medway or Thames, in the opening stages was followed soon after by the Romans crossing the Thames and making for the Catuvellaunian stronghold at Colchester, which Dio calls the 'capital of Cunobelinus'. Togodumnus died soon afterwards. This is said to have resolved the Britons to seek revenge, which can only mean he died at the hands of the Romans.

Caratacus was left to manage the resistance on his own. There is no doubt about his name and even Dio, writing in Greek, called him 'Karatakos'. In Greek the name would have appeared to mean something like 'head' or 'chief', but whether it meant this also to the British is unclear. The Celtic *caero* means a 'ram', perhaps appropriate when Cunobelinus was based on the word for a 'hound'. Either way, the name seems suitable for a leader. 'Caraticus' turns up as a graffito on a piece of samian ware from Richborough, and the Fossdike Mars was a votive gift from two brothers, one of whom was called Caratius, but otherwise the name is rare. The few types of coins that appear to name him show that he seems to have been as Romanised as his father in that sense. Hercules, an eagle and Pegasus appear on his issues. But they emulate the types of Epaticcus so much that we have to ask if being called a 'son' of Cunobelinus necessarily means what we think it means. It is probably more accurate to regard the 'sons' of Cunobelinus as a mixture of men he had fathered by more than one woman, nephews, adopted sons, cousins and kin. Given that we know sharing wives was customary, it was quite possible for one woman to bear a child by a man, and others by his brothers, and even his sons.

Our Caratacus need not even be the CARA- of the coins, who might simply be another man with a similar name and perhaps indeed a son of Epaticcus. So there is no need to try and stick to a rigid reconstruction of Cunobelinus and his lineage. The mysterious 'AGR' has already been mentioned. Is it too much to suggest that Caratacus was called Agrippa as a young man and designated philo-Roman successor, but threw off this name and reverted to something more British once his father was dead? We cannot possibly know. In the aftermath of the battle against Ostorius Scapula (see below) Tacitus tells us *Carataci fratres*, 'the brothers of Caratacus', surrendered (*Annals* xii.35). Evidently there were more 'brothers' than Adminius and Togodumnus, but how many we have no idea.

Caratacus resolved to maintain his opposition to Rome. It is interesting that he seems to have behaved differently from everyone else. Most of the ruling houses in southern Britain capitulated, and provided Claudius with the submissions he could brandish on his arch in Rome. At some point Togidubnus was made a Roman citizen, adopted the names Tiberius Claudius, and sat out the rest of the first century AD in reliable loyalty to his masters while enjoying the status of *rex magnus*, 'great king' (if the restoration of the Chichester inscription is correct), the ultimate British 'confederate with the Romans'. Togidubnus had perhaps already been schooled at Rome. In 47 the Iceni opted for a localised rebellion, but it was quickly suppressed. So, for the most part the British tribes and their rulers stayed where they were. Caratacus, on the other hand, moved west.

It is worth briefly staying with Togidubnus, since he was in every sense an anti-rebel. A realist or an opportunistic quisling, Togidubnus signed on the dotted line when it came to Rome. He accepted the deal, which was status and esteem in a Roman context. He was the Roman equivalent of African and Indian princes educated at Eton and Oxford to mould them into a British imperial vision of reliable local leaders. We know nothing of his origins since he never struck any coinage, which makes it likely he was a lesser family member, perhaps of the Atrebates, without a 'past', plucked out and fashioned as a puppet client king. This incidentally leaves us none the wiser about his name. Tacitus calls him 'Cogidumnus', while the Chichester inscription calls him '[..]gidubnus'. The restored form 'Togidubnus' is based on the known Celtic names of the period and considered to be more likely, though the truth is there is no verification of it. The inconsistent use of 'b' and 'm' in the name is incidentally due to Latinising a Celtic name with consonants and pronunciation which had no perfect Latin equivalent. To this day in Greek the paired consonants 'mp' are used to represent the sound 'b', while 'b' itself is used for the 'v' sound.

Togidubnus remained loyal throughout the first century and when he died the kingdom was subsumed into the cantonal districts of Roman Britain. He represents the ideal textbook client king. There were few like him. Publius Ostorius Scapula replaced Aulus Plautius as governor of Britain in the year 47. Ostorius Scapula proceeded to prosecute the war in the west. Perhaps he knew where Caratacus was, but for the moment suppressing an Iceni rising (see chapter 3) compromised his efforts and showed him he could take nothing for granted in the war in Britain. With this behind him, Scapula turned back to the west and moved into northern Wales and the territory of the Deceangli. It is a moot point whether this really formed part of the long-term Roman strategy, or whether the withdrawal of trou-blemakers into the highlands made following them the only expedient solution to crushing resistance. Even so it was inevitable that Scapula left determined pockets of resistance behind him.

The Roman army found it impossible to bring the Britons to a battle, though otherwise the campaign was said to have been successful. Instead, the Welsh hills provided the Britons with a bolthole and allowed the Romans to extend themselves more and more, and thus expose themselves in the rear. Part of the purpose may have been to pave the way for an attack on Anglesey and the Druids. If it was, that would have to wait until the exploits of Suetonius Paullinus (see next chapter). The legion, probably the XX and until then theoretically based at Colchester, had been brought up to the front to reinforce the advance. A coup in Brigantian territory was easily suppressed in the middle of this, but only because the Brigantes were a client kingdom (see chapter 4), and for the moment a tolerably reliable one.

The Silures of south Wales were altogether a different kettle of fish to the Deceangli. It is as well to appreciate that the further west the Romans moved, the more they found themselves facing tribes for whom the finer points of Mediterranean civilisation were of utterly no consequence. This was not a region where coinage circulated, or where tribal leaders posed as Romanized monarchs and willingly accepted jobs as puppet kings. Even something as banal as pottery was a novelty and large proto-urban settlements like the *oppida* of the south-east were unknown. So, there was no local predisposition to Roman ways. In other words, the Coca-Cola culture of the Roman world simply did not impinge on Silurian consciousness. The Silurian mindset was completely different and, as Scapula discovered, neither *atrocitate* (severity) nor *clementia* (clemency) made any difference to their determination not to capitulate (*Annals* xii.32). As many powerful states before or since have discovered, the prospect of brute force does not necessarily persuade an enemy to give up overnight.

If anyone was already aware of this, it was Caratacus. Capitalising on his reputation for sustained resistance, he had been popularly elevated to a stature way above that of other British leaders in spite of the fact that he had not won a single battle and had consistently retreated. But while Caratacus might have suffered defeat, so far he had evaded capture and avoided the easy option of client status. Like most British serial failures he was more popular then ever. The Silures took Caratacus to their hearts and he had been galvanising them against the approaching Roman army. But southern Wales is considerably more accessible than the rest of the region thanks to its suite of parallel valleys accessed from the southern coastal belt. So Caratacus pulled his Silurian supporters back further into central Wales and the territory of the Ordovices. This capacity for organising inherently disorganised peoples marked Caratacus out as a different sort of leader. The traditional route for the Britons was to divide themselves up amongst tribes and thus guarantee their eventual defeat in a self-induced Machiavellian divide-and-be-conquered suicide bid. Had Caratacus been able to assert himself more effectively from the outset, things might have been very different for him. For the moment though he was still doing remarkably well, and by creating a multi-tribe resistance he offered the most effective bulwark against the Roman invasion to date.

Caratacus resolved to trap the Romans. He found a place where he and his supporters could hold the high ground, and to attack them the Romans would have to cross a river. This would mean the Romans would be sitting ducks, stuck between the river and the Britons hurling missiles down on them. Some believe this site to have been below the Iron Age hillfort at Llanmynech, close to where a Roman vexillation fortress and supply-base of around this date was built at Rhyn Park, just around 20 miles west of where a legionary fortress was later built at Wroxeter. It is impossible to be certain, but this does not affect the graphic account of the battle or its outcome. Any intermediate high ground was kitted out with a stone rampart and defended. The battle resembled a kind of miniature Omaha Beach on D-Day. The Roman forces were obliged to cross the water and face a thoroughly defended embankment. Tacitus says the combination of a galvanised enemy and the challenging terrain *obstupefecit* Scapula, 'rendered senseless' (*Annals* xxxv.1). Scaling the heights to grapple with the Silurian and Ordovician defenders meant facing a hail of lethal missiles and a high rate of casualties as a result. But just as in 1944, in spite of the casualties, the sustained assault eventually created a gap, allowing the Romans up and over and able to demolish the rest of the defences. The Britons withdrew to the defended higher ground. The battle had opened with a territorial advantage to the Britons. Now the criteria altered to the simpler one of hardware. The Romans liked it when this happened, since when it came to hardware they were bound to win. Lacking the armour to withstand the effects of swords and spears, the Britons of this part of the world also lacked either the terrain or equipment to intimidate the Romans with chariots.

Caratacus seems to have made a quick getaway; so quick in fact that he ungallantly left his wife and daughter behind, as well as more of his 'brothers'. He fled north-east and for some bizarre reason now made a critical error of judgement. He appealed to Cartimandua, queen of the Brigantes, for protection. He might as well have presented himself at Ostorius Scapula's tent on his knees. He was promptly arrested and handed over to the Roman authorities in the year 51 when Cartimandua seized the opportunity to enhance her standing with the invaders. Caratacus can scarcely have been unaware of Cartimandua's inclinations, but given the tempestuous nature of Brigantian politics he may have been aiming at another Brigantian faction and fell into the wrong hands. Or perhaps he had no choice. Either way it was the last choice he made. From now on he was an irrelevance apart from providing the Romans with publicity.

Caratacus was astonishingly successful in his campaign against Rome. He seems to have had a striking ability to absent himself when things went the wrong way, only to pop up again somewhere else. He was evidently prepared to sacrifice friends and family along the way if there was no other choice except to surrender. He lasted an outstandingly long time. He fought the Romans throughout nine campaigning seasons, while a decade later the celebrated Boudica scarcely managed one. His capture was celebrated in Rome as one of the all-time greatest and glorious events in Roman military history. But Tacitus suggested this was a mistake. In elevating the defeat of Caratacus to such heights, the illusion was created that the war was won, while at the same time reinvigorating the Silures with a desire for revenge (*Annals* xii.38). The Silures nearly wiped out the Roman occupation of their territory. It was hardly surprising. Scapula had ordered the Silures be wiped out or forcibly moved elsewhere. It left the tribe with nothing to lose, and no choice but to fight to the death. The ensuing hostilities wore Scapula out and he died in post. It took another governor, Didius Gallus, to calm things down. It was an episode that might have helped the planners of the Iraq War of 2003 weigh up whether defeating Saddam Hussein would be an end, or just the illusion of one.

In his later years, pardoned and a resident in Rome, Caratacus was said to have wandered around in awe at the city's buildings and magnificence, wondering why a people who had so much had wanted the miserable bivouacs in which he and his people had lived. Caratacus of course missed the point. It was that very poverty, and barbarian outlandishness, which allowed the Romans to trumpet their munificence and generosity of spirit. Paradoxically he seems to have realised that the mercy shown him enhanced Claudius as an emperor – this, in truth, was all part of the same thing. The very fact that Caratacus had challenged Rome provided Rome and her historians with the opportunity to examine the price of Rome's success. By embodying Rome's ancient virtues of bravery and leadership, Caratacus was a gift to a Roman state in crisis. Like other rebels who came after him, he helped Rome search for what had made her great. In this sense he simply invigorated her.

Caratacus also failed to appreciate that he was on the whole a dinosaur. While he maintained his resistance he found the only place he could do so was amongst people who had no idea what Rome amounted to. There is no evidence that any of the Catuvellauni followed him to Wales. In the meantime, many of the other tribes of the south-east were busy selling their souls to the Roman way of life. The Boudican Revolt (see chapter 3) represented a catastrophic disruption of the process but it is crass to fail to realise that most people, given half a chance, opt for stability and security – whoever provides it. Nevertheless, Caratacus represents a more human side to the resistance to Rome. We have no idea when or where he died, but he presumably faded away quietly in a house in Rome like the Confederate leader Jefferson Davis, a decaying object of fascination to those who could remember who he was and what he had been, and a trophy of the victor's munificence. The Welsh remembered him as he was, and he survives in their lore as Caradawc, and the king handed over thanks to the treachery of a queen they called Aregwedd Foeddawg.

3

Bleeding from the Roman Rods

BOUDICA

East Anglia is a prominent and distinct part of England. Neatly defined by its long, curved, eastern coastline and its extensive tracts of low-lying land, it contains few natural obstacles apart from marshes and long coastal inlets. Today it remains predominantly rural and relatively isolated from the rest of Great Britain since no motorway has yet been built to carry traffic all the way in. The later history of Roman Britain saw settlement develop across the region, and it has in recent years become the source of some of the most exceptional treasures of the whole Roman world. But relatively few villas have ever been found here and, apart from Colchester, it only ever had one significant town. The regional capital Caistor St Edmund, *Venta Icenorum*, was always small and got smaller as time went on. Today that town is simply open fields, thanks to Saxon and later settlement moving a few miles north to Norwich. It seems remarkable now that East Anglia could once have been the source of what was perhaps the most violent rebellion in all of British history. It is also the one about which we have the most information at every level, including brutal archaeological evidence for the violent conflagrations visited by Boudica and her hordes on the Roman towns she attacked.

⋙◆⋘

When in the year 61 the last blood-caked British body slumped to the ground the soldiers of the *XIV Gemina* and *XX* legions, and their attendant auxiliaries, had good cause to celebrate. The battle against Boudica and the Iceni, perhaps the Cenimagni who had surrendered to Caesar in 54 BC, had come nearly a generation after the Roman invasion of Britain. Had the day been lost the efforts of eighteen campaigning seasons would have been in vain, and Rome's prestige across the known world would have been tarnished forever. It is no exaggeration to say that if Boudica had won, then rebellions throughout the Empire might have broken out.

Nevertheless, the victory was not a moment that Nero and his advisors chose to savour. The Roman Empire was still considerably less than a century old, and a defeat by a barbarian woman could have permanently dented its prestige, as well as leaving the administration totally perplexed. As Herodian noted nearly two hundred years later, as a general observation, 'barbarians are liable to be easily roused – even for quite erratic reasons' (I.iii.5). Nero's reign had begun in 54, following the suspicious death of his cousin, stepfather and predecessor Claudius. Nero was to be the last of the Julio-Claudians, the short-lived first imperial Roman dynasty. Nero could at least trace his ancestry right back to Augustus, his great-great-grandfather, unlike Claudius who was descended from Augustus' sister Octavia, and Augustus' wife Livia by her first marriage. But at this midway point in his reign, Nero had only just escaped the influence of his mother, Agrippina the Younger. It was largely thanks to her that he was emperor at all, since she had made her second marriage to Claudius in 49 when Nero was about 12. In 54 Claudius died, probably killed on Agrippina's orders. Nero succeeded, supplanting Claudius' son Britannicus who was conveniently murdered in 55. In 59 Nero had his mother murdered too, but for the moment he remained under the restraint of Seneca and Burrus. He was earning a reputation as a sadistic, self-indulgent maniac. This image would provide the historians with the perfect device in their tales of the catastrophe to come.

Britain presented Nero with a dilemma precisely because of its connection with Claudius. Nero had mercilessly ensured his own grip on the throne at the expense of Claudius and Britannicus, but could not afford to discredit his predecessor. Claudius was, after all, his adoptive father and this seems to have been why he abandoned the idea of giving up Britain even though he had no territorial ambitions of his own. Nero was vastly more interested in his theatrical and gaming activities, interspersed with episodes of monumental cruelty and admiring his own appearance with particular emphasis on the first shaving of his beard.

By the late 50s Britain had absorbed the efforts of four legions and probably another 20-30,000 auxiliaries, in total an army of around 50,000, for more than a decade. This was handy in the sense that troops thus occupied were less likely to provide support for an imperial usurper or focus their attention on grievances. But there came a time when Britain started to look like an expensive and futile indulgence. The Boudican Revolt came very near to making the decision for Nero. In spite of its defeat, the fact is that the Neronian garrison of Britain came within an inch of losing everything. It could have been the greatest Roman military catastrophe since the loss of Varus and three legions in Germany in the year 9. Britain was not even the only military disaster – the Roman army was defeated in Armenia, and Syria was almost lost too.

The Boudican Revolt has always been a big deal in the history of Roman Britain and even in the greater history of Britain, where it is constantly cited as a kind of primeval Battle of Britain. In the great scheme of antiquity the victorious outcome for Rome meant it could be treated as almost a side show, avoiding further embarrassment. So, there were no explicit victory coins, no victory parades, and no celebratory monuments. At least we know of none, either from the sources or from the wreckage of Rome's public buildings that survive. Some rare gold *aurei* of 60/61 had reverses

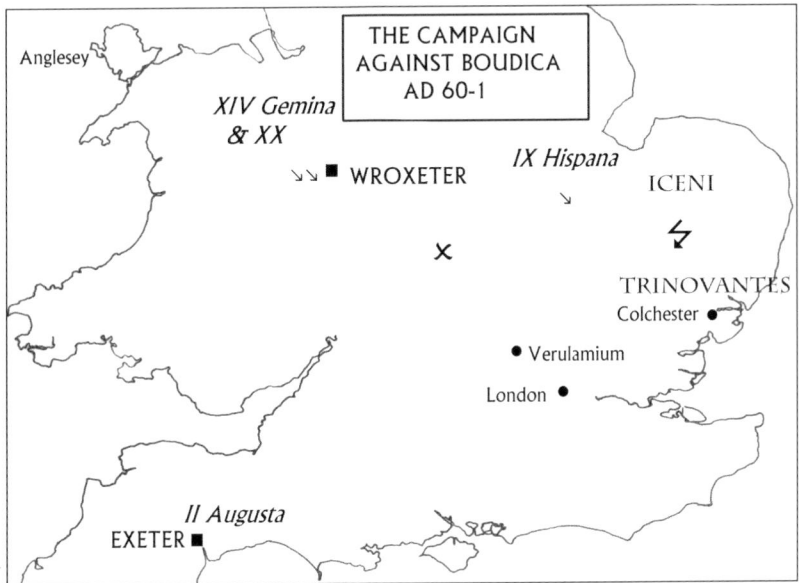

2   The Campaign against Boudica AD 60-1. The rising in East Anglia was first attacked (unsuccessfully) by *IX Hispana*. The revolt then sacked Colchester, London and Verulamium, while the governor, Suetonius Paullinus, retreated to meet the *XIV* and *XX* as they marched south-east from Anglesey. A decisive battle (X) somewhere in the Midlands ended the campaign. *II Augusta* took no part

showing Roma with her foot on arms, and others with *Virtus* (valour) doing the same. But the legends were stock imperial titles – there was no specific reference to Britain. However, Nero rewarded the victorious legions, or at least it seems he did. It must be from this moment that *XIV Gemina* added *Martia Victrix* to its titles, which it certainly had by 66 (see chapter 5). The *XX* became *Valeria Victrix* in a cryptic gesture of alliterative balance. To be fair though, we cannot be certain when these awards were granted other than that they existed by the end of the first century.

The episode seemed catastrophic by any measure. The battlefield might have been strewn with British dead but three towns lay devastated and thousands of people had been killed with a reckless viciousness that would echo down the centuries. On the other hand, Boudica did the Romans a huge favour. Had she sustained a guerrilla campaign she could have made life unremitting misery for the Romans by tying down huge numbers of soldiers, and consistently disrupting every, and any, attempt to Romanise Britain. Instead, she played all her cards at one stroke. By gathering her forces together in a single straggling army, she presented the Romans with an enemy that could be targeted in a way that virtually guaranteed defeat for her. All she offered her own people, in the end, was mayhem, starvation and despair.

Nevertheless, for the Roman historians who recalled the Boudican Revolt, there was a paradox in the crisis that illustrated perfectly the troubled Roman identity in the Empire. The Boudican hordes were admired for their ancient dignity as noble savages, defending their own to the death. Meanwhile, the Romans who had come from similar origins and won an Empire thanks to their own mastery of war, government and power, had lapsed into decadence. The contradiction coloured the Roman perspective but when the Revolt broke out, a more practical response took priority.

The events of the drama pivoted around two key personalities: Suetonius Paullinus, the governor of Britain, and Boudica herself. But we need to be careful. The juxtaposition of these two leaders is a literary device used by Tacitus and Dio. It is a very effective way of constructing history in a way that generates a readable story, and provides hooks on which to hang characteristics, moral judgements, and the dynamic of leadership. In the background lay the personality of Nero, who provided another dimension to the literary choreography. We can see the same thing in conventional tales of the English Civil War (Charles I versus Cromwell), or the Second World War (Churchill versus Hitler, or Stalin compared to Hitler). At the same time the emphasis on key personalities can obscure the broader issues, or even other personalities who exerted colossal influence but whose personalities are so opaque and low profile that they can be omitted from the story altogether. When it comes to ancient history, these secondary players are marginalised out of the record we have, leaving the historian with no option but to go with what is left.

Gaius Suetonius Paullinus was Britain's fifth governor, but his predecessor Quintus Veranius had died in office only a year after arriving in 57. Suetonius Paullinus took charge of a Britain that had experienced rapid change in a fantastically short space of time. At this relatively early date in imperial history, it was not surprising this senator's family origins were Italian. He was a major establishment figure. Paullinus enjoyed a popular reputation as a military strategist and was determined to seize his chance to prove himself in major campaigns.

So Paullinus was not chosen by chance, though of course he may have used every contact he had to make sure he was offered the post. Britain was, after all, almost a plaything for those with military ambitions. Caesar had managed to turn his own limited achievements over a century before into box-office successes and Paullinus will have spent much of his adult life hearing about the progress of events since 43. He had himself been a praetor before the year 42 when he led a campaign against the Moors in north-west Africa (Mauretania). The campaign had come about because Caligula had killed the client king Ptolemy, son of Juba, who had been placed on the throne by Augustus. The fighting took Paullinus across the Atlas Mountains and deeper into the Sahara as he chased the rebels. This turned out to have been useful experience when he came to Britain nearly two decades later. Perhaps with Caesar's publicity machine in mind, he seems to have published an account not just of the fighting but also the landscape he fought across.

We have no idea what Paullinus did in the intervening years. He had to have been at least 30 to serve as a praetor and must therefore have been born close to the end of the reign of Augustus (AD 14). When he arrived in Britain Paullinus was at least in his late forties and will have heard endless accounts of the highs and lows of the campaign from his peers. He will also have had comprehensive access to public and private documents tabulating the progress of the invasion. He may also have visited or served in Britain in some capacity, though we have no verification of that.

Of Boudica's origins we know nothing at all. Even her name might be more of an epithet than a personal one. It certainly proved durable. More than a century later Dio calls her 'Boudouika', which is simply a variant form of the name in Greek letters. In other words, it might have been a title posthumously awarded by her erstwhile followers, or even by the Romans for dramatic purpose. Even if it was contemporary, it might have only been a name coined in the Revolt, either by Boudica herself or by her followers. *Boud-* and *Bod-* are well-known as components of place-names and mean something like 'victory'. Around the time of the Roman invasion, the Dobunni (whose territory crossed the Mendips and Cotswolds) issued coins in the name of Boduoc or Boduog, perhaps short for Boduocus, which is a masculine variant of the form. In fact, it takes little imagination to work out that 'Boudica' is very possibly a classicised version of a name that might have been in reality 'Boduoga'. Caesar had earlier defeated a Gaulish tribal leader called Boduognatus (*Gallic War* ii.23).

Boudica was thus a British Victoria in almost every possible sense of the word. She was an individual whose reputation was made by circumstance. A thousand years before she might have lived as a tribal king's wife or concubine and, regardless of her personal qualities, died without trace. It is the Roman world that has preserved her for us, in a mixture of awe and horrified disdain, thanks largely to Tacitus and Dio who recognised the symmetry and tabloid appeal her personality provided their tale. This of itself raises the fascinating question of just how authentic she was. More intriguing than anything else, as we shall see, is her total disappearance after the final battle of the Revolt.

Boudica was probably around thirty years of age in the year 60, but she may very well have been older. There is no verification of her existence, or her name, apart from the mentions by Tacitus and Dio. Suetonius mentions the event, but not Boudica. Boudica is never called a queen by Tacitus though this generates an interesting subject in its own right, where the Romans seemed to prefer its use for tribal monarchs who supported them but denied it to their opponents (see chapter 4). Indeed, Boudica is specifically described otherwise, in ways that show she was connected with the ruling family but not a ruler herself. Tacitus calls her the *uxor*, 'wife', of Prasutagus, *Rex Icenorum*, 'king of the Iceni', and as *generis regii*, 'of the royal line'

(*Annals* xxxi, and *Agricola* 16). Dio describes her as a 'British woman of the royal family' and allows her to call herself *Basileuousa*, 'queen', in his version of her speech (lxii.6.4). In part this was due to Roman historians ascribing a formal rank as a monarch to those men and women approved by Rome. The ambiguity is plain enough from those tribal kings who called themselves *Rex* on their coinage, and may ultimately have derived from Roman recognition of their status. The ordinary Britons probably made no such distinction. Certainly it is difficult to see how or why they would have regarded Boudica as anything other than a queen, or as a female king.

Boudica is invariably discussed along with the two daughters she seems to have borne Prasutagus. Their fate, as we shall see, formed the catalyst for the rebellion, at least in the accounts we have. Given what we know from other accounts of British tribal habits, it is theoretically possible Boudica was only one of several 'wives', and these daughters only two of many children of Prasutagus by a variety of women. But Prasutagus specified these two daughters as his heirs, along with Nero, which suggests he had no other children unless he was deliberately excluding them. Dio also says Boudica had unusual intelligence for a woman. Leaving aside the damnation with faint praise for a moment, it starts to become clear that Boudica need not have been the only woman to be humiliated by the Romans after the death of Prasutagus. Indeed, Dio even claims that on the battlefield Boudica said she was acting on behalf of all violated women and girls of the Iceni. Tacitus refers in a general sense to the abuse heaped on the relatives of Prasutagus and the manner in which his family were treated like slaves. It is entirely possible it was only Boudica's dramatic personal response to the situation that brought her to the forefront, condemning other women of the Iceni royal household to anonymity, though as we shall see it is even possible that the Boudica of history never really existed at all.

Prasutagus was originally thought to have appeared on a silver coin issued by the Iceni, with the legend once read as SVB RII PRASTO, and on the reverse ESICO FECIT. It appears to mean, 'under King Prasto, Esico made [this coin]', on the assumption that *Rii* was some sort of Celtic form of *Rex*. However, the numismatist Jonathan Williams has shown that more legible coins recently found in a hoard from Fincham (Norfolk) read SVB ESVPRASTO. That doesn't solve the issue as he goes on to explain, because 'Esuprastus' is otherwise unknown, and the use of *sub* ('under') is without parallel on Celtic coinage. Moreover, coins of the Corieltauvi do include a number with the name ESVPRASV, who was probably the same person. Finally, a new hoard from Silsden (Yorks) has shown that the Icenian Esuprasto coins might have been dated too late – this of course was originally based on the assumption they referred to Prasutagus.

To cut a long story short, what this means is that we have no verification of Boudica or Prasutagus from the coins of the period. They exist solely in the Roman written record. The similarity of the name on Corieltauvian and Icenian coins might even mean that the Iceni had a far less well-defined identity before the Revolt period. The conundrum arises from the simple fact that all our historical accounts are Roman, and Celtic coins were issued by people who adapted a foreign alphabet to represent names in a language that had no written form.

Like many late Iron Age British coins, the 'Esuprasto' design had been derived from Roman models. Together with the use of Latin words the coins mark a change from the earlier tribal coins with their distinctive 'Celtic' designs. Some of these tribal silver coins have a metal composition so similar to Roman *denarii*, it seems they must have been manufactured by melting Roman silver down. Esuprastus, like many contemporary Celtic rulers, was exhibiting himself to his people in a Latinised and Romanised image. Such coins are unlikely to have played much part in day-to-day transactions – the value of each unit was too high – but instead perhaps served as donatives for warrior loyalty. Whether the silver used had been stolen, or had been supplied by the Roman state, we have no idea, but given Prasutagus' will it seems likely he had been the recipient of Roman hand-outs or loans to buy his amenability and that of his supporters. If they were loans, they might have been part of the money-lending that would return to haunt the Romans.

It is impossible to distinguish any early Roman coins found in Iceni territory as part of the Roman cash injection rather than later losses, but hoards offer slightly stronger evidence. The Norton Subcourse (Norfolk) hoard of 113 Roman silver *denarii* was made up very largely of first-century BC Roman Republican silver coins, but it also included a few imperial coins with the latest being two *denarii* of Claudius struck in 41-2 (one of which was a forgery). The hoard was therefore not buried before 42. So little Roman silver was struck from 37 until 64 that the hoard could easily have been deposited at any time in the late 40s or 50s. Everyone, Roman or provincial, was dependent on using old silver from the Republic and it is routine to find first-century AD hoards that have a very high proportion of coins a century or more old dating from the Republic.

The Norton hoard, unfortunately scattered in a field, was also associated with two Icenian silver coins. At first this seems hard to explain unless the owner was someone happy to store his wealth in local and Roman coinage. Such a mixture does not fit the usual pattern of hoards but the Icenian coins are hard to explain otherwise. Bullion did not enter Icenian territory only in coin form. The Hockwold-cum-Wilton hoard of early first-century silver plate is one of several bullion hoards from the region, but the only one to be exclusively Roman. Several decorated two-handled silver wine cups with pedestal bases made up the hoard, but all of them had been deliberately dismantled and hammered flat. Whoever owned this silver was only interested in the bullion, not in using them or selling them as aesthetic objects. Other hoards from the area of the same period, like Crownthorpe, were made of Roman and native products, though the Crownthorpe collection is particularly interesting in appearing to include a pair of cups made locally in bronze as copies of Roman silver cups.

Needless to say, we have absolutely no idea *why* such hoards were buried and not recovered or whether they belonged to wealthy tribesmen or Roman soldiers. But they certainly fit the historical context of a client kingdom exposed to injections of Roman bullion. On the other hand, Dio's 'version' of Boudica's battlefield speech includes a specific grievance about the Romans taxing the dead, in other words the Roman equivalent of death duties. She is said to have complained that since none of them had any money and nowhere to get it from, how could they have paid? This of course contradicts the bullion evidence (if it was tribal property), and the reference to loans being called in (see below), as well as specific evidence for the injection of cash in other provinces. The reality though was probably that very few ordinary tribal people had access to cash, however much their leaders benefited from subsidies.

By the end of the 50s south-eastern Britain had become a semi-urbanised province. While the Thames had once been a tribal barrier, the river had now become a highway for commerce and development. This was a critical factor in the transformation of Britain into a single entity from an island fragmented into tribal areas. From nothing, London grew so fast that by the time of the Revolt it was a heaving mercantile centre in spite of no official attempt having been made to found it.

To the north-east, Colchester had become the symbol of Roman victory in its Temple of the divine Claudius. Once a tribal capital, part of the former *Camulodunum* had been made the site of a legionary fortress and then a colony for military veterans within five years of the invasion. The original native settlement was far more extensive and diffuse. The colony was now a mass of opportunistic ex-soldiers bent on exploiting everything they could from the region. For the local people, the Romans merely represented a new variation on exploitation. Before 43 the Trinovantes had been absorbed into the Catuvellaunian empire across the north Thames basin. The coastal area had probably been an attractive prospect for the Catuvellauni, whose leaders coveted commercial and social contact with the Roman Empire.

It was from *Camulodunum* (Colchester) that 'King Cunobelinus, son of Tasciovanus' (as he styled himself) ruled south-eastern England in the last thirty-odd years before the invasion. Many of his coins carry the legend CAMV for the tribal capital. It was thus entirely appropriate that Colchester served as the primary target of the invading Roman army, which even waited for Claudius to arrive in Britain to lead the approach in person. It was here that Claudius received the surrender of British tribes, ordered their disarmament, and provided instructions for the rest of the campaign.

Archaeology has provided the physical evidence for a legionary fortress on the site that was probably built in 43 and 44. We can only assume it was the XX legion. Apart from an undated tombstone there is no verification of its presence. In any case, part of the legion, whichever it was, will have been on campaign until its permanent withdrawal in or around 49. But the area was not so settled it could be left unsupervised. The classic Roman solution was the colony of veterans. Ostensibly a demonstration of Roman civilised urban living and a means of familiarising the locals with their responsibilities and obligations as Roman provincials, it also acted as a block of reserve troops. The plans were characterised by a ludicrously negligent level of complacency and over-confidence. No new defences were built while the colony was built in, around, and over the old fortress. It would turn out to be a catastrophic lack of foresight.

Iceni territory corresponded to what we now call Norfolk and part of Suffolk. Prasutagus died around the year 59 but had already made plans for his estate in the naïve belief that he could guarantee his people a stable future. The Iceni had a poor record in Roman eyes. In 47 they had revolted during the governorship of Ostorius Scapula, in spite of already acceding to the terms by which they had become a client kingdom, exposing Roman over-confidence. The ensuing battle demonstrated that the Iceni could operate as a significant challenge, and it was a close-run thing. The governor's son, Marcus Ostorius Scapula, was decorated for his efforts in saving a Roman's life.

The client kingdom was a handy political device, supposed to provide the Roman government with reliable allies on its borders. Not only had the Iceni torn up the deal, but they had also organised other tribes into the rebellion. But critically, the Romans did not end the region's client kingdom status and this can only mean that the rebellion was geographically restricted and only involved a faction within the Iceni. Nevertheless, a fort was built at Saham Toney in the heart of East Anglia and was probably just one of many. But at around the same time a large native complex covering more than 30,000 square metres was laid out on Gallow's Hill near Thetford. It consisted of concentric ditches and ramparts surrounding a central enclosure. Although a building stood in the central enclosure it is entirely unknown whether the site was religious, commercial, military or social in purpose. The site probably served all of these in some way, but its sheer scale means that it is easily interpreted as having played a significant part in galvanising the tribal resolve to rise against Rome. But the truth is we do not know. It is just as possible that it was originally an attempt by Prasutagus, in his role as client king of the Romans, to create a centre where tactful offerings to the Roman imperial cult could be made.

In or around the year 51 a triumphal arch was erected in Rome to commemorate the conquest. Claudius had another three years to live, so of his thirteen years as emperor, the conquest occupied eleven. It was his single greatest military achievement and played a defining part in consolidating his tenuous grip on the throne. The arch was a permanent, but traditional, record of the achievement. It was depicted on the reverse of the only coin series to record the invasion. By a lucky chance part of the inscription from the original arch has survived. Typically for a Roman imperial inscription it is dominated by trotting out imperial titles, though these have the advantage of dating the arch. We know from Dio that another arch was also erected in Gaul. It too will have carried the announcement that Claudius was the first to bring barbarians across the sea under Roman control, and that he had received the submission of eleven British kings. Or at least that is how the text is normally translated. The 'eleven British kings' and the claim that the campaign had been 'without loss' are beyond doubt but the inscription is incomplete. 'Submission' is inferred. In other words it might have been defeat or submission or both, or something else. No individual king is mentioned. We can only assume that Prasutagus was one of them, perhaps renewing his capitulation after the revolt of 47. He ruled in the south-east and we know he was apparently a client king. During this time he was probably given and lent money, and even some Roman military security, to guarantee that Iceni territory remained stable while the conquest proceeded in the west.

Whether or not Prasutagus was provided with funds does not affect the point that many British tribal leaders were certainly lent money. For some reason the money was recalled by the procurator Decianus Catus not long before the Revolt broke out. We do not know why he did this. It is possible that the calling in of loans was a preamble to abandoning Britain. Tacitus described how the Britons saw the procurator and the governor of Britain at this time as a pair of exploitative monarchs, whereas in the past they had only to put up with a single king per tribe (*Agricola* 15.2). The procurator specifically *in bona saeviret*, 'wreaks his fury on [their] prosperity'. Another possibility is the coinage reform of the year 64, when Nero started to issue coinage in abundance once more but with the silver and gold at reduced weights. Until that point, imperial coinage was relatively limited and erratic in availability. Whoever planned the reform would have wanted to build up stocks of metals. Recalling existing coinage with its superior level of purity was an essential part of that. Under Trajan, for example, a specific directive that old worn coin be melted down is recorded by Dio (lxviii.15.3). Private individuals had also lent money in blatant attempts at speculation. Seneca, Nero's tutor, was after a good interest rate. His loan of ten thousand *denarii* was equivalent to the annual pay of around forty-four legionaries, a relatively modest amount, which means there were probably many more like him. But crucially, the Britons were said not to be interested in the money. This suggests that there was some compulsion to take on loans, perhaps easily enforced if the reluctant debtors had little idea of what their obligations would be when it came to interest and repayment.

Meanwhile, the new governor was thoroughly diverted by a campaign in Wales. This was a critical strategic mistake and must have been based on the entirely fallacious assumption that the south-east was secure enough to be left largely in the hands of veterans and administrators. Suetonius Paullinus was hell-bent on wiping out the Druids, whose psychological and practical support was galvanising resistance to the Roman conquest. There was also the utter revulsion felt by the Romans for the way Druids sacrificed human beings so that their entrails could be used to interpret divine intentions. As we saw earlier, Caratacus had found a power base in southern Wales. Now the remote hills and valleys provided a magnificent and intimidating buffer between the Roman province and the island of Anglesey, where the Druids had their stronghold.

It is very easy to take the naïve view that the Druids represented some sort of unadulterated native force of natural and righteous power, now under threat from the vicious and totalitarian Romans. In reality the struggle was much more equal. The Druids exercised unchallenged religious, legislative and military power over the British tribes. They enjoyed the sort of immunity that the medieval church did from secular power and restraint. As a separate caste they were also, to all intents and purposes, detached from tribal identities. In other words, the Druids had their own special type of liberty and it was potentially at the expense of almost everyone else in Britain – especially the human victims they used for sacrifice. They even had a monopoly on literacy, that final bastion of independent thought. From a political, social or military perspective their continued existence was totally unacceptable to the Romans, but it is a moot point whether the Druids were necessarily better or worse than the invaders. 'Better the devil you know' might have been the Britons' perspective to begin with, but Druid popularity seemed to wane remarkably quickly after 61. In fact they disappeared.

Britain already enjoyed a captivating reputation for being the home of magic and superstition. This fascinated the Roman world, but it enhanced the Druids' image as enemies of the state. To Suetonius Paullinus, the prospect of wiping out the Druids must have looked like a guaranteed fast-track to success. Considering that his life seems to have been remarkably quiet since his Mauretanian exploits of 42, the opportunity to take over after the unexpected death of Quintus Veranius must have seemed the gift of a lifetime.

Anglesey presented one very obvious obstacle: it is an island, and so it was then. While the Menai Straits are not broad or particularly dangerous, they had allowed Anglesey to accumulate an indigenous population that willingly harboured anyone escaping the Roman army. Suetonius Paullinus marched against the island with *XIV Gemina*, and part of the *XX*, as well as auxiliaries. That left the rest of Britain held by *II Augusta* in the south-west, *IX Hispana* either at Lincoln or divided up amongst several bases, and the rest of the *XX* in south Wales somewhere. Obviously auxiliaries were dispersed here and there, but we have no idea of how many and where.

The disposition of the Roman forces was to play a vital part in the unfolding events. So enthusiastic was Suetonius Paullinus to set out on his campaign that he exposed himself to attack in the rear, while his remaining forces were simply too far apart to take on any rebellion. So, we can only assume that he either took it for granted that there was no chance of a rising, or that he grossly underestimated the scale of any potential opposition. Part of the problem is the exact timescale. The climax of the rebellion took place in 61, but it is very likely that the critical sequence of events began the year before.

First of all, the recall of debts presented the creditors very probably with people unable or unwilling to pay and added to an accumulated body of general grievances about the Roman colonists and their behaviour in East Anglia. The next event was the death of Prasutagus. Far from his will guaranteeing a seamless transference of power to Nero, it was as good as torn up on the spot. There is no mention of Suetonius Paullinus being directly involved in what happened, perhaps because he was already in Anglesey. Centurions started to lead the systematic exploitation of the territory. The men involved will have been centurions drawn from each of the four legions across Britain and detached to act as government agents in a variety of administrative, legal and police duties. This was entirely normal. Marcus Favonius Facilis at Colchester, whose tombstone is so invariably interpreted as cast-iron evidence that Colchester was originally a fortress of his legion, the *XX*, may very well have been one of these men. We do not know, but a plausible scenario is that he was sent to Colchester while the rest of his legion was in campaign in the west.

Another Norfolk coin hoard, from Eriswell, closes with an unworn silver *denarius* of 55, but overall the hoard had 72 Roman coins and 255 Icenian silver issues. Not only does the terminal date fix it very close to the rebellion, but also the high numbers of local coins means it is perhaps either the accumulated wealth (and borrowings) of an Icenian, or perhaps a collection of coins seized by some of the Romans bent on ripping off the area. We have, of course, no idea. The hoard is as likely to have been abandoned by an Icenian physically prevented from returning to it in the aftermath of the Revolt by death or restrictions on movement, as it is to have been buried by a retreating Roman soldier during the outbreak of the Revolt. It is equally possible it belongs to after the Revolt when someone had the wit to hoard the superior pre-64 coinage before it disappeared from circulation when the coinage was debased. That person could simply have failed to recover it because he died from illness. Either way it reflects a context in which there was loot to be had in East Anglia though in general there is little evidence for wider enjoyment of material goods. Pottery, for example, was restricted to simple handmade wares while tribes in the south-east were producing considerably more technically impressive wares. This is a reminder that tribal Britain was highly stratified when it came to possessions, something which would prove to have defining consequences in the longer term.

The kind of abuse meted out probably included tribute payments, as well as the stated confiscation of aristocratic estates. One of the scams, still being operated twenty years later, was to sell local people the grain they need to pay their tribute liability. The grain itself never moved anywhere, but individuals had to travel miles to locked granaries, hand over cash for the grain, and then leave it there to be treated as their tribute-paid. It is unlikely that the centurions themselves engaged in much of the direct negotiations. Centurions were sufficiently well-paid to have their own personal retinue of slaves and freedmen, but this of itself caused considerable offence. To the Britons the idea of dealing with a slave was insulting and objectionable, while the concept of a freedman was beyond them – he remained, in their eyes, a slave in all but name, which in a sense was true. On the other hand it is hard to see exactly how a Briton was effectively 'free'; the reality was that the Britons were really fighting for the freedom of their masters, which in the end meant their chiefs and ultimately the Druids.

The finer points of freedom were lost on the Iceni who not only found themselves subjected to a variety of insults, but also saw what remained of their ruling house humiliated in the worst way possible. The daughters of Prasutagus were raped, and Boudica was flogged, and the remainder of the population dealt with as if they were slaves. The Romans responsible seem to have acted in a foolishly haphazard and opportunistic fashion because there was no obstacle to the Iceni immediately resorting to armed conflict. The implication is that this was a leaderless cavalcade of brutal intimidation, conducted by men whose sole concern was self-gratification and the curious pleasures brought by humiliating others.

Is this plausible? Yes and no. It is entirely possible that individual Roman officials operated unilaterally in a manner that would inevitably lead to violence. From elsewhere in the Empire we know that corrupt governors could provoke appeals to the rule of law, and that taxes were raised from moneylenders who thereby acquired the right to enforce collection (at a profit) from those liable to pay. One of the other theories is that the recovery of burned einkorn grain in London from destruction levels dated to the Revolt indicates a poor harvest that year or the year before, forcing grain to be imported (einkorn apparently only grew further south), and therefore making it harder for tribal Britons to pay their tribute in kind. This is fantastically tenuous and a typical example of trying to get history out of archaeology by following one track, and ignoring other possibilities. The burnt einkorn might be a fact, but grain could be imported for a variety of reasons, including convenience and taste. Shipping grain to London via the Rhine or via the sea around Gaul might have been a good deal cheaper and easier than carting it down to London from inland Britain in a scarcely-developed province, and have nothing whatsoever to do with tribute payments and poor harvests. Importing food carried on long after the Boudican Revolt.

In any case, it is difficult to believe that corruption in eastern Britain was quite as wholesale as the stories of the Boudican Revolt suggest. The Romans were far from incompetent imperialists. On the contrary, they were on the whole extremely effective at delegating power to established locals and integrating communities into regional versions of Roman society. The Empire depended on compliance, and generally the improvement in standard of living, peace and security meant it was usually forthcoming, however begrudgingly. It is unlikely that Togidubnus would have remained loyal in the south had he and his people been subjected to continuous abuses. The Revolt turned out to be a catastrophe but it was distinctly limited in its take-up, with only the Iceni and Trinovantes implicated. Either way no one had the wit to imprison or otherwise restrain Boudica, which can only mean a failure of leadership or quite simply a freakish combination of circumstances and personalities that drifted out of control before anyone had realised what was happening.

Boudica turned out in every sense to be equal to the moment, but then perhaps that was how the story was written. As far as the Iceni were concerned, they had been presented with a simple choice: it was all or nothing, and therefore they had nothing to lose. There is no mention of Boudica's role as a leader at this point in Tacitus, but Dio places her firmly at the helm from the outset. Dio describes her as a tall woman, with a harsh voice, a mass of red hair, and dressed in a multi-coloured tunic with a mantle fixed with a brooch, and with a gold torque around her neck. Of course Dio, who wrote so much later, had never seen her, and nor could he have known anyone who had. Tacitus never provides anything so specific, which must mean that the description was one developed over time to present Boudica as an appropriately baroque and terrifying, but rational, obstacle to the Roman war machine. One might compare the treatment of legendary heroes, long after they lived, in cinema. Robin Hood is unlikely to have resembled Errol Flynn or Kevin Costner, both of whom appeared in films that reflected their own times more than the period or people they set out to portray. Had

Boudica been an insignificant nonentity, the story of her defeat would lose its exotic appeal and any value as an achievement. She is, in every characteristic, the opposite to the image of Roman leadership and this was an essential symmetry to the story, just as Fletcher Christian and William Bligh have always provided the similarly opposed forces in films of the famous mutiny on HMS *Bounty* in 1789, and have been suitably caricaturised in films of the episode as required.

Nevertheless, Boudica presented the Romans with a direct challenge to their own self-image. The reigns of Tiberius, Caligula, Nero, and to a lesser extent Claudius, had created a dilemma. The victorious growth of the Roman Empire was seen as a direct consequence of Roman virtues, the political and legal system, and the qualities of the Roman spirit enshrined in the ascetic personalities of Republican heroes like Cato the Elder. In other words, the Empire was a just and righteous reward for superior virtues. But the price seemed to have been a dizzying spiral into decadence and grotesque self-indulgence, where leadership was replaced with corruption, frantic sexual free-for-alls, and a rollercoaster of reckless spending and destruction of everything Rome was supposed to stand for. Caligula's reign had already demonstrated how bad things could get. Writing when he did, Tacitus had the benefit of hindsight and could look back across the first century to add the last four years of Nero's reign, and all of Domitian's, to the image of Roman moral decline. Dio had all this to ruminate on, and compound it with the horrifying events of the reigns of Commodus (180-92) and Caracalla (211-17).

Boudica was therefore presented to the Romans as an enemy, but one with many of the qualities Rome was losing. Dio composed a speech for Boudica – a routine device that allowed the writer to set up opposed camps as each side declaimed its point of view. Dio's Boudica bolstered her forces with the reminder that the Romans could not cope with physical hardship and depended on effete comforts like oil and wine, while engaging in homosexual relations with boys. This was unlike the

Britons who could live off anything and endure any amount of discomfort. Writing in the early third century, Dio perhaps had in mind the experience of Septimius Severus' forces on the Caledonian campaign of 208-11, who found themselves hopelessly outclassed and outwitted by the northern tribes whose tolerance of the frightful conditions in northern Britain left the Roman army bewildered, frightened and disoriented.

Dio also utilised Nero's ambivalent sexual identity to present a more subtle contrast. Dio had Boudica describe Nero as a woman, and thus appropriate to the Romans with all their decadent inadequacies. Nero was a man with all the weaknesses of a woman. Conversely, Dio's Boudica is a woman with all the strengths of a man. Like so many of Rome's rebels, Boudica forced the Romans to look in the mirror. Boudica became a literary mouthpiece for Rome's evolving crisis of leadership. She was presented as a worthy, albeit barbaric, opponent whose virtues included fighting for liberty at the head of a wholly committed population prepared to throw everything and anything into the struggle. The Romans could not help but admire that, and wonder where their own spirit had gone.

After appealing to the goddess Andraste for protection, the Iceni burst out of East Anglia to the delight of the Trinovantes. Not only content with pushing the Iceni into a corner, the Romans had also done a brilliant job of guaranteeing allies for the Iceni in their rebellion, though it must be stressed that this was limited. The Trinovantes had found their farms and homes confiscated purely for the benefit of the veterans at Colchester. This land, the *agri captivi*, could theoretically have eventually involved an area of more than 250 square kilometres (about 100 square miles) around the colony in an ongoing process of appropriation from the date the colony was instituted.

The imperial cult at Colchester was considered by Tacitus to have symbolised domination. His next sentence, *delectique sacerdotes specie religionis omnis fortunas effundebant* (*Annals* xiv.31), is usually translated to suggest wealthy Trinovantians, obliged to serve as priests, were forced to waste their wealth on the temple and its cult.

As so often, closer examination of the Latin shows it says less. The passage means literally, 'and the chosen priests were blowing fortunes on the pretence of religion'. It does not say they were 'bound' to do so, and nor does it say that the Trinovantian wealthy were the priests, though one could be forgiven for believing it did say both those things if one had only read two currently available translations. Actually, that it implies both is a very reasonable inference but that is not the same thing and there is more than one way of looking at the passage. Each interpretation constitutes an opinion, but in archaeology and ancient history opinions have a habit of turning into facts to make up for the limited supply of the latter.

For a start, it was normal for wealthy Romans to integrate official religious duties into their careers. They donated money to the cult and the city in order to beautify it, edify the citizens and enhance their reputations. Some of the priests are bound to have been colonists and traders. If so, they were only 'wasting' their fortunes in the sense that the town was about to be destroyed. Even if local people were obliged to join in, it is unlikely that everyone objected to taking part. Some of the local aristocrats are bound either to have hedged their bets, or sided with the Romans. This would not be so very surprising. Roman government depended on those prepared to work within the Roman system, and awarded them enhanced status, often at the expense of those who would not. Tiberius Claudius Togidubnus in the south is the classic example of just that. Yes, if wealthy Trinovantians had been signed up as priests of the cult it is very possible they were 'wasting' their fortunes, but *whether they thought so at the time* is altogether a different concept. They might very well have considered it an essential investment in their future status and not necessarily resented it at all. So, on the whole the cult's role in provoking the rebellion was more likely to have been just that it was there at all, rather than because its priests joined the Revolt.

There is no meaningful way of knowing how large the rebellion was, or what proportion of the regional population became involved. Some of the Trinovantes might have been directly exposed for long enough to the Romans to think better of bothering to rise up against them. Some might well have become integrated into, and dependent on, the new provincial economy. By the time of the final battle the Boudican forces were said to be around 230,000. But that was from Dio who wrote around 150 years later and we know that army figures from antiquity are usually meaningless in our terms. Only when units of known size, like Roman legions, are specified can we have anything approaching the correct figure. In any case, the numbers included dependants, and others who joined along the way. At this early point the numbers must have been very much less, while others watched to see which way the tide turned before deciding who to back.

The colonists retreated to the low hill that is Colchester and found themselves with nothing more than a half-built town to defend. The town itself had a senate-house, a theatre and a vast classical temple surrounded by houses, old barracks, and shops though it would be a mistake to confuse this with an elegant Mediterranean city. Colchester was probably more like a frontier town of the Old West, replete with pretentious establishments made out of wood and surrounded by ramshackle housing. It had little chance of acting as an armed compound. Some of the old legionary defences must have still been in evidence but more than a decade after they were abandoned, the ditches were half-choked with backfill, rubbish and undergrowth. The excavations that demon-strated the ditches had been backfilled also showed that the rubbish included human remains. Several skeletons have been recovered from here, some of which show signs of a violent death. This sort of evidence is very difficult to interpret because it is so tempting to link it directly to the history. But we know that the Roman army routinely displayed the heads of its victims so it is perfectly feasible that some of the remains had been originally posted along the early fortress' ramparts. As such they will have acted as a reminder of the sanctions facing anyone else prepared to resist the Roman army. But the Celtic tribes were equally happy to indulge in the same habits so there was nothing about this that made the Romans worse than anyone else. Either way, the revenge would be more than adequate.

An emergency message was sent to the procurator Decianus Catus. He was probably in London and sent a miserably inadequate 200 troops who now stood fast in the temple compound with the small Colchester garrison. In the meantime, news reached the *IX Hispana* legion somewhere in Cambridgeshire and Lincolnshire and its commander, Petillius Cerealis. Women and children were sent away, leaving Colchester to the men. They did nothing to reinforce their last stand. This was no Rorke's Drift, when in 1879 a tiny British force defended a hospital against thousands of Zulus in South Africa and won a clutch of Victoria Crosses in the process. The rebels destroyed the town in the first assault and in the second wiped out the defenders after a two-day siege. Only now did the proverbial cavalry arrive in the form of all or part of the *IX Hispana*. The rebels turned about and massacred the legionaries, while the legionary cavalry – a body of troops numbering no more than about 120, unless it means auxiliary cavalry attached to the legion – fled back to their base with Cerealis.

In fact not all of the *IX Hispana* can have been wiped out, as we shall see later. Cerealis could not possibly have risked his whole legion on a rebellion, both because of the stupidity of such a decision and because it is extremely unlikely the legion was all in one place. Nevertheless, at this stage, the loss of even a part of the legion was a terrifying disaster. While Colchester burned, a straggle of women, children, old men, animals and slaves staggered towards London in the full and complete knowledge that they could do nothing to defend themselves. Decianus Catus considered the situation, and took the chance to pack his bags and leave.

It cannot have taken more than a week for news to reach Suetonius Paullinus who had by then reduced Anglesey and its inhabitants to surrender. With admirable presence of mind he abandoned the mopping-up instantly and moved south-east. He is said to have moved 'through the enemy' to reach London. Perhaps just a generic reference to the Britons, it might also mean that the Revolt had already become characterised by a diffusion of its forces across south-eastern England. But Paullinus was probably on horseback with a small unit of cavalry. His infantry were coming up in the rear from north Wales, but slowly. As an aside, one of the legionary tribunes was a young Gnaeus Julius Agricola, probably serving with XX (which he was given command of a decade later).

Paullinus resolved to abandon London to its fate – it was, after all, unfortified and way beyond his resources to defend – and took the ruthless decision to move off only with those who could manage the retreat. Everyone else was left behind, and the same applied to Verulamium. Colchester, London and Verulamium are the only towns specified in the sources but Chelmsford appears to have suffered the same catastrophic level of burning found at the other three. The layer of destruction is unequivocal and is up to 60cm thick in these places. Filled with the burnt remains of wattle-and-daub buildings, pottery and even carbonised foodstuffs the burnt layers bear witness to catastrophic firestorms in each town. It goes without saying that isolated farmsteads and small villages will have been destroyed when and where they were found, but that these are never going to be as evident in the archaeological record. The house at Park Street, near Verulamium, is an exception. It was burned around this time, though destruction by fire of single buildings can never be reliably attributed to an historical incident.

Tacitus is fairly brief in his account of what went on in the towns, and only says that the work included killings, executions and burning. Dio was less restrained. His version is much more macabre, providing a more vicarious account of sadistic brutality on an epic scale. According to him, the noble women were hanged, followed by amputation of their breasts, which were then sewn to their mouths. Then they were skewered. This apparently took place while a kind of religious orgy went on in the name of the goddess Andate (perhaps a variant on Andraste). This kind of psycho-sexual humiliation and violence often forms part of third-hand accounts of wars from antiquity into modern times. But first-hand accounts of atrocities in, for example, the Vietnam War show that such things can and do happen in war, especially when there is a vast cultural gulf between perpetrators and victims. An Icenian coin of the mid-first century BC depicting a grim-faced female might even portray the goddess. However, the type has no lettering to verify the fact and it does not appear again.

None of the accounts specify a time of year. But Suetonius Paullinus can only realistically have moved into Anglesey in the summer. With the south-east in flames, another potential crisis loomed: the harvest. Everyone involved in the Revolt will have paid little heed to the year's crops. If the Revolt had been planned for a while, perhaps back in the spring, even sowing the fields might have been abandoned. The march of destruction will have wiped out a lot of what was planted, together with stores, as well as the infrastructure of warehouses, vehicles and roads. The Roman forces found themselves compromised by the severance of supplies and the prospect of hunger. Even so, this should not be exaggerated. During the Hundred Years' War it is known that settlements in France only a few miles from the path of armies could escape depredations and elevated food prices almost entirely.

The only logical route for Suetonius Paullinus to withdraw along was Watling Street, but this does not mean it is the only possibility. Watling Street leads into north Wales and this perhaps was the road along which the infantry were now advancing while he retreated from the flames to meet them. By now, Boudica's forces had supposedly reached a gaggle of 230,000. In theory, the rebels ought to have been confident about winning. But their real strength lay in a chaotic guerrilla campaign, which was almost impossible for an organised army to confront effectively. Unfortunately, this was where Boudica's leadership failed. Instead, she resolved to pursue the Roman army, obliging it to turn and face her. In a pitched battle numbers mean less than tactics and hardware. Boudica had little of either. She also led an army compromised by over-confidence, dependants, loot, and possessions. In liberating her people, she had also freed their mercurial lack of coordination and discipline.

Suetonius Paullinus, on the other hand, had an army of professional soldiers battle-hardened from a major campaign. He had around 8,000 legionaries, plus auxiliaries. The force could have amounted to 15,000, somewhat less than he had hoped thanks to the *II Augusta's* failure to respond to the call for help. Obviously this was tiny compared to the Britons, but the assessments of the Boudican forces are really no more than hearsay. The numbers of Romans, on the other hand, can be tied down with much more certainty. The battle speeches appear at this point in the accounts of the Revolt, and some of their content has already been discussed. Tacitus utilised the image of Boudica's soap-box to depict her with a mixture of misogyny and admiring disdain. She comes across as a kind of dominatrix who presented a direct challenge to Roman masculine power and sexuality – her victory would prove the destiny of a woman 'that men might live and be slaves'. The message was clear: to be defeated by Boudica would amount to symbolic castration.

The Romans turned to face the Boudican hordes. Paullinus chose a spot where his rear was defended by a wood, and ahead of him the Britons could only approach through a narrow gap. This compromised the advantage of numbers, and prevented an all-out frontal assault on the Romans. Instead the Britons had to pass through and form up on a plain below the Romans, where there was no cover. Paullinus divided his army into three solid blocks and waited. The Britons hurled themselves forward, and used up a dangerously large amount of their ammunition in a long-range flurry of missiles and spears. Curiously, at Gettysburg in 1863 the tide of the American Civil War turned in a similar way. It was the highpoint of the Confederacy, with the Army of Northern Virginia further north than it would ever be again and poised to march on Washington. The Confederates bombarded Union positions on higher ground, prior to and in preparation for what would be the celebrated catastrophe of Picket's Charge. They almost ran out of munitions in the process. Picket then charged across open country toward the barely-scratched Union positions on higher ground, for his exposed men to be systematically wiped out in a hail of bullets and shells. Around three-quarters failed to return. Gettysburg ultimately cost the South the Civil War, but the battle at the climax of the Revolt cost Boudica everything at a stroke. The Romans waited until the Britons had spent most of their energy, then advanced and broke straight through the rebels who found themselves unable to escape, not only because of the terrain, but also because their own baggage train was in the way.

Needless to say, Tacitus suggests the battle was little more than a turkey shoot with a ludicrously small number of Roman dead at 400 and an amazing 80,000 Britons wiped out. Neither is really believable, and only machine-gun fire on one side would really allow such a result. But even 400 Roman dead, and the same number wounded, shows there was significant resistance. Considering that the Britons were playing for the highest stakes imaginable, and also had the benefit of using chariots in the field, this ought to be expected. Dio's account is of a much more protracted struggle that lasted most of the day, and with many British casualties being those people waiting by the wagons.

This brings us now to the curious mystery of the end of Boudica. Her fate is not really very clear, surprising given the prominent role both historians give her in the preamble. Tacitus says she 'ended her life with poison'. Dio says that in the aftermath of the battle, when many of the Britons escaped and prepared to regroup, Boudica grew sick and died. Boudica's demise is so perfunctory and inconsequential that it scarcely seems credible that such a critical personality could wither away so fast unless, having served her literary purpose, she was written out as quickly as possible. It is interesting that the two accounts of her death are so radically different in their significance. Tacitus ought to have been the more accurate, since he wrote closer to the time, but suicide was also how Nero ended his life eight years later, and it was the way the disgraced camp prefect of *II Augusta* escaped punishment. Given her personality, as described or created by the Roman historians, it is scarcely credible that she would end her life in so ignominious a fashion. So, it is quite possible that when he came to write the *Annals* (published around 116) suicide suited his dramatic purpose. In the *Agricola*, which he wrote nearly twenty years before the *Annals*, Tacitus attributed the revolt's demise to *socordiam*, 'indolence'

(31.4), and made no mention of Boudica's end. On the other hand, Dio's account of her withering away and dying from an illness sounds more like a convenient way of removing her. Surely, if she really had committed suicide, Dio would have known about it?

We really need to ask whether Boudica's real role in the whole Revolt was ever really very significant at all, and just possibly whether she actually existed. Even if she had existed, there might have been little known about her apart from the name. Her treatment works as a ritual literary device, which explains its prominence in the story. If the rape and flogging really happened, their significance was perhaps more symbolic than anything else. The truth is that Boudica may only have been one among many leaders of the Revolt, but whose personal image and experience at the hands of the Romans made her a perfect figure to hang the story of the rising around. It is even an extreme possibility that Boudica is a fabrication, at least in the form recorded. At no point does she seem to have been seen or spoken to by any recorded individual Roman. Of course this could simply be a failure of the records, but it means to the Romans she was as much a symbolic image as she is to us. However, Dio indicates that it was her death that dealt the fatal blow to the Revolt, and implies that had she not died then there was a real chance that it could have carried on. If that is true, the battle was really much harder and less conclusive than Tacitus claims.

In the aftermath there were winners and losers. Obviously, the Britons lost hand over fist, though doubtless those like Togidubnus who remained loyal looked even better than they had before. Roman loser number one was Poenius Postumus, *praefectus castrorum* (camp prefect) of *II Augusta*. When news reached him that his failure to mobilise the legion had cost his men a chance to share in the glory of victory he fell on his sword. The *II Augusta* remained plain old *II Augusta* till the end of its days. Conversely, this may have been the time that the *XIV Gemina* became the *XIV Gemina Martia Victrix* and the *XX* added *Valeria Victrix* to its name. The *IX Hispana* was reinforced when two thousand legionaries were sent across from Germany, thus demonstrating that not all the legion had been wiped out. Eight auxiliary infantry cohorts and a thousand cavalry came too.

Suetonius Paullinus both won and lost. In one sense he was a hero, and certainly Tacitus admired him. In another, his judgement was called into question in letting the Revolt break out at all. For the moment he kept the army mobilised to mop up the aftermath, but Suetonius had already been the victim of a whispering campaign. The new procurator, Gaius Julius Classicianus, was a Gaul by origin and seems to have registered quickly that settling the province was being compromised by Suetonius' interest in pursuing private feuds at the province's expense. Quite what these feuds were, we have no idea. It might mean feuds with tribal leaders, or it might mean infighting amongst the Roman leadership. Classicianus put it about in writing that the war was going to carry on until Suetonius was removed. No doubt Classicianus had his own agenda, and when the imperial freedman Polyclitus was sent to find out the truth, it seems Suetonius was partly vindicated, though it is clear his harshness had compromised the path to reconciliation. Mud sticks and when a few ships were lost, the pretext was found for relieving him of his command. In came Petronius Turpilianus to take over, and from thereon the Revolt was to all intents and purposes over.

Since we have no British perspective on the Revolt we can only wonder whether Boudica and her followers became the subject of folk myth and hero worship in Britain. If they did, they apparently did nothing to stimulate any imitators in the years to come. Boudica never became a William Wallace or Joan of Arc. Unlike Caratacus, she had no impact on the folklore of Britain until modern times. Andate, and Andraste, are never heard of again. The substantial Romano-British epigraphic record mentions many dozens of different gods, but not these two. If Boudica achieved anything it was to present the bulk of the population with a stark choice: either they opted for the Roman way, or they opted for chaos. In this sense, Boudica did the Romans an enormous favour by showing everyone that all she had to offer was destruction, mayhem, death and ruin. She had not intended to offer them that, but that was how it turned out. Hitler, after all, promised the Germans the world but delivered them into a whirlwind. Caratacus, it ought to be remembered, had to retreat to a part of Britain where Roman living was a meaningless concept. Boudica fought across territory where plenty of people had had a chance to make a more informed judgement.

The proof is in the pudding. There was no tribal rebellion of any kind in southern Britain thereafter and the physical evidence everywhere is that the Roman way was widely accepted rather than imposed. It is facile to believe that the disappearance of revolt after 61 was exclusively due to Roman oppression. The Romans were good at oppressing people, but not that good. Judaea, for instance, remained a hotbed of discontent, rising in 66, and again in another great rebellion under Hadrian. There is no evidence of sustained military occupation in Iceni territory, and had rebellion continued to simmer we can be sure that East Anglia might have remained home to a legion, or at least a handful of permanent auxiliary forts, as the north and west were. The unavoidable fact is that either the rebellious Iceni and their allies had given up, and sunk into disconsolate apathy, or that some of them had never been very committed in the first place and actually preferred a world in which tribal wars had been consigned to history. The destroyed towns were rebuilt, and in the short term grew even more prosperous. In any case, a man or woman's loyalty is often first to the homestead, crops and livestock. During the American Civil War even the dedicated and fanatically loyal Confederate army was constantly compromised by bouts of desertion so that men could return home to sow crops, bring in the harvest and mend roofs.

Even in the Iceni heartlands a civitas capital was built at *Venta Icenorum*. But it never grew beyond a modest size and bears all the hallmarks of a backwater. Like other settlements in the region it had low levels of imported Roman goods in the decades after the Rebellion. Perhaps that was also Boudica's legacy: condemning her people to being generations of second-class members of the Roman world. The site at Gallow's Hill, Thetford, was systematically dismantled. It was never allowed to rot away in peace. Ramparts were shovelled back into ditches. Timbers were pulled out of their holes, indicated by the absence of any rotten wood in the postholes, and big posts pulled out by digging bigger holes around them. Fragments of Roman armour suggest soldiers were present, but whether they just stood around forcing the Iceni to do the demolition work for them, or set to themselves is impossible to say. In a remarkable piece of irony, the late fourth- or early fifth-century Thetford Treasure was found just yards away in 1979. Its most striking feature was the series of references on the silver spoons to an ancient Roman woodland god called Faunus. Whoever the Faunus sect worshippers were, they looked back to a Latin Roman tradition for their religious revival rather than the ancient Iceni gods of the region.

Had Boudica won, would it have been different? In the long run, probably not. Just like the slaves in the revolt of Spartacus in Italy well over a century before, it was easy for the Boudican rebels to see what they hated but it was much harder for them to see beyond that. Once they had smashed everything up, there was nothing left to do except wonder what they were going to eat next and where they could go. This was no War of Independence on the American model, or the English Civil War. Boudica had no bill of rights, no alternative constitution, and no agenda of reform. Of course it was scarcely an age of political idealism – that lay seventeen centuries ahead – but in the end few rebellions succeed in creating a genuine alternative to the system they seek to annihilate. In truth, the beguiling glamour of revolt creeps away into the shadows once stomachs start to rumble, and as the nights draw in when winter looms.

4

Damned in a Fair Wife

VENUTIUS

⟫◆⟪

Venutius was the husband of Cartimandua, queen of the Brigantes. Unlike the tribes of southern Britain, the Brigantes never produced any coinage – at least not any that we know about. That means that we have absolutely no verification of the names, personalities, or lineages that ruled the Brigantes apart from what the Roman historians tell us. It's an unavoidable handicap, but the volatile relationships and personalities at the heart of the Brigantes provided all the ingredients of a political crisis, with a grand passion and a husband scorned. It fascinated the Roman historians, and thus the story survives.

⟫◆⟪

The Brigantes dominated what we now call northern England, meaning really Yorkshire, Lancashire and beyond. Appropriately the name suggests an upland folk since *Brig* seems to have meant a high place in ancient British. In modern Welsh the word means 'top', and the similar Welsh word *bryn* means 'hill'. In the years to come, the region would be controlled from the legionary fortress at York. From here, the Roman military high command administered those parts of northern Britain under Roman control and was only able to do so through a network of roads and forts that controlled valleys, passes and river crossings throughout the challenging terrain. Even today the Stainmore Pass is often closed in winter. For most of Roman Britain's existence control extended across the territory up to and around Hadrian's Wall. At other times, Roman power extended into Scotland. But in the middle of the first century AD, northern England was only just beginning to drift into Roman consciousness.

The Brigantes first became a cause for concern in 47-8 when Ostorius Scapula took up his post as governor, replacing Aulus Plautius. He had put down a localised revolt amongst the Iceni with some difficulty, and then proceeded to take the campaign further west into Wales. At this point, the Brigantes dissolved into *discordiae* (*Annals* xii.32). There is no suggestion, either from the history or the archaeology, that Brigantian territory had been subjected to any Roman military intervention or conquest. At any rate the Romans felt able to ignore them for the moment. But the tribal territory was large and sprawling and it is inconceivable that any one ruler or faction was able to guarantee compliance. The *discordiae* must then mean some sort of breakdown amongst the tribal aristocrats. Considering future events, this clearly involved pro- and anti-Roman factions. It is possible that the Romans had attempted to sign up a Brigantian cabal, posing as representatives of the whole tribe, as a client kingdom and that rival factions took exception to this.

Ostorius Scapula was obliged to abandon his Welsh campaign and return to deal with the Brigantes, though Tacitus makes this look as if he was being thoroughly professional about the whole thing. Scapula was resolved to shelve new conquests until the previous ones were secured. One might ask why he had not made sure of that before he set off west. The solution to the Brigantian problem was to organise 'the execution of a few' that had taken up arms, and a pardon for the rest. Wiping out the faction this way must have presented the Brigantes with a very clear message: comply or die.

The suppression of Brigantian discord seems to have benefited Cartimandua. At least, she was in power around three years later but whether she was the one who called in Roman support, or was put into power by them as part of the solution we have no idea. We have already met Cartimandua. She was the Brigantian ruler who handed over the fleeing Caratacus to the forces of the governor Ostorius Scapula in the year 51. The event is doubly significant. Tacitus mentions this fact in retrospect, while explaining the background to the Brigantian civil war (*Annals* xii.40). He says that Cartimandua was specifically a queen, *regina*, a status that he never ascribes to Boudica.

Tacitus says that the Britons made no distinction between their rulers on the grounds of sex (*Agricola* 16). The most conspicuous Roman usage of the term *rex* or *regina* is when the individual, like Prasutagus, Togidubnus or Cartimandua, was a Roman supporter. It seems more likely to be omitted when the person concerned is an opponent. As we shall see, Venutius is never any more than Cartimandua's consort, and at the battle of *Mons Graupius* in 84 when Agricola defeated the remote tribes of Caledonia the leader of his opponents is Calgacus, described as just the most prominent of *plures duces* 'many chiefs' (*Agricola* 28.4). So, calling Cartimandua a queen is probably Tacitus' way of stating the Roman-approved legitimacy of her power. She only technically existed as a monarch when Rome acknowledged it.

The handing over of Caratacus enhanced Cartimandua's status in Roman eyes, since it provided Claudius with a thoroughly satisfactory climax to his victory parade in Rome. This is said to have made her wealthier. If so, the wealth was probably rather modest. Unlike the Iceni area, where a number of coin hoards leading up to the date of the Boudican Revolt have been found, there is no such phenomenon in Brigantian territory. In fact the area is conspicuous for a virtual lack of hoards terminating under Claudius and Nero, which suggests either a lack of Roman cash injections, loans or bribes, or Roman authorities – or both. Only a generation later under Vespasian (69-79), when the Roman army occupied the region, do hoards appear. The closest we get is with the ill-recorded Halifax hoard of 1828, which ended with coins of Caligula. To be fair, imperial silver and gold of the early principate was so erratically struck that any hoard buried before 64, when Nero began a great increase in coin production, is likely to be dominated by Republican coins. But in this region only the Pudsey hoard of 1775 falls into that category.

This is an interesting perspective on Brigantian royal self-aggrandisement. In other areas it looks as if Roman bullion was being supplied as subsidies, for it to be melted down and reissued as tribal coinage, or for it to be hoarded. Some of the Iceni hoards contain a mixture of both tribal and Roman coinage. It seems that in Brigantian territory either Roman subsidies were not paid, or if they were then Cartimandua pocketed them. Perhaps that is to read too much into far too little, but there is no shortage of hoards in the region from the late first century onwards, so we could very reasonably assume that more like the Pudsey hoard might have been found by now. In the last few years East Anglia has continued to yield more hoards from before the Boudican Revolt. The Brigantian region has produced none like these, but several more from later in the first century and afterwards, like the Skellow (S. Yorks) hoard ending in 81. In spite of this conspicuous divergence from the aristocratic habits of the southern tribes, the Brigantian high command was still able to construct a vast settlement at Stanwick in North Yorkshire, and stock it with the kind of imported material Cunobelinus and the others had been enjoying back in the 30s and before.

The archaeology of the area certainly exhibits a distinct hierarchy in death in a long tradition stretching back across the first millennium BC, especially in East Yorkshire. A small number of the dead were accorded special treatment in the form of 'warrior' burials, with the earliest including the remains of chariots. One of the best-known, and most recent, discoveries is the Wetwang chariot burial, deposited some time between 400 and 200 BC about 20 miles east of where York was later established. Given the role played by Cartimandua in the mid-first century AD, it is interesting that the body was identified as that of a middle-aged woman. She was accompanied by a dismantled chariot, which survived mainly in the form of the iron fittings like the iron tyres, the horse bits and terret ring. At another, found at Garton Station nearby, it was possible to 'cast' the wheels from traces in the ground.

By 51 then Cartimandua was firmly established as a sort of northern female Togidubnus – a loyal client monarch who had demonstrated that she would betray a British leader in support of Roman interests. This compliance with the divide-and-rule policy operated by the Romans was marvellously convenient, and it proved the undoing of the Britons. We know that the Brigantes had already demonstrated their ability to fragment, and we also know that at some point before this Tacitus had had cause to mention Venutius. We do not know why, or what the context was because that part of the *Annals* is lost; all we have is Tacitus telling us that he had already mentioned his Brigantian lineage.

Unfortunately, at this point the chronology of the Brigantian saga becomes a tad more complicated. Ostorius Scapula had died in post as governor of Britain. He was replaced in 52 by Aulus Didius Gallus, who remained until the year 57. During the interregnum the Silurian tribes took the opportunity to return to war and defeated a legion. From later dispositions we can take it this was either *II Augusta* or the *XX*. The spin put on the significance of the events is not relevant to our story here, but Tacitus makes it clear that it was Venutius of the Brigantes who was now the most significant practitioner of war in Britain.

Tacitus says that Venutius, Cartimandua's husband – but interestingly he is never specified as a chief or king – had 'long been loyal', and had received Roman military support. From this we can infer that he was involved in the handover of Caratacus, and had perhaps also been threatened by the breakaway Brigantian faction back in 47. Of course, another way of looking at this is that by helping to get Caratacus out of the way Venutius had the opportunity to become more important and supplant him as the most prominent British chieftain.

Venutius and Cartimandua's union began to dissolve into irreconcilable differences. They divorced, the tribe split into factions and a war broke out. This was scarcely in Roman interests, since a client kingdom was only of any use if it was stable and secure. Instead, Venutius' men invaded Cartimandua's territory spurred on, says Tacitus, by the fear of being done down by a woman (*Annals* xii.40). This is an interesting comment, since the general picture in Celtic society is of a much more resilient sense of equality amongst men and women and a tradition of accepting women as military leaders. But the problem for us is that Tacitus inserts this reference into the part of the *Annals*, his history of the period 14-68, where he is talking about the events of 52-7 and it makes it sound as if this was when the Brigantian ruling house started to fall apart. However, he also specifies that it is out of context, which explains why the same process appears later in his account of the period 68-9, in his *Histories*, which covered imperial history from 68-96. It is almost certainly the case that the version in the *Annals* is displaced, and that Tacitus is referring to the same episode and not two different occasions.

In any case Tacitus is more expansive in the *Histories*, but now the tale of Cartimandua and Venutius is firmly slotted into the events of the year 69 (*Histories* iii.45). This makes more sense because he talks about Cartimandua gradually developing a sense of self-importance and grandiosity that went hand-in-hand with developing a loathing for Venutius. She then made a disastrous error of judgement. She embarked on an affair with Vellocatus, *armigerum* (armour-bearer) to Venutius. One published view of their names is that Cartimandua means 'sleek filly', Vellocatus means 'fighter of the good fight', and that Venutius' meaning is unknown though no explanation of the derivation is offered (Birley 1979, 27). But if Vellocatus is based on Latin words, it could be taken to mean either the 'sly shaved one'; or the 'clear-sighted fighter', if *Vello* is actually from *Bello* (a Latin reader would read *Bello* as *Vello*). In other words, nobody really knows what the names mean.

In every sense, embarking on an affair was an act of reckless misjudgement. It took no account of Venutius' popularity and exposed Cartimandua to the wrath not only of her husband but all his many supporters. To begin with, the problem was an internal

Brigantian one, but it bore all the hallmarks of a Borgia-esque Italian Renaissance feud as a family dissolved into infighting. Cartimandua captured Venutius' brother and relatives but this only upped the ante.

Cartimandua immediately found her kingdom in meltdown as Venutius raised support from within and without the tribe. The broader historical perspective also makes 69 a much more credible time for the fracas than the 50s. Since the death of Nero in 68 the Roman Empire had been convulsed in a catastrophic Civil War as a series of emperors fought it out. By 69 Vespasian had emerged as the victor but along the way Roman government had been compromised. Also, one of Britain's legions, the *XIV Gemina*, had been withdrawn to eastern Europe and was an active participant, while vexillations from the other three were also involved. So, Britain's garrison was significantly denuded, perhaps by as much as a third. If Venutius was the master of war Tacitus says he was, then he knew now was the time to seize the day.

Cartimandua's pro-Roman affiliations, and the implications that it was she and not Venutius who was the sponsored Roman client, polarised Brigantian loyalties. Venutius had become a rebel against Rome in spite of his earlier position. Cartimandua was plucked out of the deteriorating fiasco by Roman forces by the governor Marcus Vettius Bolanus, installed by Vitellius, briefly emperor during the Civil War of 68-9. The soldiers used were *cohortes alaeque*, '[auxiliary] infantry and cavalry', probably because they were closest to the action. We don't know the exact date, but given the absence of legionary vexillations on the continent it is unlikely there was much choice. It would certainly not have done to risk a legion, or part of one, in an unpredictable theatre.

The Roman army removed Cartimandua but this was no unopposed surgical extraction, executed in the dead of night by commandos dropped from metaphorical helicopters. They had to fight Venutius and his forces several times before succeeding. Apparently, the son of Vettius Bolanus fought in a British war around this time, recorded in a poem by Statius. It is always difficult to take this sort of thing too literally. The verses say forts were built, and a breastplate seized from an unnamed British king, but such references are as likely to have been routine poetic licence. Venutius was left in sole command of the Brigantes. Rome's buffer state had gone and Cartimandua disappears from the record. We have absolutely no idea what happened to her.

Venutius had only a short time to enjoy his new-found position as ruler of the Brigantes. In 71 Quintus Petillius Cerealis arrived in Britain, sent by Vespasian (to whom he was related), to take over from Vettius Bolanus. It consolidated the change of regime and opened a new chapter in the history of Roman Britain. Cartimandua was the last Romano-British client monarch, and Venutius had no chance of succeeding her in that role. He had sealed his own fate. Vespasian and Cerealis had already seen what a rebellious tribal chieftain could do. In 61 Cerealis was commander of *IX Hispana* when it was humiliated in the Boudican Revolt. In 71 he was fresh from leading the campaign against the revolt of Civilis in Germany. Civilis was a Batavian chieftain who had served with success in the Roman auxiliary forces. Falsely accused of treason, Civilis, like Venutius, capitalised on the Civil War of 68-9. Initially posing as a supporter of Vespasian, he mobilised German tribes to attack Roman units loyal to Vitellius before finally declaring himself a rebel against Rome. Cerealis defeated Civilis at the Battle of Vetera. He probably brought *II Adiutrix Pia Fidelis* with him, restoring Britain's legionary contingent to four after the departure of *XIV Gemina* in 70. The new legion appears at Lincoln, apparently replacing *IX Hispana*, which seems to have been moved forward to found York.

During the next three years Cerealis prosecuted a sustained campaign into Brigantian territory, presumably managed from York and Lincoln. The implication is that the work covered much of northern Britain, and certainly the discovery of marching camps across the Pennines, and military buildings at Carlisle made of timber felled in the early 70s support that. It is very unlikely that the campaign ever climaxed in a single decisive confrontation. Tacitus describes a series of battles, 'some of them bloody', which left most of Brigantia under Roman control (*Agricola* 17).

Venutius also disappears from the record, but by 74 most of Brigantian territory had been declared part of the Roman province. It would remain permanently a militarised zone until the end of Roman Britain's days, but in the short-term Cerealis had laid the foundations for the Agricolan campaigns of 78-84 that took Rome right into Scotland. Over the next thirty years a network of forts and roads, which still partly define northern England today, were established.

Note

In the *Agricola* Tacitus mentions the female leader of the Brigantes as burning a colony and storming a fort, in the speech he ascribes to Calgacus. This is evidently a mistake for Trinovantes (most likely) or the Iceni, as he obviously means Boudica and not Cartimandua (*Agricola* 31.4). The error can be attributed either to Tacitus himself, or the copyists through whom his work has come down to us.

5

Band of Brothers
XIV GEMINA MARTIA VICTRIX

In the year 70 the general Petillius Cerealis called the *XIV Gemina* legion 'the conquerors of Britain' during the campaign in Germany against Civilis (*Histories* v.16). Till the end of its days the legion had the name *XIV Gemina Martia Victrix*, which means 'the *XIV* made from two legions, the warlike and victorious', though its members did not always brag about it. The legion had one of the shortest 'permanent' sojourns in Britain, though vexillations of units like *VIII Augusta* and *XXII Primigenia* made far briefer forays. In spite of its triumph on the field against Boudica, the legion also made a nearly disastrous decision to back the wrong man less than a decade later when civil war broke out in 68.

The *XIV Gemina* is first testified in Britain in accounts of the Boudican Revolt. It formed the backbone of the army led by the governor Gaius Suetonius Paullinus in north-west Wales in 60, and stood fast against the chaotic final charge in the last battle of the

Boudican Revolt. It had little choice. The Boudican hordes lay between it and the south-east and an escape to the continent if need be. Tacitus explicitly says that the legion was there – an important point because the legion's activities in the years beforehand have to be inferred from this reference. It almost certainly formed part of the invasion force in 43, but we cannot be absolutely certain. It could actually have been sent in at any point between 43 and 60. It could also have been sent over in instalments, in the form of vexillations. That does not affect the point that the legion had invested a great deal of its prestige in the conquest of Britain by 68.

Before it came to Britain the *XIV Gemina* was at Mainz, *Moguntiacum*. We have no news of what it did between arriving in Britain and the campaign against Anglesey. Conversely, we can assume it was sent north-west across the Midlands and into the Welsh marches to a site near where Shrewsbury is now. It is something of an archaeological tradition to track the paths of legions along main roads toward the legionary fortresses where they are testified. This is a dubious pastime since it creates the impression of rigid linear advance by a legionary column. For the *XIV Gemina* this must have meant passing via Mancetter, Kinvaston, Wall and Red Hill to reach Wroxeter, a route probably established in part during the campaign against Caratacus under the governor Ostorius Scapula (47-51). But these days no one thinks any more in terms of the progression of a legion from Base A to Base B. The reality was a constant stream of comings and goings, the formation of vexillations, and dispersal of vexillations and individuals to different campaigns and different duties every year. It is impossible to reconstruct these movements, so all we can do is appreciate that the presence of a legionary's tombstone tells us nothing more for certain than that this was where he was buried. It does not mean the whole legion was with him when he expired and even if it was, that legion could have been a hundred miles away a week later.

Nevertheless, it only takes a casual glance at the map of Roman forts and roads in Britain to see that Wroxeter emerged as a pivotal site soon after the middle of the first century, with construction probably beginning during the governorship of Aulus Didius Gallus (52–7). The site was a hub for traffic from the east and south and from here roads radiated north, west, and south-west, and controlled the crossing of the Severn. A few miles to the east the old Iron Age hillfort of The Wrekin could now be supervised. At the same time native social and economic activity was diverted to the Roman military market at the new fortress. It was a familiar enough process and took place at numerous locations throughout Britain.

Wroxeter would later become the town called *Viroconium Cornoviorum*, a name of uncertain meaning but it was evidently the cantonal capital 'of the Cornovii', the tribe of the region. Two tombstones of legionaries from *XIV Gemina* seem to show that the legion had some sort of presence; strictly speaking though they could very easily have been there with a vexillation or even in detached individual capacities. There is no inscription of the legion acting as a whole. We do have the tombstone of Titus Flaminius, from Faventia, who was 45 when he died at Wroxeter after twenty-two years' service. This could easily mean he had personally witnessed most of the early conquest of Britain. Marcus Petronius, from Vicetia, lasted eighteen years in the army before dying at the age of 38. Although both men served in the *XIV Gemina* this is not the only unit testified at Wroxeter. Other stones name a soldier of the *XX* on the governor's staff, and a trooper from an auxiliary cohort of Thracians. Wroxeter's fortress will have accommodated troops as required, in an unending series of comings-and-goings.

Neither of the Wroxeter tombstones is dated, and neither carries the titles *Martia Victrix*. It isn't the demonstrable rule that the stones must pre-date the Boudican Revolt because there are plenty of examples of inscriptions of the *XIV Gemina* from the continent of a later date that lack the titles, and plenty that have them. But there are no inscriptions of the legion from anywhere else in Britain apart from the late second-century (or later) tombstone of a man set up by his heir, a veteran of *XIV*. Consequently, it is impossible to avoid the conclusion that most of the legion at least was in the area when the Anglesey campaign was begun, and thus formed the core of the legionary component. Nevertheless, it must be the case that many members of the legion were dispersed across Wales and beyond, with some centurions detached to civilian administration and taxation duties, and the command of auxiliary units, while individual soldiers were sent off here and there on a wide range of work that included serving on the governor's staff.

The *XIV Gemina* legion made its name under Nero, thanks to the fact that Suetonius Paullinus took it to Anglesey as the centre-piece of his campaign against the Druids. This happy chance gave the men of *XIV Gemina* a front-row seat to history in the suppression of the Boudican Revolt (see chapter 3), and made it one of the most celebrated legions in the Empire. Unfortunately, despite the historical record of the legion we have no names of any of its officers or commanders, but a legitimate speculation is that Paullinus had once commanded it, or served in it as a tribune. Later Agricola would honour his old legion, the *XX*, in a similar way. Nero subsequently declared the men of *XIV* his *potissimos*, 'most important' (*Histories* ii.11), which only served to enhance their glory and encouraged the legion to consider itself a mark above the rest. In a sense, the *XIV Gemina* was a cut above most other legions, but circumstances soon led it to gamble everything.

The *XIV* left Britain for the continent within a few years of the Revolt because Nero had recalled them at some point during the 60s, so great was their reputation (*Histories* ii.66). In 66 a tribune of the legion called Marcus Vettius Valens set up a dedication at Rimini, and recorded that he had been decorated in a British war, apparently confirming the fact that the legion had been moved. He gave the full titles, Gemina Martia Victrix, proving that it had been awarded by this early date but of course it was still Nero's reign and therefore nothing to be ashamed of.

By 68, just seven or eight years after the suppression of the Boudican Revolt, Nero's dizzying decline into decadence had brought the final act in his life's performance to an end. The narcissistic, sadistic and perverted aesthete killed himself as his power crumbled around him and challengers began to march on Rome. One of the first up was Servius Sulpicius Galba, then over seventy years old, and governor of the province of *Hispania Tarraconensis*. In March 68, Vindex, governor of *Gallia Lugdunensis*, led a revolt against Nero. Tacitus mentions that Nero had detachments of troops gathered from Germany, Illyricum and also Britain, for another campaign but sent them against Vindex (*Histories* i.6). *XIV* may have been part of this, but vexillations of the other British legions could have been involved too. Vindex was soon killed by Lucius Verginius Rufus, governor of *Germania Superior*, but Galba had already thrown in his lot with the Vindex revolt. When Nero killed himself, Galba seized the day and by the summer of 68 he was emperor in Rome.

Once in the hot seat Galba earned instant popular loathing for trying to institute reforms, for failing to pay the Praetorian Guard the cash hand-out promised, and for his own greed. The pace of power politics started to run out of control when he passed over his own chief supporter, Otho (then governor of *Lusitania*, part of Spain), as successor. Otho took advantage of the Praetorians' disaffection and used their support to topple Galba in January 69. Otho, it seems, enjoyed the support of the *XIV* which, like so many of the legions, were now starting to takes sides in Rome's near-catastrophic Civil War. On the Rhine, the legions of the German frontier had decided to support Vitellius, a man who Galba had made governor of *Germania Inferior*. The odd exception was Britain, where the three legions that remained after *XIV's* departure (*II, IX* and *XX*) found their enemies amongst the Britons rather than other parts of the Roman world. The barrier of the sea also inhibited any impulsive moves, and limited news from the continent.

Not only did the legion become embroiled in the fighting that nearly destroyed the Roman Empire before its first century of existence was up, but it also fell out with its Batavian auxiliaries who too decided to back Vitellius. The legion marched in an army headed by Annius Gallus for Otho. Otho's army did little to cover itself with glory. They looted as they went, destroying farms and sacking the town of *Albintimilium* (Ventimaglia). The climax, for the

XIV, came at Bedriacum in April 69 when Vitellius defeated Otho. Not that this seems unduly to have bothered the *XIV*, whose soldiers simply bragged that only a few veterans of the legion had been defeated and that the rest of them had not even been there at all. Evidently, no one in *XIV Gemina Martia Victrix*, heroes of the Boudican Revolt campaign, was going to admit to being defeated on the battlefield.

Vitellius punished the legion by sending it back to Britain away from centre-stage, and humiliating it by ordering the legionaries to march alongside its Batavian auxiliaries. This was a crass decision that nearly led to another battle. The Batavians and the legionaries hated each other so much, only the support of two Praetorian cohorts forced the Batavians to step down. The two units were separated once more and the *XIV Gemina* was despatched back to Britain on its own, though its men toyed with the idea of sacking *Vienna* (Vienne) in Gaul en route. It was a paradox that some of the soldiers who had wrought revenge on Boudica for destroying three Roman cities in Britain could even think about burning a Roman city to the ground.

The Civil War had a while to run yet. Vitellius was doomed too, since throughout this time Titus Flavius Vespasianus, former commander of *II Augusta*, had been leading his own campaign. A popular soldier of great acclaim, Vespasian had been sent by Nero in 66 to suppress the Jewish Revolt in Judaea. His supporters galvanised those opposed to Vitellius, and capitalised on the disaffected troops defeated at Bedriacum. Letters were sent to several legions, including the *XIV* then in Britain, inviting them to support Vespasian's march on Italy.

Was the *XIV* legion really a rebel against Rome? After all, the *XX* caused trouble in the aftermath of the Civil War and hesitated before accepting Vespasian as emperor. But of all the legions at any time in Britain, *XIV* was the only one ever to play an active part in the power politics of the rest of the Empire. Its role in the Civil War was not decisive, but it played an important part in contributing to a series of chaotic and destructive campaigns that almost wrecked the Roman Empire. In the end, Vespasian restored order and his reign marked the beginning of a long period of relative stability. For the legion there was one final gesture in the disruption. In 70 Vespasian pulled the *XIV* out of Britain to take part in the campaign against the Revolt of Civilis in Germany. It never went back, but for the rest of its history that time in Britain was its climax, and that role in the Civil War its most notorious. Curiously though the battle honours were not always remembered. Sometime between 222 and 235 a dedication in Italy recorded the legion as *XIV Gemina*, but omitted Martia Victrix. Perhaps a title won under Nero was not necessarily something to celebrate.

Vespasian was no fool. He could see the *XIV* was a dangerous legion with ideas above its station. In Britain, with three other legions available, there was the possibility that the province could act as the power base for another challenger. With the *XIV Gemina* removed, in its place arrived the recently formed *II Adiutrix Pia Fidelis*. With different loyalties, and a reputation to win, it owed more to Vespasian. Its time in Britain would be short too, and by the second century Britain was home permanently to just three legions though even that, as it turned out, was no guarantee that the garrison of this volatile province had been neutralised.

6

The Fog and Filthy Air
THE NORTHERN TRIBES

Some time in the second century a legionary legate called Lucius Junius Victorinus commemorated a sortie beyond Hadrian's Wall on an altar. He said he had been to a place called *trans Vallum*, literally 'across the frontier', where his achievements had been 'successful'. Passing 'across the frontier' to Victorinus and all his soldiers meant travelling into the hinterland of the Roman Empire. Technically, at least so far as the Romans were concerned, this was also part of the emperor's domain even if in every practical sense northern Britain had a distinctly variable experience of Roman power. Various tribal groups, and other references, pop up in our sources across the centuries. Many were probably ethnically the same, and not surprisingly some of the names are really just generic or cryptic references to amalgams of peoples, such as the 'Maeatae' between Hadrian's Wall and the Antonine Wall, and the 'Dicaledones' to the north. Ptolemy for example names the Selgovae and locates them north of the Brigantes, but south of the Damnonii, and east of the Novantae. Beyond the Novantae, along the eastern coast of the southern uplands of Scotland were the Votadinii. Whatever the reality of these groups the Roman experience of them was certainly similar. They presented the Romans with an intractable problem: an unorganised enemy that had no collective interest in becoming part of the Roman world.

Over a period of 250 years at least three major campaigns took the Romans into what we call Scotland, but none resulted in permanent occupation. In this remote territory the Romans were dealing with peoples who maintained a tradition across generations for resisting conquest. In every sense the two sides were poles apart. The classical world was meaningless to the tribes, and the Romans were equally bewildered by their inability to bring these impetuous and fickle warriors to heel. Both fought totally different sorts of war, so even a proper battle was almost impossible. Roman troops were constantly faced with all the erratic fluidity of disparate bands of tribesmen that disappeared into the mist and marshes they had sprung from. To begin with an uneasy stalemate formed on the northern frontier. In the last century of Roman rule, the deep north became a source of incursion and invasion as the garrisons of the northern forts were decimated by the ambitions of usurpers and adventurers.

Cartimandua's Brigantian domain was the remotest British tribal kingdom that the Romans were able to integrate permanently into their system of frontier sidekicks, though its fragmented political state meant it proved unacceptably volatile. Beyond her domain Britain was all that the Mediterranean civilisations considered the end of the world. Northern Britain was a land surrounded by dangerous seas and where savage and unpredictable weather ravaged a mountainous and bleak landscape subject to relentless long winter nights.

It was not until the governorship of Gnaeus Julius Agricola (c.77/8-83/4) that the Romans first really encountered the people of the far north. It's unlikely that Agricola ever imagined that more than 200 years later Roman military campaigns in this region would still be undertaken. In fact early in his governorship Agricola had already unwittingly created much of the infrastructure of the eventual limits of Roman Britain. He spent most of the rest of the time campaigning beyond in territory that, for reasons including political expediency and the elusive tribes, never became permanent parts of the province.

Agricola's activities gathered new data about northern Britain, though this added to a canon of information accumulated by traders, geographers and others. But when Tacitus claimed that it was during the governorship that *nunc terminus Britanniae patet*, 'now the end of Britain is exposed' (*Agricola* 30), he had some justification for the statement. Agricola explored the eastern lowland zone of what we call Scotland and what he knew as *Caledonia*. Valleys were surveyed, places for forts selected, rivers negotiated and the coastline explored. His ships circumnavigated the island to confirm a fact already known. We can be sure that throughout every one of the campaigning seasons, Agricola's military scouts and planners scoured the landscape for information to archive. It is sad that we only have Tacitus' panegyric of his father-in-law's achievements because, while it is remarkably detailed by ancient standards, it mentions places and regions that cannot always certainly be identified on the ground in today's Scotland.

Agricola was permanently confronted throughout his campaigning by 'the enemy' (*hostium*). Although the war eventually culminated in the battle of *Mons Graupius* this was very unrepresentative of how the fighting had been conducted along the way. The tribes withdrew further into the north (*Agricola* 22). Tacitus perceived this as a forced retreat, but he never considered that the Roman forces were being drawn further and further into regions that challenged their supply routes, their reconnaissance and even their confidence. It was a classic trap that barbarian tribes were expert at setting. Likewise Tacitus interpreted the lack of any irritating skirmishes or guerrilla tactics as evidence the enemy was terrified of the Romans. The enemy had no need – after all, as Tacitus acknowledged, the Roman army was being subjected to vile conditions. The natural superstition of Roman troops only added to the unease. Vicious weather, intimi-

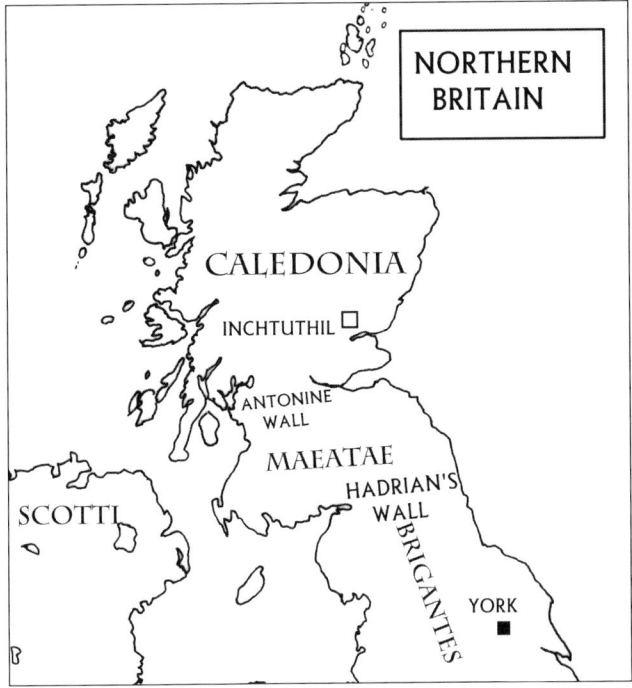

3 Northern Britain. Inchtuthil was briefly occupied c.83–9.
York remained the principal control centre from the
beginning of the second century

dating terrain, and an enemy that flitted like shadows in and out of
the gloom provided a suite of bad omens.

It took considerable leadership to compensate for the environment.
Agricola's solution was a textbook example of Rome's characteristically practical approach to the worst places. Forts were established, or
so the story goes, to provide bastions against the conditions and to
hold territory in the winter months. Agricola was also initially helped
by the time-honoured tribal tradition of fragmenting into factions. A
chieftain joining him provided a hostage, and intelligence (assuming
he fed Agricola with reliable data). The capture of prisoners revealed
the fact that the Roman fleet, then constantly supplying the army at
landing points up and down the east coast, fascinated and terrified
the Britons.

The consequence of the Roman advance, and the realisation that the Roman army with its fleet was an unparalleled threat, provoked a certain amount of unification amongst the tribes. This capacity for ragged and unpredictable bouts of co-operation was potentially disastrous for the Romans and it emerged occasionally to present them with an insurmountable challenge. The combining of forces very nearly ended the Agricolan advance. Assaults on forts were arranged, and a night attack on the *IX Hispana* could have destroyed the unit without the timely arrival of the cavalry.

In a throwaway line Tacitus passed over the secret of the northern Britons when he said 'if it had not been for the marshes and forests hiding the fugitives, that victory would have brought about the end of the war' (*Agricola* 26.2). What he was actually saying, without realising it, was that without the all-powerful secret weapon of the Britons, the Romans would have won the war. The Britons' secret weapon was their ability to disappear into the wilderness. Tacitus failed to appreciate that since there was evidently nothing the Romans could do about that (and Agricola certainly couldn't) there was no chance the war could be won by them. The only option in the meantime was to bring the Britons to a set-piece battle, which took place at *Mons Graupius* in 83 or 84. Somewhere in northern Scotland, the location is now unknown for certain, though the importance of the event means a fair amount of scholarly energy has been expended on trying to identify it. Needless to say the result was generally inconclusive, though a more practical suggestion based on aerial photography and surveying produced the suggestion that *Mons Graupius* is Bennachie, a few miles west of Inverurie in Aberdeenshire and thus close enough to the Roman route up the east coast to make sense. But there is no means of being certain now.

The speech Tacitus put into the mouth of Calgacus, leader of the Britons at the battle, is a revealing record of how a Roman historian perceived the reality of imperial rule though he awarded it a kind of pseudo-credibility by stating that *in hunc modum locutus fertur*, 'it is reported he spoke this way' (*Agricola* 29.4-32.4). Calgacus 'told' his warriors they were not only *servitutis expertes*, 'untouched by servitude', but also their remote location had saved them from even having to see its effects elsewhere. Faced now by the Romans, *raptores orbis*, 'robbers of the world', the only alternative to fighting was accepting the *solitudinem*, 'devastation', that the Romans called 'peace'. On the face of it this is a damning comment on the Roman abuse of power. It was a future defined in terms of enslavement, made worse by the cycle of tribute that meant Britain fed her own slave-masters. In contrast, Agricola's speech is little more than a conventional general's rallying cry. Of course, Tacitus' purpose was to illustrate what Rome had lost through her greed and ambition for riches and power, but at the same time he showed that the Romans were sufficiently sophisticated to see beyond their own immediate goals.

In a very real sense, what Tacitus says skirts remarkably close to our own time. We wring out hands with imperial guilt, but do all we can to minimise our loss of power. The speech raises all sorts of interesting questions about Tacitus and his motives. It is scarcely credible that he was seeking to denigrate Rome, but in showing his ability to empathise with the mind of the enemy he created a vastly more credible scenario than a puerile account of a stand-off between a heroic Roman general and a vicious barbarian would amount to. The ambiguity in his judgement made for a far more compelling account. The same point could just as easily apply to Boudica. However, when it came to Calgacus, Tacitus was also interested in drawing attention to his father-in-law's qualities as a firm but fair and humane Roman governor and leader of men. Calgacus thus became the medium through which the old Roman order in Britain could be described, in contrast to the Agricolan way, and also by extension the Empire of the mid-first century compared to the second century when Tacitus wrote.

Winning the battle at *Mons Graupius* did nothing for the Romans in their attempt to consolidate control of the region. A turf and timber legionary fortress was built at Inchtuthil further south, and other forts were established. The abandonment of the conquered territory by Domitian a few years later was castigated by

Tacitus, who rather dramatically called this the time when *perdomita Britannia, et statim missa*, 'Britain, having been conquered throughout was immediately let go' (*Histories* i.2). In truth Domitian and his advisors were aware that the deep north was going to tie down too many soldiers for too long in a futile attempt to confront an enemy that spent its time disappearing into marshes and forests. It was a pity for Septimius Severus more than a century later that either he failed to read the *Agricola* or ignored its contents.

In the meantime the most memorable description of the Britons comes from a writing tablet found at Vindolanda, dated to the very end of the first century or around fifteen years after the battle at *Mons Graupius*. It has all the careworn tone of an inconclusive war of attrition, a futile and relentless series of skirmishes and squabbles which gave both sides a purpose for living, and at the same time an unending excuse for cynical indifference. One letter includes the word *Brittunculi*, a derogatory Latin form that we can only translate with adjectives like 'wretched little Britons'. It implies the frustration and irritation of being plagued by mosquitoes or vermin. Whether it means enemy hordes, or Britons hired as Roman mercenaries, is a moot point, but the latter seems unlikely in the context.

In 1868, General Philip Sheridan was in charge of the Department of the Missouri in the American West. He was determined to end Indian resistance, and received this support from General William Tecumseh Sherman, hero of the recently ended US Civil War. 'I . . . will use all the powers confided to me to the end that these Indians, enemies of our race and of our civilisation, shall not again be able to begin and carry out their barbarous warfare on any kind of pretext they may choose to allege.' The names might be different, but the attitudes would have fitted seamlessly into the northern frontier of Roman Britain. Today we would call this racism, and recognise that it provided the necessary hatred to 'legitimise' extermination of unwanted lesser beings.

1 The Battersea Shield. Dredged from the Thames at Battersea, this late Iron Age ceremonial and highly decorative shield is a tour-de-force example of tribal military display equipment. It had undoubtedly been a water offering, and many other deposits of military equipment have been found in such contexts. About 350-50 BC

2 Snettisham (Norfolk). One of the gold torcs from the nine hoards found close together, and dating to around 70 BC. Although nothing is known about the owner, the use of false-bottomed pits to conceal the richest goods suggests the burial was for protection and eventual recovery rather than ritual. Like **colour plate 1** the material is evidence for the substantial personal wealth and status held by late Iron Age tribal leaders in Britain like Cassivellaunus, which some of their descendants did their best to hold onto during the Roman conquest

3 Boudica at Westminster in London. This Victorian statue is today the best-known depiction of Boudica with her daughters, at the reins of her war chariot. But how much of this image is based on fact, and how much is the invention of Roman historians?

4 Celtic coin art and its origins. *Left*: a bronze coin of Philip II of Macedon (359–336BC). *Right*: a gold stater of the Corieltauvi (East Midlands and Lincolnshire), struck in the mid-first century BC. The obverse of the latter is an abstract development of Philip's hair, but the face has been dispensed with entirely. The horse on the reverse is more obviously derived from the Macedonian prototypes. The Celtic stater shown here is similar to many other varieties struck in southern and eastern Britain in the first century BC

5 *Left and right:* Claudius (41-54) and Nero (54-68) on *sestertii* struck at Rome in 41-2, and Lyons in 64 respectively. During these reigns, Britain's conquest was begun and sustained, despite the resistance led by Caratacus, and the Boudican Revolt

6 The tombstone of Gaius Julius Alpinus Classicianus from London. His post as procurator of Britain in the aftermath of the Boudican Revolt during the 60s was recorded by Tacitus, and confirmed by the text on his funerary monument. The restored text is based on work by R.S.O. Tomlin

7 The replica military granary at the Lunt fort, Baginton near Coventry. Built shortly after the Boudican Revolt, this multi-phase fort was in use for only about twenty years. The building is raised off the ground on posts to protect grain from rodents and damp. Such granaries were probably used to store the tribute grain that provoked so much resentment in early Roman Britain

8 View across the Lunt replica timber fort from the *gyrus* (exercise yard) to the east gate. Short-lived earth-and-timber forts were scattered across southern and central Britain during the conquest phase

9 Bullion. Roman soldiers obeyed the emperors who paid them in gold and silver, which was also vital for paying off and bribing barbarians on the borders. *Clockwise from top:* gold *aureus* of Nero (65-6), reverse of a silver *denarius* of Hadrian depicting a Victory (127), reverse of a silver *denarius* of Trajan depicting military trophies (103-11)

10 Roman military might. The reconstructed west gate at *Arbeia*, South Shields, to the east of Hadrian's Wall and on the south bank of the Tyne. The height is hypothetical, but the work gives an outstanding idea of the physical presence of Roman stone forts that proliferated across the north in the second century AD

11 *Top four coins:* Britannia on coins. *Clockwise from upper left: as* of Hadrian struck about 119 depicting Britannia; *sestertius* of Antoninus Pius struck in 143 depicting Britannia; *as* of Antoninus Pius struck 154 with Britannia; *as* of Septimius Severus recording British victories in 209–11

Bottom four coins: The Gallic Empire. *Clockwise:* double-*sestertius* of Postumus (259-68) over-struck on an old *sestertius* of the late first or early second century; bronze radiates of Postumus, Victorinus (268-70), Tetricus I (270-3). The radiates are from the Normanby (Lincs) hoard of 1985, consisting of 47,912 coins, more than 33,000 of which were Gallic Empire issues

12 *Top:* Obverse and reverse of a bronze radiate of Carausius (286-93), struck at the 'C' mint. The reverse is an unusually fine representation of a war galley, reflecting the basis of his power as a naval commander

Bottom three coins: The ideological battle was advertised on coinage. *Clockwise from lower left:* reverse of a bronze radiate struck by Carausius (286-93) with the legend *Expectate Veni*, 'the awaited one is come', alluding to a line from Virgil's Aeneid, and mintmark *RSR*, representing a line from Virgil's Fourth Georgic, meaning 'The Golden Age is Back'; reverse of a follis of Constantius I (struck 296-305) with the legitimate Empire's slogan, 'The Genius of the Roman People'; reverse of a follis of Constantine I struck at London 307-25 with the slogan, 'The Undefeated Companion Sun-God'

13 Lullingstone (Kent). Autumn, as depicted on the fourth-century mosaic that covers the floor of the villa's main room. Autumn's hair is filled with ripe crops, symbolising Britain's abundant agricultural produce, that made losing Britain to usurpers impossible to contemplate

14 Charioteer on a mosaic from the villa at Rudston (Yorks). Other panels depict the Four Seasons, and peacocks. Dated on style to c.325-50, and a remarkable illustration of a sport scarcely otherwise known in Britain, but found in an area with a prehistoric tradition of chariots as part of the equipage of tribal aristocracies

15 Marble bust, from the villa at Lullingstone, Kent. Although it was deliberately sealed in an underground room c.250, it was carved somewhere around the middle of the second century. The style and appearance means it must be a portrait of a man of some status and importance, either in Britain, or an ancestor portrait brought to Britain by a new owner of the house

16 The remains of the theatre at Verulamium. Although it occupied a key position in the centre of the town and played a major part in pagan religious activities, by the fourth century it was derelict thanks to official suppression of paganism by the Christian emperors of the period

17 Burgh Castle (Norfolk) looking west. One of the best-preserved of the shore defence installations, Burgh Castle belongs to the late third century. Its bastions were added after construction had already started. An extensive settlement existed alongside, so the site may have served as a fortified port on what was then a much larger estuary than it is today

8 Caistor St Edmund (Norfolk). The sole surviving bastion of the late(?) third-century defences of *Venta Icenorum* still stands 3m high. It was probably added with most of the other bastions in the fourth century. The walls enclosed a much smaller area than had originally been laid out, perhaps reflecting insecurity in the period, or a town that had never lived up to expectations thanks to the stigma of the Boudican Revolt

9 Magnentius (350-3) and Constantius II (337-61). *Left to right: centenionalis* of Magnentius with a Chi-Rho reverse; *cententionalis* of Magnentius with a reverse depicting the Victories of Augustus (Magnentius) and Caesar (his brother Decentius); gold *solidus* of Constantius II who organised the ruthless pogrom amongst Magnentian supporters in Britain through his agent, Paul

20 Brading (Isle of Wight). Winter, depicted on a fourth-century mosaic. In 343 Constans had to make a winter emergency trip across the Channel in foul weather to deal with an unknown problem (see chapter 11)

21 Small bronze head of a girl from Silkstead, near Otterbourne (Hants). The concept of representation this way is classical and Roman, but the treatment of the eyes belongs to a more primitive provincial tradition. Height about 12.5cm

2 Carrawburgh (Hadrian's Wall), temple of Mithras. The rise of Christianity was just one facet of mystery cults that grew steadily in popularity from the first century AD onwards. Mithras also promised rebirth and redemption, but in being only open to men it lacked Christianity's inclusiveness. It seems to have been deliberately destroyed in the fourth century, perhaps on official orders to suppress paganism, especially a cult that seemed to ape Christian practices in its ritual meal and use of the basilican building form

3 Magnus Maximus (383-8), as depicted on a bronze coin struck at Arles in Gaul. Although conventional in design, the coin is relatively crude. The reverse shows Maximus 'recovering' the state

24 Brantingham (Yorks). One of several busts depicted on a large fourth-century floor. The busts appear to be portraits and they may commemorate ancestors of the household or living members posing as Muses. If so, they represent a rare glimpse of how the villa-owing élite saw themselves. These were the people most affected by the disruption that the episodic rebellions of the period caused

25 Gold *solidus* of Honorius (393–423), struck at Milan 393–402. His reign was challenged by the revolt of Constantine III and saw the formal end of the Roman Britain. The reverse shows the victorious Honorius, an image that was at variance with the truth

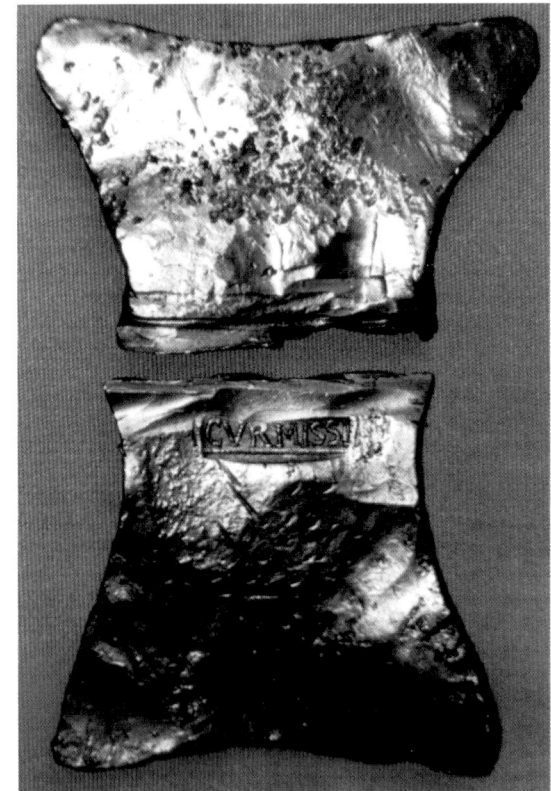

26 Lullingstone (Kent). Late-fourth-century wall-paintings from the house-church depicting Christians in an attitude of prayer. The extent of Christian activity in Britain at this time is unknown. Not only were pagan cults enjoying a certain amount of revivalism in this remote part of the Empire, but Christianity was itself still struggling with heresies, factionalism and liturgical rivalries that reached their most dangerous extent yet with the arrival of Pelagianism

27 Coleraine (N. Ireland). Silver ingot from a hoard of late Roman plate, interpreted as bullion stolen by, or paid to, Irish raiders in Britain and cut up as required. It bears the stamp of a bullion official, Curmissus. Buried in the early fifth century. Original height about 16cm

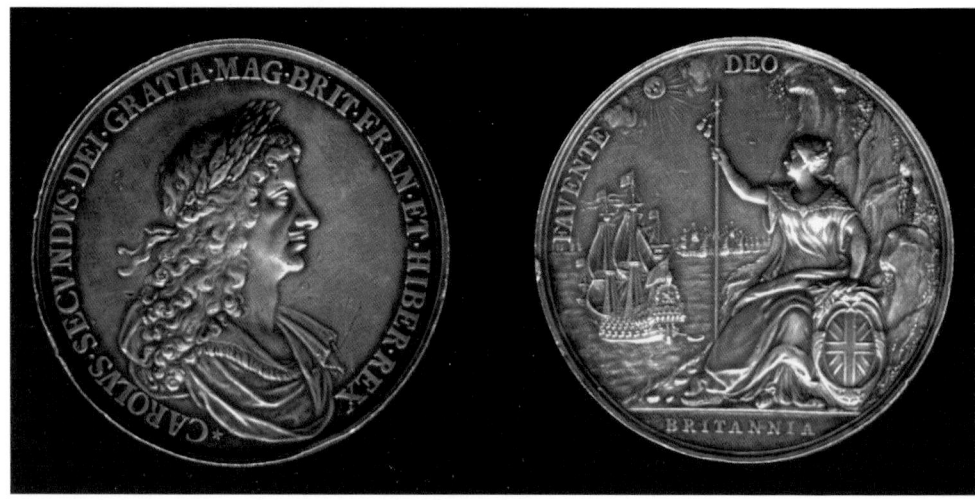

28 Lullingstone. Painting of the Christian Chi-Rho from the house-church

29 Charles II (1660-85) on a medal struck early in 1667 to commemorate the naval build-up in the Second Dutch War. The king is shown in the dress of a Roman emperor, and on the reverse the Roman figure of Britannia has been revived with a slogan meaning 'God is propitious'. Around the edge (not visible here) is the legend *CAROLVS SECVNDVS PACIS ET IMPERII RESTITVTOR AVGVSTVS*, 'Charles II Augustus, Restorer of Peace and Order', adopting themes and titles from Rome. The piece, by Jan Roettier, perfectly illustrates the preservation of the Roman image of power in later regimes

We can also take it as read that certain Britons were only too happy to act as guides, interpreters, fifth columnists, and sexual partners, in return for Roman silver. In a curious way the relationship must have served both parties rather well. The Roman soldiers had the opportunity to engage in battles where they could bag a few Britons, burn the odd village, and return home to the fort to sharpen their swords and muse on the repulsive cultural inferiority of their enemy. It is a curious paradox that often those most given to such superciliousness often turn out to be closest to those they loathe. Most of Britain's frontier troops came from provincial backgrounds that meant they were only first- or second-generation Romans themselves. Meanwhile, the Britons could forget their traditional internecine differences and coagulate into loose and casual alliances under the leadership of local warlords. Wiping out the odd Roman patrol provided them with the chance to acquire Roman equipment, and supplied them with anecdotes to brag about till their dying days that, on the whole, were not likely to be very far off.

Part of the problem was that Trajan (98-117) seems to have been entirely indifferent to Britain. He was far more interested in his Parthian and Dacian wars. After the end of the Agricolan campaigns, Britain is all but silent to us until the arrival of Hadrian in or around the year 119 except for the Vindolanda documents. If the army in Britain was anything like the army in Germany, it had quietly declined into Easy Street where officers built kitchen gardens and lolled around in undisciplined indifference, safe in the knowledge that the Emperor was a metaphorical million miles away. Hadrian was unlike any other emperor though and, a stickler for military discipline, was not inclined to tolerate frontier frolics and spent his reign touring the Empire and setting slackers to rights.

The wars and wall building of the next forty years or more are not really part of this book, but they marked out an effectively permanent abandonment of Roman ambitions in the far north. We know very little about how the northern tribes were regarded since we do not even really know how Hadrian's Wall was supposed to function. It was evidently not a barrier as much as it was a sequence

of conduits that funnelled traffic into control points at the milecas-
tles and forts. This suggests a certain amount of coming-to-terms
with the *realpolitik* of the region, but if the tribes of the Wall region
had accepted some of the reality of the Roman presence, those
further north had other ideas.

The Maeatae appear only in the writings of Dio Cassius. Dio is very
specific, and tells us that the 'Maeatai' lived 'near the Wall that splits
the island in two' (lxxvi.12). He was referring to the end of the
second century, and the beginning of the third, so it is interesting
that the name does not appear earlier. The name seems to be a
conflation of two elements. The second part, -*atai*, is considered to
be some sort of generic term suggesting a people or group, qualified
by the first part. The *Mae-* component is believed to be linked to a
Celtic form connected to the Latin *major*, and the Welsh *mwy*, which
both mean 'large'. So that produces 'large people' which, it takes
little to realise, does not tell us very much at all unless we remember
that Dio also said Maeatae was an umbrella term for several different
tribes operating together. Indeed, he even said that other tribal
names had been absorbed into the Maeatae, and the Caledonians
beyond. These presumably include parts or all of the Damnonii,
Novantae, Selgovae and Votadinii.

In other words, the Maeatae are the *Brittunculi* to all intents and
purposes. Dio provides us with a potted description of how they lived.
It is probably a mixture of fact, half-truth, and generic all-purpose
barbarian 'attributes' that depicted them as appropriately uncivilised.
Dependent on their flocks of animals, what they could hunt (except,
strangely, fish, which they spurned), and the wild fruit they could
gather, the Maeatae seem to have been a nomadic people who lived
in tents and who had no clothing. There seems to have been little
sense of family grouping, with women being shared, and everyone
taking responsibility for the children. As might be expected, tribal rule
was exercised through a hierarchy of warriors, but decisions seem to

have been formulated by groups rather than a single individual. In war they used chariots, and infantry, arming themselves with a shield, short spear, and a dagger. On campaign they were prepared to tolerate any conditions and could survive indefinitely on roots and bark, supplemented by emergency rations that they carried with them.

The sources are silent on names for most of the second century, but the 'British war' that was 'threatening' in 163 probably involved them (*Life of Marcus Aurelius* viii.7). A generation later in 184, 'the tribes in the island crossed the Wall that divided them from the Roman soldiers and did a huge amount of damage', which included killing a legionary commander with his troops (Dio lxxiii.1). The latter event was important enough for the Roman victory in Britain to be commemorated on a huge series of coins struck that year by Commodus. There is no obvious reason why the invasion should have happened then in particular, and indeed there may have been none apart from a cycle of breast-beating and a new generation of warriors anxious to prove themselves, perhaps at the behest of a charismatic new leader. Of course, particular circumstances or opportunities might have contributed to the rising about which we know nothing. For example, it is entirely possible that climatic conditions contributed to a tribal food shortage, or perhaps a local Roman commander had decided to throw his weight around in an especially offensive manner. We have absolutely no way of knowing.

In 197 the Maeatae, or the confederation of Wall-side tribes, became more organised. They involved the Caledonians to take part in their next rising. By this date, the civil war of 193-7 (see chapter 7) had just passed its climax. The governor Clodius Albinus had been defeated and killed after challenging Septimius Severus for the Empire, and had taken a huge quantity of Britain's garrison on campaign with him. This was the first time that had happened, and it presented the northern tribes with a magnificent opportunity. The new governor, Virius Lupus, was faced with an emergency. Rather than risk more troops, and what was possibly a neglected military infrastructure, on revenge, he bought the Maeatae off with bribes. Over the next decade under Lupus and his successors Gaius

Valerius Pudens and Lucius Alfenus Senecio, a number of inscriptions show that fort buildings and facilities were repaired, rebuilt or built from new.

During the governorship of Alfenus Senecio (205-8), word seems to have reached Rome of a fresh barbarian rising in Britain. At least that was what Herodian wrote down, while Dio just reported that Severus was on top of things in Britain when it came to warfare. Perhaps it was just the pretext Severus used to come to Britain to fight a new northern war, supposedly to conquer Caledonia, though in fact it was because he wanted to get his sons (and putative successors), Caracalla and Geta, away from their undesirable recreational practices at Rome. Caracalla and Geta preferred to spend their time in decadent, drunken rowdiness, but Severus wanted to harden them up into more respectable emperor-material. The upshot was that for the rest of his life Severus led the new British war that took the Roman army deep into Caledonia, until he died at York in 211. Over the next year Caracalla, who Edward Gibbon called 'the common enemy of mankind', promptly abandoned the advance bases and any territory that had been taken.

Caracalla had other distractions but there was no doubt that the British war had been costly and inconclusive. Legionary vexillations had been brought over from the continent to assist, including probably *XXII Primigenia*, and part of Rome's Praetorian Guard. The revision of South Shields as a supply base seems to have belonged at least in part to this time. Septimius Severus had been initially confounded by the response of the northern tribes. Presented with a full-blown Roman campaign bent on a trophy war, the tribes simply decided to offer a peace treaty. Since an effortless peace was not what Severus wanted, he refused to accept the favourable terms and started the war anyway. He might as well have walked into a booby trap.

The Maeatae and the Caledonians were experts at fighting in their own part of the world. Roman soldiers were not, especially those brought into Britain to take part in what they hoped would be an exhilarating turkey shoot. Weighed down by equipment, armour, and their aged emperor's baggage train, the Roman forces were easily drawn deeper and deeper into the twilight fringes of the known world they feared so much. The tribal warriors were perfectly content to lurk in marshes and swamps up to their necks, creating the impression they were retreating all the way. The Romans were hopelessly compromised by trying to prosecute a war in a nightmare confusion of forests, swamps and river-crossings. They did their best to cut down woodland, drain the swamps and build bridges, but this only added to the delays. They were also roundly tricked when the enemy let loose flocks of cattle or sheep. The Romans wasted time rounding up and chasing the animals and were just led on deeper into the wilderness. Like the weekend hunters in the film *Deliverance*, they had lost the initiative to a wild, fearful and inscrutable foe.

Forcing any enemy to have the common decency to face the Romans in a set battle proved impossible. Instead the Roman army had to be broken up into detachments of only a few troops and were easily ambushed by tribesmen lurking in the waterlogged undergrowth while the Romans struggled with their armour and weapons. It was futile, especially considering that the tribes concerned evidently found the prospect of Roman culture entirely an irrelevance. Lacking the tradition of long-term subliminal exposure through the indulgence of their leaders, they were simply too detached from the concept of material culture, roads, urban settlement and housing to see any potential for selling out.

The reality of the war, as recorded by Dio and Herodian, flew in the face of the triumphant coins Severus issued in his own and those of his sons. *Victoriae Brittannicae*, the legends announced on all denominations, and the three men added 'Brit' to their personal titles in spite of huge losses of men. The war was pursued in spite of the setbacks, and by 210 the forces had reached the north-eastern part of Caledonia. On the face of it, the Romans had overcome the problems and were delighted when the Maeatae and Caledonians accepted a peace deal. That just bought the tribes time and the following year they returned to the war, challenging the over-stretched Roman forces once more. But time had run out for

Severus. He did not live out the winter, and the war or what was left of it became Caracalla's responsibility. Caracalla was not in the least concerned with fighting in Caledonia so he made a peace deal with the tribes, withdrew the army, abandoned the forts and returned to Rome where his short, reckless and brutal regime ran its course. The rebellious Maeatae and their associates had proved totally intractable opponents to the end. But once left to their own devices they evaporate from history.

Curiously, the tribes of the remote north disappear from the sources for most of the following century. This is almost certainly no more than a function of the existing record. There was no third-century historian to match Tacitus, Dio or Herodian, and in any case the main events of the Roman world were taking place elsewhere. A long period of reconstructive work followed in Britain's northern forts, as a series of inscriptions over the next thirty to forty years testify. But even that record gives out in the late third century, and the new forts of the Saxon Shore are frustratingly bereft when it comes to inscriptions that might tell us who built them and why.

It is not until the fourth century that the peoples roaming the territory north of Hadrian's Wall return once more to the record. In 305-6, Constantius I took an army deep into the north again. He was said to have occupied the 'forests and marshes of the Caledonians and the Picts', as well as Ireland and other islands. In 306 he died at York, like Severus a century before, presumably having returned to the rear to pass the winter in comfort. The account comes only from a panegyric in his name and tells us nothing about the process of the war, or whether it had been provoked by tribal incursions during the reign of Carausius (see chapter 10). The *Picti* means 'painted ones', and with a basis in Latin literary tradition it is likely the name was a Roman colloquial term for people who decorated themselves with tattoos, rather than representing a new ethnic label. Another panegyric, for the year 297, adds that the Picts went about half-naked – an essential sartorial style if their tattoos were to be evident to anyone else.

Perhaps then the Picts were just the Maeatae and Brittunculi once more. It is impossible to say, but whoever they were they continued to provide a source of irritation and harassment. Writing about the late 360s, Ammianus Marcellinus refers to the *Areani*, a body of irregular frontier scouts or spies whose job was to keep on the move and watch out for anyone bent on operating a raid across the border. Crucially, he tells us they had been in use 'since early times', though this is the first reference we have for them. 'Early times' could mean anything from the first century up to the early fourth.

The Picts appear again in 360, forming a conspiracy with the Scotti, to attack Britain. They broke a peace agreement they had already made and caused havoc in and around the frontier. The Scotti were of Irish origin, but took advantage of the short sea crossing from northern Ireland to attack Britain by land from Caledonia. Eventually of course their name would supplant Caledonia. In 367 a catastrophic invasion of Britain followed, led by the Picts, Attacotti and Scotti. At least the event is always described as catastrophic, but there is a curious lack of any evidence for wholesale destruction at towns and forts. In other words, if there was no historical evidence, it is unlikely anyone would have inferred the event took place from the archaeology of the period. This is in marked contrast to the Boudican Revolt, and it does mean that the incursion may in fact have been very localised and limited in extent. Nevertheless, the *dux* (duke) of Britain, Fullofaudes, was ambushed and imprisoned. Ammianus provides a sort of confirmation that the name 'Picts' was just a convenient label by stating that they were made up of two tribes, the Dicaledones (denoting two groups of Caledonians) and the Verturiones. Another incursion followed, says Gildas, the fall of Magnus Maximus in 388. Picts and Scots moved in to take advantage of an enervated Britain, and it took a 'legion' from Rome to expel the invaders.

The picture of who was really involved in invasions of Britain from the north, their numbers, and whether they supplanted local people or integrated with them is impossible to unravel. With so little physical evidence for the barbarian hordes of the north, it is impossible for us to really know who they were and which groups were the same as others. There are no inhumation cemeteries that would allow analysis of skull forms, build and physique, or grave goods. They exist mainly in the Roman literary tradition, and represent just part of the problem faced by the rulers of southern Britain for centuries.

By contrast southern Britain is a relatively easy place to co-ordinate and control, and this played a huge part in the physical disparity between the urbanised south of Roman Britain with its farmland, villas, roads and resources, and the military north. Dissemination of cultural influence is simply far easier in terrain where communications are comparatively simple to arrange, and where people come regularly into contact with one another. Exactly the same factors contributed to the development of medieval England, and the tensions that arose in the efforts to try and subdue Scotland. This cultural, linguistic and conceptual divergence continued to result in violent repercussions right up until 1746.

Virtually the only real evidence we have for any of the Roman wars in the remote north, apart from the literature, are traces of forts in Scotland, coastal fortifications, and occasional finds of Roman material and coins. Some of this is almost certainly bullion handed over as bribes to buy peace, or bounty paid to tribal bands that were prepared for a while to work in Roman interests. The most convincing is the Traprain Law hoard made up of the so-called *Hacksilber*. Unlike a normal hoard of plate found within the Empire, and buried for both its bullion and aesthetic value, *Hacksilber* is what it sounds like: hacked-up silver, and treated thus because the only concern was its bullion content. The Traprain treasure included more than a hundred broken-up silver vessels, including flagons, goblets and spoons. Functional items, despite their decorative nature, they were rendered into useless lumps of metal because they had no use to the people who now owned them. A similar hoard was found at Coleraine in Northern Ireland, the region from where the Scotti came. It is more than possible that some of this bullion was requisitioned by force from the Romano-

British by their own officials. Perhaps the Hoxne (Suffolk) hoard, not buried before 408, represents an attempt by a family or families to protect their wealth from compulsory seizure. Long afterwards, the *Anglo-Saxon Chronicle* preserved a memory of the kind of precautions taken. For the year 418 it says that 'the Romans' (meaning the Romano-British) collected up all the treasure they could, burying some and taking the rest to Gaul.

We do not know when or where the hacking-up of the Traprain loot occurred. Perhaps the silver was commandeered within Roman Britain in the latter years of the province's history, and weighed out into standardised packages, which were then used as bribes to try and control incursions across the frontier. Alternatively, the silver could easily have been stolen as loot by raiders, bagged up and then removed across the frontier for storage as bullion wealth. There is a long historical tradition of bullion that originated in controlled conditions being favoured in places where such controls are non-existent. Roman silver *denarii* had earlier circulated widely beyond Rome's frontiers, sometimes manufactured with serrated edges to demonstrate the bullion's integrity. Tacitus states that German tribes preferred serrated *denarii* to any others for this reason (*Germania* v.5). One example is the Birnie (Moray) hoard of Severan *denarii* found a few metres from a roundhouse, and conceivably some of the bribe money paid during or after the Severan expedition. The silver thalers of Maria Theresa of Austria (1740-80), first struck in 1780, were considered so reliable a means of storing wealth in the former Abyssinia (now Ethiopia) that they were struck for trading purposes well into the twentieth century. Preparations for the Italian invasion of Abyssinia in 1936 included the striking of replicas in Mussolini's Rome for use in the war zone. Today the British gold sovereign is valued throughout the world because of the guaranteed level of fineness at 91.67 per cent. But as far as Roman Britain was concerned, the supply must have dried up quickly. That which could be requisitioned, or stolen, was, and that which could be buried or secreted away disappeared. Very little Roman plate or coin trickled in afterwards.

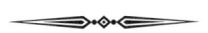

By the early 80s the Roman army had wended its way as far as the northern tip of Scotland, looked across the Irish Sea, and circum-navigated Britain. Between around 140 and 165 the Antonine Wall cut off the Southern Uplands of Scotland from the north. In the early third century, and the early fourth century, two more imperial campaigns took Roman soldiers all the way into Caledonia once more. Throughout all this time, even northern England remained perpetually a military zone. Few civilian towns existed apart from the settlements that clustered around the forts and near to Hadrian's Wall like Carlisle and Corbridge. Aldborough, as *Isurium Brigantium*, was the sole civitas capital of the north. But most had so little inherent durability that they faded when the forts were given up, and often in fact evaporated before that took place. In other words, Roman 'settlement' in the north was entirely dependent upon, and inter-woven with, the army economy. This was somewhat different from the south where a more developed rural Roman landscape meant towns functioned in a more sophisticated economic environment.

Perhaps the writing was on the wall from the outset. The tribes of the south mostly capitulated in every sense to Roman rule, though the extent to which they benefited or were assimilated varied consid-erably. The absence of rebellion after the Boudican Revolt shows how much had changed. But in the south there was already an awareness of what the Roman world meant. Given a choice, most people seem to have acceded to the new state of affairs. Tribal rebel-lions receded into an historical oblivion, and when Roman Britain came officially to an end, strenuous efforts were made for future generations to lead a Romanized way of life together. In the north, the tribes had far less sense of what Roman life was. In every respect they spoke a different language to the classical world. Socially, linguis-tically, technically, and legally, the dialogue broke down – or perhaps never even began. Wholly different mindsets acted as a far more effective boundary than stone walls.

7

Ambition's Debt is Paid
CLODIUS ALBINUS

When Septimius Severus died at York in 211 he had enjoyed remarkable success as a usurper to the imperial throne. He had held onto
power for nearly two decades and his family members would
continue to hold the throne until 235. In the chaos that followed, that
seemed a considerable achievement but to begin with it was touch
and go. Severus had to play a dangerous game in which he played off
his rivals, including the governor of Britain: Clodius Albinus.

On 31 December 192, the mercurial emperor Commodus was
killed in an attempt to finally bring to an end a reign that had
veered wildly between terror and indulgence. Since Commodus
had been murdered, the coup succeeded in its primary purpose but
it offered no path to a safe and secure future for the Roman
Empire. The result was a civil war that set the tone for the next
hundred years. One of the key players in the immediate aftermath
was Clodius Albinus, governor of Britain. Anyone who could
control such a remote and turbulent province was worthy of admiration. Britain was a place where he could make or destroy his
reputation. Many of the incumbents were carefully selected from

the most experienced senatorial professional soldiers and administrators the Empire had to offer. On the other hand, Britain was the
sort of place where it could all go horribly wrong. In the distant
past this had had more to do with trying to conquer and hold the
place. By the end of the second century the Roman world was in
a new state of disarray. Britain's vast and isolated garrison made it a
tempting power base for men who would be king.

Clodius Albinus, governor of Britain at the death of Commodus,
was one of a new breed of Roman administrators. As a young man
he was thought well of. Marcus Aurelius recommended him as 'a
man of experience, strict in his way of life, and respected for his
character . . . do encourage him to make himself known to the state,
because he will be rewarded as he deserves' (*Life of Clodius Albinus*
x.7–8). On the other hand, Albinus later earned himself a reputation
as a tyrannical husband, master and general, noted for his gluttony,
drunkenness and violent temper. His name meant 'the White One',
and later it was believed he had very white skin and thus he was
named, though it is equally likely that the name was responsible for
the skin story. Nevertheless Albinus was also described as having a
broad brow and unkempt curly hair, which accords with the image
on his coins, though of course the coins could have been the source
of the description in the first place.

As the provinces became ever more integrated into the Roman
world, so whole generations of the provincial élite became integrated
into the Roman ruling senatorial class. As it happens, Britain seems
to have been particularly unusual in being excluded from this but for
the upper classes of Spain and North Africa a seat in the senate was
becoming par for the course. For a few, this was not enough and they
set their sights on the ultimate goal. In the mid-190s a reckless new
civil war was played out between two North Africans.

The second century was a freak of history when it came to
benign rulers. Just as it ended with a murder, so it began with the
murder of Domitian, almost a hundred years before in 96. Domitian
was paranoid and cruel, and ruled with terror, though in other
respects he was a conservative and competent emperor. Nerva was

chosen as his successor. Nerva served as a consul under the Flavians and earned himself a reputation as a lawyer. Already in his mid-60s, Nerva moved quickly to nominate his own successor during a short reign that was distinguished by reform. Roman law made it easy to adopt a son, and for that adoptive son in every way to succeed his new father and to be accepted as such. Nerva made a brilliant choice in Trajan (98-117). Although Trajan was committed to military expansion, prosecuting a series of wars in Parthia and Dacia, he followed Nerva in restoring the prestige of the principate.

It was the Empire's good luck that Trajan also had no son. He adopted Hadrian (117-38) who in turn was followed by his own adoptive son, Antoninus Pius (138-61). Pius adopted Marcus Aurelius who succeeded him to rule until 180. The period came to be regarded as the age of the five good emperors and it derived almost entirely from the fact that until Marcus Aurelius, none fathered a son who survived to adulthood. The only alternative was choosing the best man for the job. Few monarchs enjoy such a privilege and it could not last. The run of good luck faltered with the accession of Commodus in 180, the natural son of Marcus Aurelius. Of course, it could have been the case that Commodus would turn out to be the man for the job. But in every sense he was the most unsuitable candidate around: easily led, violent, indulgent, perverted and unpredictable.

The accession of Commodus had spectacular repercussions, especially in Britain where from the outset an unusually large garrison had spent its time engaged on the intermittent, but relent-less, warfare that characterised this strange and remote province. Britain was really a time bomb since she was fully equipped to mount a major imperial rebellion when the imperial throne was being disputed. Back in 68-9 the *XIV Gemina* legion, one of four then stationed in Britain, had been a star player in the Civil War. Had all four taken part the result could have been decisive and altered the course of Roman history.

The generation of soldiers in Britain between around 170 and 192 had no opportunity to take part in morale-boosting and triumphant wars of conquest. Ever since the abandonment of the Antonine Wall in the decade before, they had been on the defensive. Things were far from quiet. Instead they were engaged in a perpetual bout of garrison, police and detachment duties, or at least that was the idea. Some spent their time repairing and consolidating the northern frontier, now permanently set at Hadrian's Wall. New arrivals included 5,500 cavalry supplied by a Danubian tribe called the Iazyges, who signed a peace treaty with Marcus Aurelius around 175. A major disruption to military routines and movements came with a crossing of the Wall by the late 170s that caused Marcus Aurelius to send a new governor Ulpius Marcellus to control Britain. He was left in post for a double-term, an indication that the war needed someone at the helm for long enough to bring a durable peace. In 184 Commodus issued his *Victoriae Britannicae* coins to advertise success.

The victory ought to have brought Commodus some sort of prestige. Instead, he was systematically undermining his chance for fame and replacing it with infamy. Primarily concerned with enjoying himself, Commodus handed over much of the practical side of ruling the Empire to his praetorian prefect Perennis. Commodus had a fanatical distrust of the senatorial class, and preferred to promote equestrians wherever he could. The praetorian prefecture was an equestrian post, and as such was linked directly to the person of the emperor. Commodus started making equestrians into legionary commanders, but far from this being interpreted as some sort of egalitarian gesture, it infuriated the legions since equestrians were traditionally confined to commanding auxiliary units.

The British legions, *II Augusta*, *VI Victrix*, and *XX Valeria Victrix*, took even less kindly to the idea of equestrian commanders and promptly declared one of their legionary commanders, the legate Priscus, emperor. Priscus was smart enough to see that declaring oneself emperor was a mug's game, but this did not stop a delegation of 1,500 legionaries setting off for Rome to get what they wanted. Commodus was petrified by the arrival of the British soldiers – it was, after all, a remarkable thing to do. Ever the coward,

Commodus allowed Perennis to be lynched as a sop to the rising tide of disquiet, but followed this up by sending Publius Helvidius Pertinax to Britain to sort out the agitated legionaries.

Pertinax reached Britain around the year 185. A relentless exponent of harsh military discipline, to begin with he was successful in controlling the British troops for the strangely para-doxical reason that he fitted the bill perfectly for their idea of a proper Roman emperor. So, initially they got it into their heads that Pertinax was just the man to replace Commodus, and left Priscus in peace. Unfortunately, this failed to stop a mutiny – perhaps because there seemed no immediate prospect of Pertinax challenging Commodus. The mutiny was so bad Pertinax himself was involved in the mêlée and was left for dead amongst the corpses. He punished the rebels, but soon asked to be removed from Britain. He was succeeded, in all probability, by Clodius Albinus though it is possible another governorship came between them.

The outright unpredictability of Britain's soldiers at this date was just part of the mounting hostility towards Commodus. Clodius Albinus came from *Hadrumetum* (modern Sousse) in North Africa. According to Herodian, Albinus came from a luxurious and wealthy background (ii.15.1), though he was also supposed to have included a famous Italian family called the Postumii Albini amongst his ancestors. By the year 192 Albinus was installed as governor of Britain. This instantly placed him in a decisive position. He commanded a vast and volatile garrison, which had already advertised its disapproval of Commodus the man, and Commodus the emperor.

Perhaps this was why Albinus was governor of Britain, since Commodus had at some point written to Albinus to appoint him his successor. Commodus was already aware of the gathering storm and men like Septimius Severus, governor of Upper Pannonia, who were preparing the ground and their own troops to seize power. By signing up Albinus, Commodus thought he could secure his own position. He thought wrong. Albinus turned out to be overambi-tious, but he was smart enough to see that Commodus was as good as dead and only a fool would associate himself with a lost cause.

The death of Commodus made the dreams of the British garrison come true, or so it might have appeared. On that last day in December 192 Pertinax was prefect of Rome, and seems at least to have been fully aware of the plot against the emperor. With such an ideal candidate on hand the conspirators swiftly made him emperor. Unfortunately for Pertinax he seems to have suffered from a condition known as integrity. This led him to institute reforms and curb the excesses that had characterised Commodus' reign. Laetus, prefect of the Praetorian Guard, took exception to Pertinax's use of uncompromising discipline to restore order and obedience. With the assistance of palace staff, who hated Pertinax for making them sacrifice hand-outs given them by Commodus, the guard murdered Pertinax on 28 March 193, following a reign of just 86 days.

An already bad situation suddenly got a great deal worse. The Praetorian Guard had put themselves on the spot since there was no obvious candidate available to replace Pertinax. They opted to auction the Roman Empire, and that is literally what proceeded to take place. Recognising, accurately, that they held the key to power, it seemed only logical for the Praetorians to be paid appropriately for their approval. One of the senators, Marcus Didius Julianus, offered the soldiers 25,000 *sestertii* a head. The money was roughly equivalent to twenty times the annual salary of a legionary so, as one might expect, it had the desired effect. By a strange coincidence, Didius Julianus was descended on his mother's side from a family of *Hadrumetum* and had had a successful career as a military commander and provincial governor. In 175 he had served as consul alongside Pertinax, and even succeeded him as governor of Africa. While Pertinax had always spoken warmly of Didius Julianus this did not stop the new candidate for the throne also having to guarantee to avenge the memory of Commodus to make sure his cash offer was accepted, and he also upped the money paid out to 30,000 *sestertii* a man.

The people of Rome, however, were rather less accommodating to Didius Julianus. From their point of view Pertinax had been a good thing because he had set things in order rather than indulge the army's whims. They did not take kindly either to his death or the prospect of a new emperor who might have been implicated in that death. This wasn't true, and nor was the idea that Didius Julianus had embarked on a reign of indulgence and extravagance to cock a snook at Pertinax. But it made no difference. Didius Julianus was a marked man too, but for the moment he bided his time while Clodius Albinus waited in the wings.

Didius Julianus might have been emperor in Rome, but in the east Caius Pescennius Niger, governor of Syria, had been declared emperor by his own garrison. He was not the only one. Septimius Severus in Upper Pannonia had been declared emperor by his troops too, probably on 1 April 193. Didius Julianus had suspected Pescennius Niger might rise against him but the Severan candidacy was a complete surprise to him and he was totally wrong-footed.

Lucius Septimius Severus was also an African, born in Leptis Magna. After a shaky start he had pursued a brilliant military and administrative career. The prestige he earned this way allowed him to pose as, and be accepted as, the avenger of Pertinax. Didius Julianus recognised the threat for what it was. He declared Severus to be a public enemy and sent out hired assassins to murder his rival. Severus returned the compliment. Already marching on Rome, he sent ahead to the Praetorian Guard with orders to abandon Julianus or kill him. The Guard killed Julianus on 2 June 193, following an even shorter reign than Pertinax's – he had lasted just 66 days. When Severus arrived in the city, he staged a monumental funeral and commemoration of Pertinax in a theatrical display designed to legitimise his succession.

Clodius Albinus seems to have faded into the background in this story but the truth is that events had moved so fast he was, for the moment, simply out of the loop. By the autumn of 193 Septimius Severus was in power in Rome but he knew from the outset that his position was far from secure. The main threat came from Pescennius Niger but Severus was far too astute to try and get rid of Niger without securing his rear. Not only did Clodius Albinus command a large garrison in Britain but there was also the rumour that Commodus had earmarked him as a successor. In a brilliant manoeuvre Severus made Clodius Albinus his own successor, which put the latter off his guard, in spite of the fact that Severus already had two sons: Caracalla (born 188) and Geta (born 189). Herodian described Albinus as 'vain and simple', by way of explaining his gullibility. Essentially, the gesture allowed Albinus to realise his ambition without fighting for it, and the arrangement was given widespread publicity when Severus authorised coins of Albinus in his new capacity, and approved the erection of statues.

Albinus had been well and truly fitted up but for the moment he fell for the sting. In 194 he even shared the consulship with Severus who meanwhile turned to the east. The war against Niger is not really relevant here, but it ended with Septimius Severus being in sole control of Italy and the East by 195, though Byzantium remained under siege for a while longer. Pescennius Niger had been defeated three times and made his escape towards the Euphrates. En route he was captured and executed. So much for Niger.

Septimius Severus had no intention of sharing his imperial domains, except with his own family. Clodius Albinus was not just an inconvenient nuisance. There were rumours that some senators were encouraging Albinus to come to Rome while Severus was in the east because he had a better Italian pedigree than the new African emperor. Severus had every intention of ruling without Albinus and passing the Roman Empire onto his own sons. He ruled out fomenting some sort of open dispute because that risked dividing support between himself and Albinus. So, he opted for more underhand trickery. Severus wrote to Albinus declaring that they should rule in partnership in a letter that was supposed to be read out in public in Britain by his aides. The aides were told then that they must lure Albinus into a private place on the pretext that he would be told all sorts of state secrets, but where in fact he would be murdered. The plan started out quite well. The letter was read out in public and Severus' aides then told Albinus about the need for a confidential meeting. Albinus smelled a rat the instant the aides said he had to come with them alone. In any case it was well-known that Severus had cynically courted the support of Niger's generals and then done away with them once he had no further need of them. The aides were arrested and tortured until they admitted the truth. There were no further pretences. This was outright war, and in mobilising his forces Albinus gave Severus the pretext he needed for accusing his former sidekick of treachery. Albinus was declared an enemy of the state and the Severan army set out for the north-west.

The news of Severus being on the march will have taken several days or weeks to reach Albinus. According to Herodian, Albinus was horrified when he heard the news since he had been 'idly whiling away his time in easy living' (iii.7.1). But as this was exactly how Herodian had described Pescennius Niger when Severus marched against him it may be just part of a literary convention, setting up the loser in the conflict to come.

In fact it is highly unlikely that Albinus was distracted in this way. He had already rumbled Severus' true intentions so in all likelihood he was actually involved in mobilising the British garrison. It was around this time, late in 195, that Albinus was proclaimed Augustus by his troops. He shipped his army across to Gaul, and immediately set about garnering support and money from the north-west provinces. Coins in his name as sole ruler of the Roman emperor were issued from the mint at Lyons but were almost entirely confined to silver and gold, types clearly designed for paying soldiers. If later reports are true he was probably counting on senatorial support in Rome, where senators were said to hate Septimius Severus (*Life of Clodius Albinus* xii.1). On the other hand Dio says most senators avoided taking sides (lxxv.4.2). But Clodius Albinus evidently had friends in Rome, because they paid later for their friendship. He was said to have spoken publicly in front of the British troops before this date, to praise the ancient power of the senate and regret its decline – and linking such decay with the rule of men like Nero and Domitian (*Life of Clodius Albinus* xiii.5-6). Such sentiments were bound to warm the hearts of some of the impotent and jaded senators.

We have no idea how many of the British soldiers Albinus brought with him. Removing all the troops is totally implausible. Not so long ago it was still believed that the swathe of rebuilding on Britain's northern frontier after the civil war of the 190s followed opportunistic barbarian activity in an area emptied of soldiers by Clodius Albinus. In fact, the epigraphic evidence of the next ten to fifteen years suggests repairs to set right decades of poor maintenance, unfinished building work and indifference.

Even if Britain's legions contributed only vexillations to Albinus' army, the fact remains that there was not a whisper of dissent. On the continent, support was not so easily forthcoming. Clodius Albinus was indulging in a ludicrous gamble by starting a war with a man who had already proved himself in the east. Lucius Novius Rufus, governor of *Hispania Tarraconensis*, is the only one known to have sided publicly with Clodius Albinus. Of course the truth is that the war could have gone either way, but Clodius Albinus seems rapidly to have resorted to holing himself up in Lyons. From here he manfully sent his army off without him to meet Severus.

The battle was far from one-sided. The fighting was, after all, largely between equals. Roman soldiers preferred set-piece battles, but not against men who had had the same training. Dio claims that 150,000 soldiers were fighting for each side – an impossibly large number, though Herodian says the battles of this war were exceptional for the huge numbers of participants. Severus was of course the more widely experienced general but this does not mean the battle went his way throughout. One of the Severan wings charged right into a booby trap of hidden trenches, and retreated in terror knocking over another of their units in the chaos. Albinus' soldiers took advantage of the mayhem and picked off their enemies with missiles and arrows.

Severus moved in with the Praetorian Guard to help out but he was knocked off his horse and only evaded capture by ripping off his purple cloak. In a mark of how battle tales are spun and counterspun, Dio says he was in fact spurring his own soldiers on by fighting on foot amongst them. Severus was actually in even more danger than it appears at first sight. Hearing that the emperor was down, one of his own generals, a man called Laetus, tore onto the battlefield with fresh troops to try and win the day for himself. Ironically, this lucky arrival of new forces turned the battle in Severus' favour and Laetus swiftly abandoned his spontaneous attempt to become emperor. Severan troops already on the field were delighted, put their man back on his horse and took fresh heart. Meanwhile Albinus' army were celebrating their apparent victory when they were taken entirely by surprise and routed. Lyons paid a dreadful price for being the enemy's base and the city was sacked.

It is not entirely clear what happened to Clodius Albinus in the aftermath. Dio says he committed suicide when he saw the day was lost, while holed up in a house in Lyons. Herodian says Albinus was captured and executed. Other versions suggest a slave killed him, or that his own soldiers did away with him in the hope of a bounty. It makes no difference – he was dead. Severus took the opportunity to curse his enemy in public before ordering the head cut off and sent to Rome on a pole.

The ignominy of Clodius Albinus was extended to his friends and associates. In one account senators who had supported him were executed, including those just thought to be his associates (*Life* xii.3). This seems to be verified by Herodian who confirms that Severus ransacked Albinus' archives for incriminating letters and notes from his senatorial allies (iii.8.6). Albinus' family were killed, and his own body left to rot outside Severus' headquarters (*Life* ix.5-7). Severus added to the acrimony by expending a lot of time on rubbishing his erstwhile foe in every possible respect. Of course this was normal for the time, but it contradicted other evidence from earlier times when the two men had been on good terms.

Clodius Albinus was remembered as he was by historians, simply because he had lost. He was clearly more of a man than it at first seems, or else he would never have reached the post of governor of Britain or remained a key player in the struggle for control of the Empire. Clodius Albinus was the first man to use Britain as a power base in an imperial civil war. He would not be the last. We might in theory assume the legions of Britain went home to nurse their wounds. If they did, we know nothing about that. There are no inscriptions that record reinforcements from anywhere else, or vexillations of other, more loyal, units sent in to keep the peace. Within less than ten years Septimius Severus would place his trust in the British garrison when he embarked on a huge campaign into Scotland. If anything it shows how fickle soldiers can be.

For the moment though, Severus took steps to prevent any chance of another governor using Britain as a power-base. Now, or at some point in his reign (he died at York on campaign in 211) he split Britain into two: *Inferior* ('Further Britain', the north) and *Superior* ('Nearer Britain', the south). This way, he hoped, the garrison of Britain would be split. In the south *II Augusta* and *XX Valeria Victrix* were controlled by the governor of *Britannia Superior*, and in the north the legate commanding *VI Victrix* became the governor of *Britannia Inferior*. If the idea was indeed to stop anyone else using Britain to become emperor, it might have worked for a while. But it made no difference in the long run.

8

From Here to Eternity
ST ALBAN

For all its shortcomings in terms of date and detail, the tale of St Alban is a little window into the world of Romano-British towns in their heyday. Alban was, reputedly, a resident of the city of Verulamium when he was unexpectedly drawn into imperial power politics by his spontaneous decision to become a Christian. The episode was brief and dramatic, and it echoed down through the centuries as a highlight in the Christian reverence for martyrdom. Alban's behaviour, as it was later recorded, challenged the Roman state to its core.

Christianity presented the Romans with a problem from the outset. Although inclusive, in the sense that anyone could join, it demanded exclusive devotion from its adherents. That meant rejecting in every respect the gods and traditions of the pagan past, which lay at the foundation not just of the Roman state but the whole consciousness of the Roman world. Ironically, the pagan world would have been entirely happy to accommodate Christ and his disciples, but only on the basis that Christians accept the universality of all gods and the tolerance of all religions. This was a way of life that saw no spiritual distinction between gods other than their individual powers and properties. There was a god for each place, each concept and each 'thing'. The names were infinite, the powers limitless, and the identities capable of unrestrained conflation and mixing. Christianity could not have been more different.

Britain perfectly exhibits paganism's flexibility in her multiplicity of local British and Roman gods, worshipped alongside imported deities from the Empire's more exotic regions and beyond, like Egypt and Persia. The 'system', such as it was, worked perfectly well so long as everyone who mattered was prepared to include in their worship routine adherence to the politicised gods of the Roman state. That effectively meant being prepared to worship the imperial cult, a kind of fabricated pantheon of selected deceased emperors whose posthumous deification bathed the current mortal incumbent in reflected divinity.

Christians would not play the game. To be fair, they were generally under instructions not to do so though in reality the new religion was still evolving. Orthodoxy had yet to find its feet. Even so, Christianity refuted all other religions. Of course, this led to persecution by the pagan state, or by communities, who felt their world was being threatened. Christians treated this as an elaborated protraction of the treatment dealt to Christ in the first place, so the average Christian found him or herself reacted to in a rather ambivalent way because their religion grew out of personal sacrifice in the face of pain. Being persecuted was almost a definition of being Christian; indeed, the experience of suffering proved one's Christianity and became a validation of faith. Enduring pain just served to demonstrate the strength of commitment. Not being persecuted meant missing the chance to be tested in public.

Christ was believed to have given his life so that others might be saved, and in succeeding years he might have been knocked down in the race for others to give their lives too. The more fanatical

Christians treated execution, preferably following a bout of torture, as the supreme demonstration of faith. The more pain and cruelty endured, the greater the faith, and thus the greater the glory on entering Heaven. Ideally, the episode would be recorded with lascivious detail by a church father to maximise the publicity. Violence was thus at the heart of early Christianity. It needed the pain, and was nourished by the experience of those who endured it.

This sense of exclusive primacy cut into Christianity itself. Within a few years of the religion's birth in the AD 40s, most Christians subscribed to an individual variant of Christianity that refuted all other forms of Christianity, often using physical and verbal violence to express their revulsion. By the time the state had become Christianised it too began to subscribe to one variant or another, and also exercised the same intolerance of schismatic forms of Christianity that it applied to pagans.

If that sounds perverse, it is because human religious fanaticism is perverse and irrational in all its forms. Today we are only too familiar with the consequences of this train of thought in certain other religions. Israel and the Palestinians are locked into combat precisely because of the preparedness of some people to die, not because they believe they have no hope, but because in dying in the name of their faith they believe they are guaranteed salvation. Far from being an expression of a lack of hope, dying from persecution for an early Christian was a fulfilment of hope. Not everyone could handle it. Plenty of the less committed communicants capitulated when faced with the prospect of torture and mutilation, and decided to make a sacrifice to the imperial cult. Realising that all they had to do was recant their faith, even if the recantation was totally insincere, they did so. On the whole that seems so ludicrously straightforward and lateral a solution, it just serves to emphasise how difficult it is to understand for people not integrated into the group mentality that this might be impossible for those with stronger sentiments.

Christians circulated in close-knit communities. Priests could be extremely influential, especially those who had travelled across the Empire and who had been persecuted themselves. In these groups, martyrs were venerated in tales of torture and their forbearance under the greatest cruelty. A total nonentity could propel him or herself from obscurity to the forefront of Christian fame by exposing him or herself to such experiences, and many did. Martyrdom was a fast track to an entry in the Christian *Who's Who* of major players. It is easy to see then how, in a community where so much importance was attached to a public martyrdom, individuals were prepared not just to accept it but even to solicit it. After all, to look at it the other way, taking no part in putting up with persecution was almost to deny being a Christian in the first place. It was into this psyche that Alban, resident of Verulamium, was propelled when a priest knocked at his door.

Christianity is a religion that subsists in the early record almost entirely in verbal form. Pagan cults are defined by an abundance of artefacts that portray and name the deities involved, but Christianity is not. Occasional references in the form of the Chi-Rho monogram are all we have. It took many decades for buildings to appear that can be identified by us as churches, and even longer for images of Christ to appear. Only with the legitimisation of Christianity in the fourth century does the situation significantly alter. But in a resiliently pagan place like Britain, Christianity remained even less visible. Paradoxically, it is Britain that yields one of the first images of Christ, on the mosaic floor at Hinton St Mary (Dorset), while the Water Newton Christian treasure is one of the earliest collections of Christian plate from the Empire.

Today, it is the written tradition of the early Church that provides much of the substantive information about Christianity in the Roman Empire. Alban's martyrdom is a key event in that record and was promulgated as the tale of the first Briton to die for Christ. Unfortunately for us, those who recorded the acts of the martyrs were little concerned with basic historical detail, though some of the accounts read like transcripts of actual court records. But a lack of date-conscious detail is commonplace in Christian records because this was not pertinent to the moral points being made. Even the Gospels contain extremely few references to events or authorities beyond Palestine, and it would take the excision of only a few passages to make even the accurate dating of Christ's life and works impossible. The account of Alban's martyrdom comes mainly from a fifth-century life of St Germanus, Gildas, and the writings of the seventh-century monastic chronicler, Bede. Writing at the monastery of Jarrow, Bede had access to documents that we can now only surmise existed, but he only recorded information directly relevant to his own agenda.

The name of the martyr presents its own problem. Albanus is known from a number of inscriptions to have been a familiar Roman name. Its origins lie in the word *alba*, a white precious stone or pearl, and a variety of places called Alba. Considering Alban's posthumous reputation it does look as if this was a retrospective amendment to make him look appropriately named for his destiny. On the other hand, the name might be genuine, and as such would have made it look as if he was pre-ordained for glory, thus grabbing him headlines in accounts of martyrdom.

Alban's story first appears in the *Life of Germanus* by Constantius. It has been shown that this late fifth-century account, which only turned up in 1901, can be most easily associated with the reign of Septimius Severus who was on campaign in Britain between 208-11. His younger son Geta was left in charge of the Roman part of Britain while Severus was in the north with his elder son Caracalla. Alban was condemned by 'the evil Caesar' without 'orders of the emperors'. At this time Geta held the rank of Caesar while his father and brother were joint emperors. So this corresponds with the state of affairs in 209, but it has to be said that while this is a logical inference from the evidence, corruption and conflation of different accounts make it possible that persecution under Diocletian nearly a century later was the time. Not only that, but the account by Constantius also says that persecutions ceased not long afterward – which fits a context in the early fourth century just before Christianity's legitimisation.

The next account is by Gildas in his moral tale *de Excidio Britanniae*, 'On the Destruction of Britain'. According to Gildas, who wrote in the 500s, the martyrdom of Alban occurred during the reign of Diocletian. This places it at the end of the third century or the beginning of the fourth. Alban of Verulamium took in a priest who was being chased by people bent on persecuting him. Having taken the priest in, Alban then changed clothes with the priest and then took the rap. This rather thin account does little to explain why Alban should have suddenly found it necessary to be executed on someone else's behalf, and also neatly avoids explaining why the priest was uncharacteristically reluctant to take the one-way ticket to paradise Diocletian was already generously offering him. The average zealot would have seized his chance to die in agonised and public glory at the earliest opportunity the Roman authorities were kind enough to offer him.

Bede's account is more expansive though he provides even less detailed dating material except to refer to 'pagan emperors' in the plural. This limits the possibilities to the late second and early third century, and the late third and early fourth centuries. In the Bede version Alban's unexpected houseguest engaged in an impressive bout of prayer and other routines. Eventually, Alban shared in the regimen and was converted. Not surprisingly, this did not go unnoticed and someone went to the authorities with the information that a priest was being concealed. On imperial orders Alban's house was visited, but Alban masqueraded as the priest. Although this ruse was soon uncovered, Alban's actions were regarded as all the more incomprehensible – why on earth was he prepared to take the punishment for someone he had only just met?

Alban refused to make a pagan sacrifice, and was duly tortured. Far from distressing him, the chance to be beaten up and mutilated only enhanced Alban's new found joy. His execution was ordered to take place on 22 June. Alban was led from the city, and a miracle caused the river to dry up. He was led to the place of execution up a hill, where Alban made a stream materialise. His executioner, apparently overcome by the moment and the miracles, took the chance to join Alban and both were killed. The executioner's gesture was considered great enough to exempt him from the normal qualification of baptism to enter Heaven. Just to add to the drama, the replacement executioner's eyes fell out of his head. The miracles soon caused a cessation in the persecutions, as well they might. Subsequently a church was built on the site, and now this is St Albans abbey. In 429 St Germanus arrived in Britain to deal with the Pelagian heresy (see chapter 14). His adventures included visiting the shrine of St Alban at Verulamium. Over time the shrine and subsequent abbey became the focal point of settlement, which left the Roman city to fall into ruin and serve as a handy quarry for the new ecclesiastical establishment.

If the date for the martyrdom of 209 is correct, it is remark-ably early for active Christianity in Britain. Only with the Council of Arles a century later do we have specific evidence for the existence of a Christian ecclesiastical hierarchy. Frankly, the evidence for exactly when Alban's execution took place is ambiguous, and we are unlikely ever to know exactly when it happened. The Water Newton hoard of Christian plate is also undated, except on the general grounds of style, which broadly attributes it to the third century. It encapsulates a moment in the evolution of Christianity when a group of worshippers used a collection of material that combined Christian symbols with pagan styles and practices. Christianity, prior to the legitimisation of the Church, was still hunting for its identity. Although it relied on a hierarchy and the transmission of dogma throughout Christian communities in the Empire, it was still subject to immense variation in treatment and belief. This not only contributed to schismatic disputes, but also meant there was some inconsistency in belief and practice. Once the Church became the principal religion of the Empire it became easier for the episcopal hierarchy to enforce a more universal approach – still not without enormous problems – which over time effectively suppressed not only the more overtly pagan survivals, but also any literature that did not fit into the accepted canon of religious and theological thought. Alban's story therefore survives in forms that reinforced what was considered right in the centuries afterwards. If he belonged to a variation of Christianity that was later suppressed, we would be unlikely to know about it.

A far more radical explanation for the story is that Alban really originated as a local pagan deity, and was appropriated by the Church much as actual pagan places of worship were appropriated. The trouble with this theory is that there is no demonstrable foundation for it, other than the circumstantial vagueness and convenience of the narrative. Alban's behaviour, after all, seems a little implausible at best though it does fit the context of some Christian martyrdoms. But it is easy to see how an extramural temple to a local god at Verulamium might have evolved into a Christian church, with a fabricated martyrdom tradition to 'authenticate' the new establishment. There is no archaeological verification of this, but at Uley (Glos) the shrine of Mercury might have become a very late, or post-, Roman church. In fact, both an authentic Christian martyr, and an appropriated pagan cult, could have been involved. In other words, Alban might have been a real person who did as the story tells us, but who was given a place and tradition around an existing cult that was submerged by the potent charisma of urban martyrdom.

Nevertheless, whatever the explanation, Alban is exceptional in Romano-British history as someone whose actions in life, real or imagined, were made to echo far beyond Britain and his own time. Alban symbolised the challenge Christians were presenting the Roman authorities, by refusing to back down and acknowledge the primacy of the existing power structure. It is virtually certain that he, or a cult of sorts, existed, though there can be no doubt that the story, like a snowball tumbling down a hillside, accumulated details and attributes across the decades and centuries before it was written down in the form we have. The truth is lost to us.

9

The Old Pretender
POSTUMUS

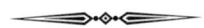

The reign of Postumus, ruler of the Gallic Empire, was a sign of the times. Postumus came to power in or about 259 as a new breed of rebel emperor, when he set up a breakaway Roman state. It was part of the Empire and outside it all at the same time. Illegitimate, it posed as a legitimate Roman Empire. It was as if a pair of alternate realities had come into existence. Postumus was a rebel emperor but he passed himself off as the real thing. Instead of setting his sights on the whole Roman world, Postumus had more regional ambitions but he adopted an ambitious programme of propaganda. His new Empire of the north-west might be hundreds of miles from Rome, but it was cast in a thoroughly conventional image. In an age of uncertainty, and destruction of 'old values', Postumus was determined to pose every inch the Roman. This was a remarkable characteristic of almost all the later rebellions. Their leaders always posed as Roman emperors – there was little sense of establishing, or asserting, a regime with a local name and identity. Instead they hijacked the Roman brand for themselves.

By the mid-third century, the Roman Empire had experienced sixty years of intermittent disruption as the imperial system imploded. The rot began with the death of Commodus in 192. Septimius Severus, victor of the civil war that followed, entirely failed to establish a durable dynasty. His sons, Caracalla and Geta, were supposed to inherit the Empire but Caracalla killed Geta in 212, only to be murdered five years later in 217, in return for his own plunge into a dark abyss of violence and perverted cruelty. Thereafter a succession of inadequates, opportunists, thugs and fanatics took their places one by one on the imperial throne. The chickens started coming home to roost during the joint reign of Valerian and his son Gallienus (253-60). Valerian, like so many emperors of the age, came to power at the head of his army. He had been summoned by the emperor Trebonianus Gallus (251-3) to bring his soldiers to help suppress a revolt by another general and would-be emperor, Aemilian. Aemilian moved more quickly though and killed Gallus. Valerian's troops made their man emperor and Valerian marched on Rome.

Valerian realised the merits of joint rule and made his son Gallienus co-emperor. With so many potential internal and external threats, in theory it was a wise move. Valerian set out for the East in 256 to deal with the Persians. Gallienus was left on his own to rule the West. He stayed on his own because in 260 Valerian was captured by the Persians. Valerian was never released and he disappeared from history. Gallienus was left to rule the Roman world by himself. But even before his father's imprisonment, the hideous problems of managing the late Roman world had become apparent. In the East Odaenathus of Palmyra held sway over much of what was supposed to be Roman territory. Although he styled himself king, ironically he actually defended Rome's interests by holding back the Persians and seems to have been recognised by Gallienus, who acknowledged that he could do nothing about it and might as well integrate Odaenathus into the system rather than exclude him.

Things rapidly deteriorated. In Pannonia a revolt erupted, taking advantage of the opportunity offered by Valerian's capture. In the west Gallienus tried to delegate some of his power by putting his son Saloninus in command of Gaul and leaving Postumus in charge of the Rhine garrisons. There seems to be some doubt over whether this was the spark that lit the touchpaper or whether Saloninus happened to be in the wrong place at the wrong time. Postumus murdered the praetorian prefect Silvanus at Cologne and added the garrison to his forces. Needless to say Saloninus was murdered, but that hardly marked him out by the standards of the day. The worst thing that could happen to a boy in the third century was being born an emperor's son. It almost guaranteed a violent death before, after, or at the same time as his father's. One version of the story is that the Gauls loathed Gallienus and were outraged at the insult of being sent a boy to rule them. Another version presented Postumus as simply an opportunist who murdered Saloninus to make sure he could seize power.

It makes no difference. Either way, Saloninus ended up dead and Marcus Cassianius Latinius Postumus was declared emperor by his troops in the year 259 or 260 in Gaul. The time was just over two centuries since Britain had become a Roman province, and around fifty years since Septimius Severus had split Britain into two provinces to prevent it being led by a rebel. Severus had never antic-ipated a large chunk of the Empire splitting away, rather than just a single province. Postumus had created a breakaway Empire, and this time no one, least of all Gallienus, was in a position to do anything about it. We know nothing about where Postumus came from but the fact that his elevation was welcomed in Gaul makes it very likely he was a Gaul himself, though his name does little more than link him to a conventional Roman identity. Cassianus is an adjectival form of the *gens* Cassius, an ancient Roman family, and means 'of Cassius'. Perhaps in remoter times his ancestors had been retainers or even freedmen of the Cassii. Postumus means 'coming after' and it too was an ancient Rome name; a Postumus had been a friend of Cicero and indeed the Cassius who had been one of Caesar's murderers had also been a correspondent of Cicero's. Marcus and Latinius were both conventional Roman names.

If his name was Roman, it fitted the style of the regime, which was fabricated as a kind of parallel Roman Empire with its capital at Trier. From here Postumus ruled Gaul, Spain and Britain. The Gallic Empire emulated the original in every way and Postumus initially proved an effective and successful pretender to the Roman throne, especially as he justified the regime as fulfilling the task he had been charged with: securing and holding the region. This gave him the credibility any Roman emperor needed. Not only did Postumus hold the Rhine frontier in 261 and secured it against further incursions, but also prevented Gallienus from recapturing the provinces in 263 though this had as much to do with Gallienus withdrawing when he was wounded.

Even when Postumus was murdered in 268 the regime managed to overcome the disarray temporarily as a short spurt of usurpers jumped out of the woodwork. Postumus had marched against Laelianus, a rival who emerged at Mainz. Postumus defeated and killed him but denied his troops the opportunity to sack the city. It was a dilemma. In his role as Roman emperor, going around sacking cities was scarcely wise, but he depended upon the support of his soldiers. They knew that, and killed him. In the interim Marius and Domitianus tried to succeed Postumus but met swift ends. Victorinus took power in 268 but the Gallic Empire started to break apart. Spain drifted back to the real Empire, and Victorinus had to suppress a revolt in Gaul. By 270 he was dead himself and one of his provincial governors, Caius Pius Esuvius Tetricus of Aquitania, became emperor. But by then Aurelian was emperor in Rome. A highly-skilled soldier, Aurelian destroyed the Palmyran kingdom in the East and then marched on Tetricus. Tetricus wisely capitulated without a struggle and was offered a dignified retirement in Rome. In 275 Aurelian was murdered too, but that is another story.

During the forty or so years before Postumus broke away from the Roman Empire, Britain had really started to come of age as part of the Roman world. By the third century her cities were equipped with the necessary public buildings. These had now for the most part been around long enough to become mature structures, many

of which were a century or more old, though it is debatable whether
many of them were actually used as intended. The administration of
the cities of *Britannia Inferior* (the north) and *Britannia Superior* (the
south) is largely silent, but enough inscriptions exist to show that in
the early 200s some men of consequence made their money on the
trade across the North Sea to Germany and Gaul. In other words,
Britain was socially and economically linked to north-western
Europe, more than to any other part of the ancient world. This is
hardly surprising. Limitations on travel and, doubtless, a sense of
regional identity cemented by language and shared traditions must
have played a natural part in reinforcing this.

Thus we have at York, Lucius Viducius Placidus, a *negotiator*
(trader) of *Gallia Lugdunensis*, presenting an arch and gate (or shrine)
to a religious precinct in the capital of *Britannia Inferior* in the year
221. We can assume that Placidus shipped goods from Gaul to
Britain, perhaps out of Bordeaux. By chance another inscription,
from Bordeaux itself, tells us about Marcus Aurelius Lunaris who set
up an altar to the goddess of Bordeaux after having set sail from York
in 237. Lunaris served as a *sevir Augustalis* (priest of the imperial cult)
at York and Lincoln. At Cologne Caius Aurelius Verus tells us he was
a *negotiator Britannicianus* (trader with Britain). A *negotiator
Britannicianus cretarius* (trader in pottery with Britain) called Marcus
Secundinius Silvanus is named on an altar at Domburg in Holland.
At London Tiberius Celerianus has just emerged from the past in a
recently recovered inscription. He was a *moritex Londiniensis* (shipper
of the Londoners?), but was a citizen of the Bellovaci. The Bellovaci
were a tribe in *Gallia Belgica* (Belgium), and together with the other
inscriptions helps paint a picture of a commercial class whose liveli-
hoods were built around commuting with the continent, and which
depended on the security of the seas.

It was the security of the seas these men, or their agents, sailed
across that had become a major issue in the third century. To a large
extent it would never go away, but the Roman world could not
accommodate the inhibition of free movement of people and goods.
Britain's military zone had rolled north in the first and second

centuries, leaving a relatively peaceable area behind it in which towns grew, and where rural settlement developed more gradually. But in the third century the army came back. The reason was simple: the North Sea and the English Channel were attracting pirates from northern Europe. It was natural enough. The sea must have been crowded with merchantmen laden with manufactured goods, food, money and men. What more could a pirate want?

Around the time that Lucius Viducius Placidus was commemorating his generosity, at least two new forts had been built to help control the seas round Britain. At Brancaster in Norfolk and Reculver in Kent, conventional forts were built in coastal locations. How they integrated with Roman naval power we have no idea. They might have served as bases for troops and look-out posts for enemy ships, but it is no less likely they protected ports and ferries or were supplied from the sea to help police the inland. Likewise, we have no idea if they were effective at all, or were just a sop to the likes of Lunaris and Placidus. We can imagine men like them bleating to the governors of *Britannia Inferior* and *Britannia Superior*, and imploring them for men and resources to protect their wealth and trade. Just how bad things became is starkly obvious at Richborough in Kent. By the mid-third century a grandly imperial triumphal arch – a marble-clad icon of Roman imperial power erected almost certainly by Domitian or Trajan to commemorate the conquest of Britain in the first century – was converted into a fortified lookout tower.

More fortified sites were added around Britain's southern and eastern shores, and similar examples were built along the Gaulish coast. Far from helping explain how the installations worked they only complicate affairs. Over the century most of the towns were equipped with full-scale defences, and it is likely the appearance of coastal fortifications belongs to the same general pattern of feeling the need to defend everyday activity. The forts at Burgh Castle, Richborough and Dover (amongst others) could easily have served as fortified ports rather than garrison posts, or both. But it would be wrong to believe this all belonged to some master plan. The appearance of coastal fortifications and town defences is too piecemeal, and scattered over far too long a time, for that to be right. Built in the 330s, Pevensey for instance is at least a century later than Reculver and Brancaster, unless some predecessor awaits discovery under the fourth-century stone walls. But the resources expended on them all can only reflect a continual belief that security needed bolstering.

It was in this broader context that Postumus came to power. It is easy to see why Britain would have accepted integration into the Gallic Empire. He was a man of substance and he had made his name in the region, and thus commanded a more powerful personal reputation amongst the influential élite in the north-west provinces. He must have seemed in every sense more real, more plausible and more relevant than Gallienus and his son Saloninus.

Postumus and his successors were largely integrated into the record in Britain as if the regime had legitimately succeeded Gallienus. Postumus held consulships in his new Empire. A few military units certainly took or were awarded the title *Postumianae* ('Postumus' own'), which they recorded on inscriptions, and he appointed his own governors. At Lancaster a baths and its basilican exercise hall were restored between 262-6, by the resident auxiliary cavalry wing *ala Sebosiana* for his governor Octavius Sabinus. Appropriately enough the *ala* adopted the new emperor's name. The troopers had become *ala Sebussiana* (sic) *Postumianae*, 'The Postumian Sebosian cavalry wing'. The *II Augusta* allied themselves at least twice on inscriptions, one from Caerleon and one from near Carlisle, with the joint reigns of Valerian and Gallienus. But by the late 260s they seem to have been manufacturing tiles with the epithet *Victoriniana* for Postumus' successor Victorinus. This also seems to have been done by *XX Valeria Victrix*, but the evidence here is even less convincing.

More specific are the milestones, or as some would have them, 'honorific pillars'. Postumus, Victorinus and Tetricus are all named on a variety of milestones in locations across Britain. Curiously though the legitimate emperor Claudius II (268-70) seems to have turned up on a single example from Wall (Staffs). It is an interesting anomaly and suggests that part of Britain's administration was less convinced about allying itself with a rebel regime, especially in the uncertainty that followed the murder of Postumus. But the stone itself is little more than a fragment. There is not a single milestone recording Gallienus, and just one for Valerian. But it is unwise to read too much into milestones. There may have been provincial, regional or even local directives to erect new stones or amend old ones, but it is quite obvious from the surviving examples that this was performed extremely erratically. Some stones could stand for fifty years before a long-dead emperor's name was replaced, with intervening rulers passing without mention despite sporadically turning up elsewhere.

For a man who came to power unexpectedly, Postumus seems to have had a clear idea of the image he wanted to present. He was unequivocally a reactionary, but he also had an eye for innovation. Postumus issued a full suite of Roman coins, some in such abundance that they are common finds today. This is in part due to the debased nature of the nominal silver coinage of the period. His coinage was also copied in such colossal quantities that coin hoards of the period often include tens of thousands of coins in the names of the rulers of the Gallic Empire.

Postumus issued coins with suitably conventional reverse legends that were supposed to evoke peace, harmony, the faithful army, and the good health of the provinces. He was 'Restorer of the Gauls', and often associated himself with Hercules, symbol of power and strength. Some of his coins name 'Deusonian Hercules', a cult based at Deusona on the Rhine. Postumus also made it clear that he fought and ruled in the name of Eternal Rome, on coins issued later in the reign and which seem to represent evolving ambitions. This contrasted with the corruption and incompetence of a succession of inadequate legitimate emperors. In a sense Postumus was really no less legitimate than many of them; the only difference was that he made no attempt to secure Rome itself. In one striking divergence from tradition, Postumus had himself depicted on some of his gold coins with a facing portrait. Amongst numismatists the gold coinage of Postumus is considered amongst the finest achievements of all Roman coinage, for both its purity and quality of execution. In fact, much of the coinage struck by Postumus (as opposed to the copies manufactured at the time) is markedly better in every sense than coinage of the legitimate Empire: the designs are better, the portraiture superior, the lettering better cut and so on. In that respect the coins symbolise the way Postumus more successfully managed the imagery of power in the Roman idiom.

So if Postumus was posing as a legitimate emperor he was in this sense doing a better job than the real one. His coinage is good evidence that was at least attempting to reform or revive the economy of the area. The mainstay was the radiate, a denomination that had started life as a silver double *denarius* under Caracalla and which was by now little more than silver-washed bronze. There is no easy modern equivalent, but Britain's contemporary £1 coin is made of base metal, while a hundred years ago the gold sovereign represented the denomination. The collapse in the buying power of the pound illustrates the point. Today the gold sovereign is worth around £60-70. The same differential would have applied in antiquity. An old silver *denarius* would have been worth many times more than a bronze radiate, even though the former was nominally half the value of the latter. What had happened was that the later radiates had a far lower *intrinsic* value than the old silver radiates or the silver *denarii*. Not only were more radiates needed to represent 'value', but the reduced value of each coin made it more easily discarded just as we abandon our coppers. The radiates of the period, minted by Postumus or those struck by forgers, constitute the vast majority of coins lost or thrown away in Britain in the latter part of the third century.

Postumus knew how significant coinage could be. Later, Carausius would achieve extraordinary results but he followed in Postumus' footsteps. Postumus tried to restore the old base metal coins of the earlier Empire. He struck brass *sestertii* in a vain attempt to revive credibility. It was rather a forlorn effort because the ridiculous situation emerged in which a radiate, nominally worth eight of the old *sestertii*, contained no more actual metal than a fraction of a single *sestertius*. To compensate Postumus tried issuing a double *sestertius*, often overstruck on old *sestertii*. He stopped short of claiming legitimacy all the way. His *sestertii* all lack the initials 'S.C.', stamped on all the old bronze and brass coins of earlier times, even the double-*sestertii* of Trajan Decius (249-51). Representing *Senatus Consulto*, 'by order of the Senate', the abbreviation paid lip service to the Roman Senate's ancient control of coinage. Evidently Postumus thought that would be a step too far.

The coinage of the Gallic Empire flooded Britain. One of the curiosities of Roman coinage was its erratic distribution. For much of the first part of the third century, Britain seems to have been excluded from regular supplies. For example, *sestertii* of Severus Alexander (222-35) and his successors are unusual site finds in Britain but not around the Mediterranean. Instead, in Britain increasingly worn and abraded second-century *sestertii* of emperors like Hadrian and Antoninus Pius remained in service until they were almost featureless discs, with some being pressed into reuse by Postumus. We can only assume that limited supplies to Britain of new base-metal coins during the first half of the third century meant they rarely circulated in a way that meant they would become casual losses.

From the mid-third century onward, coinage was increasingly susceptible to attempts at reform. This might explain the hoards of coins from the Gallic Empire in Britain, abandoned after the breakaway regime collapsed either because they had been declared officially worthless or were left in storage 'just in case' their value was restored, which in the event never materialised. The Mildenhall (Wilts) 'Cunetio' hoard of 1978 included nearly 55,000 radiates, of which more than 24,000 belonged to the Gallic Empire. The Normanby hoard of 1985 was made up of nearly 48,000 radiates, of which more than 33,000 belonged to the Gallic Empire. Hoards like these probably reflect the circulating coinage of the age and show that Gallic Empire coinage dominated but circulated alongside issues by the legitimate Empire until 273.

When Tetricus I capitulated to Aurelian in 273, the Gallic Empire slipped silently into the past. Its coins were discarded in millions, and today these are amongst the commonest metal finds from all of Britain's archaeology of all periods. New milestones and imperial inscriptions were manufactured in the names of Aurelian (270-5) and his successors. This even included extremely short-lived rulers like Florianus (276), of whom four alone have been found in Britain (out of an Empire-wide total of little more than a dozen). It has been suggested that part of the reason for this was a curious kind of regional urgency in parts of Britain to advertise support for the legitimate regime. There may have been an element of obligation involved in an area of the world that had just been part of a breakaway Empire. But to the vast majority of the Romano-British Postumus and his Gallic Empire are unlikely really to have impinged much on their consciousness. The 'system' clearly continued to function as it had before. The survival of Florianus milestones could just as easily be a distortion caused by later indifference, whereas elsewhere they were more routinely replaced. The impact will have been much more clearly felt by the descendants of men like Viducius Placidus, to whom a secure regional Empire was of far more importance than an insecure remote one. Although their sense of security must have been enhanced, the archaeology of the period shows a sustained decline in inter-province trade. By the end of the third century the great Gaulish samian industries were a distant memory. Most of Britain's ceramic requirements were catered for within the island. Trade undoubtedly continued but it seems to have been on a much smaller scale, while public building and urban development had also faded into the past.

The real legacy of Postumus was his concept of a thoroughly Roman type of rebel Empire. His sense of creating a reformed Roman world with a power base other than in Rome itself was a whole new brand of insurrection. In the past, usurpers and challengers of the imperial throne were overwhelmingly opportunist, and operated with a reckless disregard for the damage they did to Rome's prestige and sense of purpose. Self-seekers like Clodius

Albinus contrast hugely with Postumus. Postumus at least had both a sense of local responsibility, and a more expansive vision. He expended his energy on securing frontiers and presenting an effective imperial image, not on embarking on an ill-fated campaign to seize the whole Empire. He must have seemed, quite simply, more useful and relevant in the north-west. Not surprisingly, he had generated a new archetype for some of the other rebels yet to come. At the same time he had shown that in a world of destructive easy-come, easy-go rulers his vision was more than just gratuitous self-aggrandisement. Even so, the disproportionate level of military resources in the region gave Postumus the means to realise his vision. Like all rebels he suffered the usual fate, but he left more than most behind him. At least one modest sailor on the North Sea realised that. Postumus, Victorinus and Tetricus had had their day, but Mausaeus Carausius was waiting in the wings.

10

Total Recall

CARAUSIUS AND ALLECTUS

By the late third century, Rome's Augustan age seemed an almost impossibly long time ago. It was as far back in time as the reign of Anne (1702-14) and the exploits of John Churchill, duke of Marlborough, are to us. But despite the passage of time, the civil wars, the usurpers and the barbarian threats, the Roman imperial world had survived with all its institutions intact. If anything it had initially grown relentlessly. Across the provinces a myriad cities aped Rome, her buildings and her ways, and since the reign of Caracalla (211-17) Roman citizenship had been made universal. A traveller of the Roman Empire in the late 200s crossed a world in which every urban destination or overnight stop resembled each other. When Augustus ruled, Britain had no towns. In the 280s regional capitals existed across much of Britain, every one of them a miniature Rome with its local assembly, basilica and forum, street grid and defences.

There was though a qualitatively different tone to the third-century Empire. Since the death of Commodus in 192 a succession of military emperors and usurpers had transformed the image of the emperor. The idealised portrayals of Augustus had given way to unnervingly lifelike images of unshaven thugs like Maximinus I (235-8) and Philip the Arab (244-9). This was a time when a provincial soldier could rise to the top, and enjoy a brief and violent reign before his murdered body was thrown to the mob.

Not surprisingly, plenty of people regretted the way things had gone and looked back to better times, better emperors and better prospects. That had been an age of certainties about Rome's destiny, and an absolute confidence in her power. Of course, like all retrospective yearnings, the admiration of the past was based on a fantasy, but that did nothing to prevent some of the more imaginative opportunists of the age from acting out their dreams. The most imaginative of all was Carausius, or at any rate those unknown men who put him into power.

Mausaeus Carausius was a Menapian, born in the area we call the Low Countries. During Caesar's campaigns more than 300 years before Carausius, the Menapii had had to hide in the forests while the Romans destroyed their crops and villages. It was a mark of the impact of Rome on a remote provincial society that Carausius posed as a traditional Romanist and nothing else. That his heyday was in the 280s means he must have been born around the time that Postumus was running his miniature north-west Roman Empire. Carausius was said to have spent his formative years at sea, though we can only guess whether that meant he worked as a fisherman, trader, merchant sailor or as a tar in the Roman fleet.

Carausius evidently joined the armed forces at some point because he took part in the war in Gaul in 284, the year Diocletian became emperor. The war was not a conventional Roman conflict. Instead of conquering territory, or defending the frontiers, the troops faced an internal problem. They were led by Maximian against a band of dispossessed outlaws called the Bagaudae. We know little about the Bagaudae but third-century barbarian incursions and Roman political instability led to various communities and individuals losing businesses and land. Initially just forming disparate bands of the disaffected, the Bagaudae eventually coagulated into a more purposeful

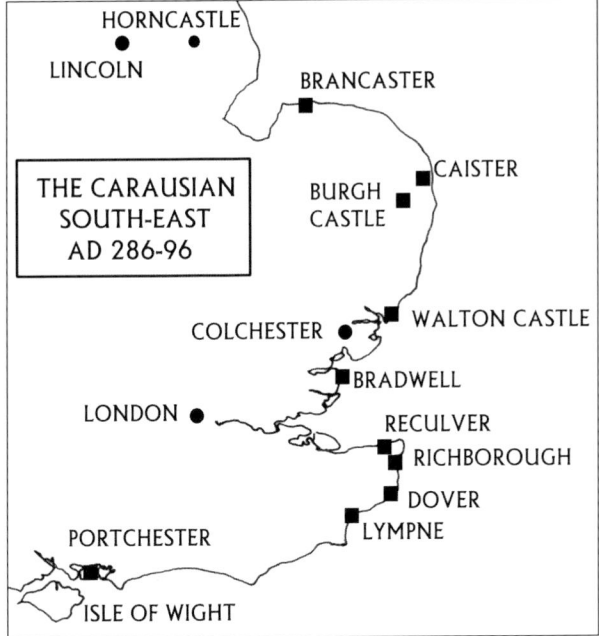

4 The Carausian south-east AD 286-96. The map shows the
locations of fortified coastal sites on the south and east. Most were
built during the third century, some under Carausius himself

rabble. It took Maximian's forces the best part of two years to
suppress them, showing how serious a threat the Bagaudae posed.

The management of the campaign itself anticipated how Diocletian
planned to rule the Empire. Mindful of the enormous pressures on
imperial administration, Diocletian was in the throes of creating a
college of emperors. From 286 he would rule the East, while
Maximian would rule the West. From 293 they would each have an
assistant, known as a Caesar, who would in due course succeed them,
and then appoint their own Caesars. And so on and so on – the idea
was to generate a self-perpetuating system that distributed imperial
initiative, influence and power more widely and was devolved through
a broader system of civilian and military commands.

In some respects the new system was designed to prevent the
problems that had helped create the Bagaudae in the first place.

Suppressing the Bagaudae did nothing to deal with the pirate threat on the North Sea and English Channel. In the chapter about Postumus, the problem of interpreting the forts that appeared around the south and east coast in the third century was raised. There is no easy explanation but like the urban defences of the same period, they combine to show that southern Britain underwent a long period of general fortification. Part of the explanation must have been a feeling of susceptibility to maritime raiding, or internal dissent, or both. By the time Carausius came to power the coasts of Gaul and Britain were equipped with a chain of coastal fortified compounds. The English Channel had become a fortified maritime rat-run. Or had it?

The physical structure of the shore forts like Portchester and Richborough, with massive walls and solid bastions designed to support defensive artillery, suggests they were defensive strongholds. They must have played a part in the Carausian Revolt but not all of them were in existence by this date. Portchester seems to be Carausian, but Pevensey was not built until the 330s, leaving a huge stretch of the south coast between Lympne and Portchester without a fort until then. With only primeval artillery at their disposal the fort garrisons would have been totally unable to fire a fusillade at pirates sailing past miles out to sea. The forts may have corralled mounted troops who rode out to challenge raiders that landed along the coast, but fly-by-night coastal pirates would probably have been and gone long before any response could be organised. Alternatively, they might have been used as prisoner-of-war compounds or as refuges for civilians. Or, they might just have been built as sops to public sensibilities and fears. Unfortunately, since the interior of the forts have yielded very little evidence for buildings it is not even possible to know for certain what sort of troops or even civilians occupied them.

We have no records of specific raids, or places that we know to have been attacked by the pirates. So the physical remains of the forts exist in almost an historical vacuum. But the threat was so severe by 286 that Maximian placed Carausius in charge of the Roman fleet in the Channel. He seems to have been alarmingly successful; alarming, that is, to Maximian who saw that Carausius rapidly accumulated popular support, instead of the imperial high command getting the credit. The region is, and has always been, a place where men have made their careers on the high seas. In the seventeenth century, the English and the Dutch were the greatest maritime rivals in the world. The North Sea and the English Channel were where those tensions exploded into violence, like the Battle of Lowestoft in 1665. That war was all about trade, and control of key routes. It merely perpetuated a dynamic that had existed for millennia, and the pirates of the third century were just another expression of it.

The means by which Carausius earned his fame was a remarkable portent, but in a world where sea power was still relatively unimportant, Britain's secret was set aside for another time. Being an island had marginalised Britain from mainstream classical civilisation, for the simple reason that the world orbited around Rome and its land-based army. Roman fleets existed, and served to good effect, but they were primarily used for landing forces and as a tactical response to maritime threats. The fleet was always secondary to the army. The commander of a fleet, for example, had traditionally been an equestrian prefect, not a senatorial legate, and thus was classified along with commanders of auxiliary units. Carausius ought to have discovered that a maritime power base in Britain provided him with the freedom to go where he pleased and to strike where he pleased. But the ships and navigation skills to realise such an ambition lay hundreds of years in the future.

For the meantime, the story circulated that Carausius let the pirates do their work, raiding villas and towns, and then ambushed them on the way home, hiving off some or all of the loot for himself. Since Carausius later appears to have had significant stocks of bullion, there may have been some truth in the story. On the other hand, Maximian might have circulated the rumours to demolish the image of Carausius as a deliverer of civilians from the pirate threat. Maximian's reaction backfired badly. He announced that Carausius was an enemy of the state. Carausius moved swiftly in a way that illustrated how he had reached command of the fleet in the first place. He announced that he was Emperor of a reborn Roman Empire, and styled himself Marcus Aurelius Mausaeus Carausius. In this way he even posed as a pseudo-descendant of Marcus Aurelius, the last emperor with an untarnished image and who had died a little over a century before in 180.

The paradox of the Carausian rebellion was its fundamentally reactionary nature. Postumus had set the tone, but he never matched the sheer unprecedented front of Carausian propaganda. Carausius rebelled against the Roman Empire by reinventing it. The ideological basis, or spin, of his revolt was that he, Carausius, had established a reborn Roman Empire in Britain and Gaul. In a curious way it anticipated the medieval 'Holy Roman Empire' that attempted to recreate a Roman Empire elsewhere than in Rome. The difference in antiquity was that the real Roman Empire was still very much alive and its rulers took exception to a provincial upstart. Of course Carausius was in a strong position. Postumus had already shown how difficult it was to challenge a popular regional usurper. But Carausius had also taken control of the seas, and he had been handed the means to do so on a plate.

Armed with a fleet, and the new fortifications along the British and Gaulish coasts, there was no one else on hand to do anything about the new Carausian Empire. If he had been filching the proceeds, plenty of the Romano-British might have regarded that as a small price to pay for stability and a vision. There is not the slightest suggestion of any popular opposition to the rebellion, even in the propaganda of its enemies. In any case, Britain had only been controlled by the mainstream Empire for the last thirteen years. Before that the Gallic Empire of Postumus and his successors would have been the principal memory for everyone in Britain and Gaul between the ages of ten and forty. At the time, that meant almost everyone. Just to add to the simmering separatist fantasies, in 280 a man called Bonosus started a rebellion in Cologne. He was believed to have been born in Spain, but to parents with British ancestry. The revolt was brief and Probus (276-82) was gracious in how he treated

Bonosus and his family. Before long Probus had another 'British' problem. One of his advisers, Victorinus, had recommended someone (whose name is unknown) to be governor of Britain. The governor led another rebellion that had to be quashed by Victorinus.

The revolts of Postumus and Carausius allowed the rebellious ruler of a breakaway Empire in the north-west to offer the landowners, the wealthy and the influential all the status, patronage and positions they craved. It is very important to appreciate that Britons, above all, regardless of their estates or local influence, played no visible part at all in imperial politics. Quite why this was is entirely unknown and in part may be due to the fragmentary evidence. But no other part of the Roman world seems to have been so marginalised from this upper tier of provincial Roman society. Some Gauls, for example, had become senators as far back as the first century. Carausius offered Britain's high-and-mighty to be major players. But those less inclined to participate saw the chance to curry favour with the legitimate Empire by being first in the queue when Carausius fell.

While this was a rebellion in any normal sense of the word, its chief protagonist took great care to operate a publicity campaign that called it the exact opposite. It is often said that Roman coinage was used as a propaganda vehicle. Many Roman coins do indeed carry news of military successes and new buildings or initiatives, alongside vast issues that just underlined an association between a Roman emperor and appropriate virtues like Felicitas, Spes, Libertas, and Hilaritas. But the vast majority conform to a relentlessly unoriginal series of stock personifications and imperial titles.

Carausius commandeered many of the usual coin types. But he also added new varieties that were at once idiosyncratic and highly traditional, as part of his quest to link the new regime with an ancient Roman mythical and literary cultural past. To add insult to injury he even managed to issue some of his coins struck on the first high-quality silver bullion used for Roman coinage for generations, and the best since Nero more than 220 years before. Some of his earliest bronze coins show that he prioritised issuing money from the outset, since they were over-struck on coins of previous reigns. Evidently there had not even been time in the opening days of the rebellion to produce blanks. Before long, the coinage became better established. Although the flans of Carausian coins vary in dimension and weight his unusual name is always spelled accurately. Die-links show that most of the coins were struck at the 'L' mint and the 'C' mint, the letters for which appear on many of the coins. L must be London, but C could be several different places such as *Camulodunum* (Colchester) and *Glevum* (Gloucester).

One of the designs has always been recognised as a radical and significant issue. *Expectate Veni* appeared on the reverse of some of the new silver denarii, and a very few bronze coins. Meaning 'Come, the Awaited One!' it alludes to a line in Virgil's *Aeneid*. This was, for many years, just speculation, but there is now no reasonable doubt of the ultimate source. Of course, it could just have been indirect transmission, but several other silver coins carry legends that echo Virgilian themes, while two of the unique medallions of Carausius give the game away. One of the medallions carries the initials RSR, and the other bears INPCDA. These correspond to the sixth and seventh lines of Virgil's Fourth *Eclogue*, one of the most famous poems of antiquity, both then and now. The lines read:

> . . . *Redeunt Saturnia Regna*
> *Iam Nova Progenies Caelo Demittitur Alto*

> '. . . The Saturnian reign returns [i.e. The Golden Age is back]
> Now a new generation is let down from Heaven above'

Together with *Expectate Veni*, the legends follow a Messianic theme. Today we associate that concept exclusively with Christ, but in the world of late antiquity the idea of a saviour was more broadly based. Christianity was not the only cult to promote the concept, and in Britain Carausius had devised a more prosaic version. Even so, he had had the sense to link his exalted position to Roman historical and literary traditions. Virgil had written for Augustus, providing an esoteric literary reflection and basis for the Augustan regime and new, post-Republic, world order. Carausius hijacked it for his own purposes, as Josef Goebbels hijacked Germany's mythical and artistic heritage for the Nazi propaganda machine, but it only worked for both because they could rely on their public recognising the themes and imagery. No other Roman emperor ever made so explicit a reference to Rome's literary heritage. Evidently the shakers and movers of late third-century Britain could be relied on to know their Virgil and, presumably, everything else respectably Roman. If that sounds unlikely, it isn't. This was an age when a relatively limited canon of literature found daily application in reading-and-writing classes. Quotations and phrases from Virgil, Ovid and others popped up in everyday speech as pieces from Shakespeare do in ours. The difference is that in the twenty-first century, most of us are too ignorant to know it – and there's the rub.

Since we know about these aspects of Carausius almost entirely from his coinage it would be useful if we knew at whom the coins were aimed. The series of silver *denarii* were surely issued for the armed forces in Britain, though there is little about them to make that explicit, apart from the *Concordia Militum* issue. Since the late second century the standard of silver coinage had been plummeting. By the 280s the legitimate Empire was producing 'silver' coinage that was little more than bronze with a silver wash. Carausius knew perfectly well that his ability to pay troops with high-quality bullion not only would ensure his path to power, but also his chances of keeping it and appearing more legitimate than the real Empire.

Carausius also issued abundant quantities of the bronze radiate coinage produced at the time. Once the radiate coin (distinguished by the imperial portrait wearing a radiate crown) had been a double-*denarius*, but from its first appearance under Caracalla (211-17) its silver purity was lower than that of the *denarius*. Like all bad money it chased out the good. People hoarded the old silver *denarius* whenever it was available, and the government used the *denarii* taken in through taxes to strike debased radiates with. It made the available silver go further, but of course in an age when intrinsic value of coinage was the key to its acceptance, inflation followed. The cycle of inflation and debasement accelerated and in the 280s the radiate was a shadow of its former self.

Carausius made good use of the radiate to promote his image and slogans more widely. The vast majority bear the legend *Pax Aug* and vary enormously in size and weight. Some specifically name the legions in Britain and several stationed on the continent, such as *II Parthica*. It was once thought that *VI Victrix* was omitted from the series in the absence of any coins mentioning the unit. This was difficult to reconcile with a single milestone naming Carausius from near Carlisle, well inside the province of *Britannia Inferior* (northern Britain), administered from York by the commander of *VI Victrix* who was also its governor. Very recently a Carausian coin of *VI Victrix* has turned up, showing incidentally how much time and paper spent on unresolvable speculation can founder when a fact, rare in archaeology, inconveniently has the good grace to turn up. It makes one wonder how much other speculation would dissipate as swiftly if only something equally tangible would materialise to resolve other problems. The radiates with the war galley reverse and legend *Felicitas Aug* might be taken to be a record of Carausius' battle fleet, but in fact they recall coins issued under Hadrian and Postumus with the same reverse type. A rare issue with the reverse *Victoria Germ(anica)* shows a conventional image of captives beside a trophy. This might be an explicit reference to Carausius' own campaign against pirates or, as seems more likely, it is just a type appropriated from earlier reigns, such as Gallienus, and which had no reference to fact. At any rate it certainly illustrates how difficult it is to be certain of the level of fiction in the Carausian coin series. Since we lack much literary verification of the reign's events it is impossible to say.

But the literary and traditional Roman overtones to some of the Carausian coins suggest that they were part of an overall package designed to appeal to a late flowering of classical aspirations amongst part of the Romano-British civilian population. The age of villas was dawning and throughout the next seventy to eighty years many of these buildings would be elaborated with mosaics depicting classical mythological and religious themes. We do not know who these people were, but as the mosaics are usually relatively crude by continental standards and the choice of themes both idiosyncratic and sometimes confused, it seems likely that they were the descendants of men and women who once might have supported Boudica and Caratacus. In other words, the upper-class Britons had achieved what the Romans had always intended. Now they saw themselves as Romans too, but along the way the Roman vision had so decayed that they saw a future with their new breed of rebel leader.

We know nothing specific about the people who supported Carausius in Britain, or whether there was an active group of people who worked against him. In fact, it is scarcely credible that everyone supported him. Such things never happen, if only because certain ambitious individuals will always gamble on a rebel regime falling and wish to place themselves in line for promotion into vacancies resulting from the inevitable pogrom that follows. A curiosity of some of the coin hoards of the period is the virtual exclusion of Carausian coinage (the same phenomenon had also been observed for a few hoards under the Gallic Empire), or was it just that the coins had become too rare or valuable to hoard this way? The Gloucester hoard, found in 1960, had 15,544 radiates. Of these, just 38 were Carausian, while there were 1,531 contemporary coins of Diocletian and Maximian. The Langtoft no. 1 hoard, found in 2000, showed a similar pattern with its 976 coins. The most intriguing aspect is the acceptance of coins struck by Carausius but in the name of the legitimate regime. At Langtoft, just three of the coins are Carausian in his name, but 45 Carausian coins struck in the names of Diocletian and Maximian were included (see below).

How can we interpret such hoards? Strictly speaking the motivation of any hoarder is entirely lost to us. But the 'legitimist' hoards do pose questions. Did the hoarder at Gloucester or Langtoft, or in any of the other cases, largely exclude rebel coin because he anticipated it might be demonetised? Or was he worried that if he was apprehended with rebel coin after the collapse of the regime, he might be implicated in the rebellion by association? A third possibility is that after the rebellion was over, the hoarder removed rebel coin to spend it fast before it was demonetised.

We cannot possibly answer these questions, but it is clear that rebel money posed an issue of sorts to some hoarders. In any case these theories are based on the idea that owning rebel money might be dangerous, and that it had become worthless – all reasonable enough, but all modern speculation. If we jump ahead through time to 9 February 1665 we find the celebrated diarist Samuel Pepys telling us that 'the Crownes of Cromwell's are now sold it seems for 25 shillings and 30 shillings a-piece'. Since the 'crown' denomination was worth five shillings (25 pence), it had now rocketed to 500 and 600 percent original face value. They had been entirely demonetised the previous March, but despite a climate in which some of the killers of Charles I were tried and executed, collectors were busy snapping up the rebel regime's illegal coinage at a vast premium (which incidentally the coinage retains to this very day). Perhaps Carausian coins, especially the silver, enjoyed a similar vogue.

Carausius had a good start. He had taken Diocletian and Maximian by surprise and, since he controlled the sea, they had little choice but to fall back. It was not all plain sailing. Carausian coins struck at Rouen show he had a foothold in Gaul but it did not last long, though he clung on to Boulogne. The coins are rare and he seems to have lost Rouen quickly and that must mean he lost the use of Gaulish ports. Thanks to the existence of imperial panegyrics and other later Roman histories we have a little more than just the coinage to go on. In or around 289 the Empire mounted an expedition to end the unseemly spectacle of a pirate emperor. Like many Roman maritime expeditions it was a disaster. Storms wrecked the fleet and Carausius was left in peace.

Diocletian and Maximian watched with horror as Carausius posed not just as a legitimate Roman emperor but even got round by the year 292 to producing coins which depicted him as the third member of their regime. With reckless bravado, Carausius approved the striking of coins that showed him alongside Diocletian and

Maximian with a legend that read *Carausius et Fratres sui*, 'Carausius and his Brothers'. The compliment was not returned. One can scarcely imagine the blind fury the coins must have occasioned, but even at this distance of time it is impossible not to admire the sheer cheek of it all. It was as if Charles Stuart, the Young Pretender, and leader of the Jacobite Rebellion had issued coins of himself alongside George II in 1745 as joint monarchs.

In 293 the tide turned, and the Empire struck back. It might have been an administrative convenience to leave Britain to Carausius. Britain was, after all, not of great importance and there were bigger fish to fry on the continental frontiers. But Carausius was an embarrassment, and altogether beyond the pale. There was no serious prospect of leaving him in place. In that year the Tetrarchy had been established. Diocletian and Maximian appointed their assistants, Galerius and Constantius Chlorus respectively. Constantius Chlorus besieged Boulogne and the city fell. The pace then quickened. Carausius was fatally damaged by this setback. We have no idea what happened behind the scenes. There is every possibility that Maximian and Constantius were operating a campaign of subterfuge. In an instant Carausius was dead, murdered (it was said) by Allectus.

Allectus is a man about whom we know nothing except that he was said to be Carausius' finance minister. Even his name is unique though it matches the participle derived from the verb *allego*, 'to choose', meaning 'the Chosen One'. For all we know he was put up to the job by Maximian and Constantius, and was promised all sorts of rewards for doing so in the way that Clodius Albinus had been conned by Septimius Severus. Certainly all the swaggering slogans of Carausian coinage disappeared in a trice. Allectus made no effort to pose as a would-be Tetrarch, though his coins recorded his peregrinations in the legend *Adventus Augusti*, 'the Arrival of the Emperor'. In contrast to Carausian coins the coins are generally well made, consistently sized and thoroughly bland. In fact, were it not for the fact that Allectan coinage only really turns up in Britain and was struck at London and the 'C' mint, he could be mistaken for a legitimate, albeit short-lived, Roman emperor. The only innovation was a small bronze coin, perhaps posing as a defunct half-*denarius* called the *quinarius* because the mintmarks are either QL or QC. Carausian silver disappeared but Allectus had enough gold left to issue good quality gold *aurei*. Two were found in the Bath spring.

Alternatively, Allectus could have been as much a rebel as his murdered predecessor but appreciated that the Carausian style had been provocative and in the end unsuccessful. Perhaps both men were just the visible face of a rebellious oligarchy that now decided to change its style. Either way the next three years were uneventful in Britain, but Allectus can scarcely have been unaware that across the water moves were afoot to terminate him. Some of his coinage has been found in Gaul so there was certainly movement of a sort, and that means news and gossip too.

By 296 the game was up. Two imperial fleets were prepared and set sail from Gaul. The praetorian prefect Asclepiodotus left from the mouth of the Seine. Masked by a handy sea-fog, Asclepiodotus slipped through the ambush set him by the Allectan fleet. Asclepiodotus landed his fleet, burned the ships to prevent Allectus making use of them, and any of his soldiers from getting cold feet, and set off inland. Allectus was totally wrong-footed by this development. It was a supreme irony. In ancient times, Britain's reputation as a fog-laden wilderness of unspeakable grimness had terrified its would-be Roman invaders. Now, 253 years after the Claudian forces crossed the Channel a British fog turned out to be the Roman trump card. Allectus fled inland, his army in disarray, and leaving behind him another wing of his naval forces. Asclepiodotus gave chase, and forced a battle in which Allectus was killed. Meanwhile Constantius' fleet was delayed but in due course made for the Thames and seized London. A great gold medallion recorded the 'Restoration of the Eternal Light' and depicted the emperor entering London to the joy of the inhabitants. It was, of course, a piece of imperial spin to present the invasion as a liberation. We can be sure supporters of Carausius and Allectus ran for cover, only to be exposed or denounced by those keen to pose as legitimists. There will have been ugly scenes of executions, confiscations and humiliation before Britain settled down as a restored province of the Roman Empire.

The Carausian revolt was an astonishing event in British history. Carausius was a refined sort of rebel. He posed as being more Roman than the Romans of the world he was rebelling against. Considering his own thoroughly mundane origins he had done incredibly well. Like most of Roman Britain's rebels his considerable personality would have made him a person of substance whenever he lived. Flamboyant, ebullient and unbelievably impertinent, he shines like a beacon out of the mediocrity of his age. Today we might regard him as a celebrity criminal. And, like today's celebrity criminals, the Roman authorities spent much of their time trying to juggle the need to deal with him while knowing that their target enjoyed a huge amount of public notoriety. Carausius had the measure of his age. He had the wit to see that his control of the sea pirates made him a superstar, and he was smart enough to offer his public a visionary future rather than the prospect of cynical exploitation. It is difficult to avoid the feeling that once he was dead, many of the Romano-British were left bereft. Perhaps it had been better being the centre of a modest Empire than a forgettable fringe component of a big one.

11

The Empire Strikes Back

MAGNENTIUS

⊰⊱◈⊰⊱

Magnentius led a rebellion in the Western Empire in the middle of the fourth century, and may even have been British in origin. He was said to have had a British father but that his mother was a Frank. He was born around the year 303, apparently in *Gallia Belgica*. The seeds of his revolt were sown in the reign of Constantine I, the Great. When he was declared emperor at York in the year 306, Constantine I embarked on a career that would change not just the face of the Roman Empire but much of the western world for thousands of years to come. Magnentius grew up almost entirely during the reign of Constantine and his sons. The new dynasty not only legitimised Christianity but also used it as a device to help hold the faltering Empire together. Once Constantine was dead in 337, his sons did their best to tear it apart once more.

The Roman world of the fourth century was a very different place from the Empire of the 280s and before. The third century was to a very large extent a crumbling, decadent and brutal version of the previous centuries. But the system was much the same, in spite of the succession of military usurpers, civil wars and volatile regimes. Diocletian recognised that the world had changed forever. The Roman system had been built around expansion, absorption and aggrandisement of territory. It was a ruthless system but it was also founded on the belief that the Roman 'way' was a better way and that this softened the blow of conquest. For the most part, the subjects of the Roman Empire conceded the point though in truth they had little choice.

A critical point had come under Hadrian (117-38) when expansion ceased as a matter of deliberate policy. From then on the Roman army was engaged mostly on frontier duties, maintaining the status quo and twiddling its thumbs. The nature of this army in the late fourth century is discussed in the next chapter (Magnus Maximus) together with the problem of identifying it in the ground. Occasional chances came for soldiers and their generals to blaze a trail across the Roman firmament, but when they came – like Septimius Severus' campaign in northern Britain – they were lacklustre and ill-starred expeditions that only exposed the futility of trying to conquer more, and the lack of commitment to hang on to it. The imprisonment of Valerian half a century later only served to show that Rome's enemies were now capable of inflicting monumentally humiliating defeats.

Part of the consequence was rebellion by men like Postumus and Carausius. They diverted their ambitions and visions to within the Empire. Instead of leading armies to greater glories across the frontiers in the name of the emperor, their frontier victories provided them with greater prestige than the incumbent ruler. To their own men, and their own regional peer groups, they were more realistic and convincing prospects as rulers. More importantly, by being 'local' they were in a position to award their followers with positions and promotion that they might otherwise have gone without. Crucially though these rebels lacked the power and support, even the relevance, to extend their power beyond the immediate provinces in which they were known.

This was markedly different from the earth-shaking events of the civil war of 68-9. Back in those days Vespasian rose to fame as a general, fighting in Britain and Judaea. When the Roman world dissolved into civil war after Nero's reckless reign, this prestige and military support brought him victory, and the Empire itself. But Vespasian never broke away from the Roman world. On the contrary he restored it, and provided the first really sound imperial leadership since Augustus himself. His dynasty was strong enough to survive his death, and even after the corrupt and violent rule of his second son Domitian in 96, it had the strength to form the basis of the brilliantly successful imperial reigns of the second century up to 180. Even in North Africa, the governor Lucius Clodius Macer who led a rebellion against Nero in 68 called himself *propraetor Africae*. In other words he styled himself in an office within the imperial system rather than establish a separatist regime. He issued coinage, but apart from one type none bore his portrait, and those that did made no mention of him assuming any sort of imperial title. Postumus and Carausius did exactly the opposite and, as such, they were effectively splitting the Empire into petty kingdoms though they posed as conventional emperors.

During the fourth century, under the new imperial system established by Diocletian, the exclusion of the north-western élite only became more pronounced. Britain was exposed to all the impositions of taxation and administrative obligations that the Empire increasingly demanded. But Britain did not enjoy the advantages of a field army, despite having to pay for it. Throughout the Empire the upper classes, the very people on whom these obligations fell most heavily, looked for a payback in the form of patronage, imperial office and influence. Unfortunately for Britain, such people seem to have been excluded from that sort of position in imperial government. No Briton seems to have become a senator, or was awarded with a provincial or military command. It is easy to see why a western usurper might have seemed more appealing a prospect, especially if his own supporters included individuals from Britain.

Just to add to the potential for discontent, Britain was also utilised as a convenient repository for undesirables though we have no specific evidence for anyone in the lead-up to the Magnentian rebellion. However, Probus (276-82) had packed off prisoners-of-war to Britain and in 361 Palladius was exiled there for his support of Constantius II who had died earlier that year. These were not the only examples. Such gestures can only reflect a perception in the centre of the Roman world that expulsion to Britain was a way of publicly humiliating political enemies, and that Britain was about as bad a place as one could be sent to. The consequences can only have been to corrode loyalty to the state in Britain, as well as quite literally provide potential manpower and leadership for rebellions. In eighteenth- and nineteenth-century Britain, Ireland was used in much the same way and with similar results. When someone like Magnentius ran his own rebellion, it is not altogether surprising that Britain was prepared to play along.

Constantine was the son of Constantius I Chlorus by his first wife, one of the two original junior members of Diocletian's college of emperors who died in York in 306. The year before, Diocletian and Maximian had abdicated to be replaced by Galerius and Constantius respectively who were promoted as had been expected. Naturally enough, two new junior emperors (known as Caesars) would now be appointed. The trouble was that Galerius chose both of them. In the West, Flavius Valerius Severus would assist Constantius, and in the East Galerius was joined by an inexperienced relative of his, Galerius Valerius Maximus.

Constantine took exception to being sidelined in favour of a man chosen by Galerius. He immediately set off to join his father, then on campaign in Britain. Along the way he was placed under arrest by Galerius, an interesting move since it demonstrated to Constantine exactly what the stakes were. In other words, it was going to be all or nothing. Constantine reached his father and was present in York when Constantius died. It was only natural that the soldiers of his army would elevate their master's son to the purple, and they did.

Constantine then embarked on a series of wars that eventually brought him total control of the Roman world by the year 324, wiping out Diocletian's new system in its infancy. The machinations are far too complicated to go into here, but they even involved Maximian indulging himself in two comeback tours as emperor. One of the battles fought along the way was the one Constantine won at the Milvian Bridge in 312. He followed that the next year with the Edict of Milan, which declared religious toleration and thus legitimised Christianity.

Just to add to the problems Constantine had four sons: Crispus by his first wife, Minervina, and Constantine II, Constantius II, and Constans by his second wife, Fausta. Fausta resented the seniority of Crispus over her own sons so she put it about that Crispus was planning something treasonable. Constantine fell for the ruse and had his son put to death. When he discovered Fausta's scheming he had her executed too. That left him three sons to deal with on his death. Unlike Diocletian he went for the routine dynastic solution, and appointed them as his Caesars, adding a couple of nephews to this family imperial college by 335.

Constantine had only a short time to wait. He died in 337. The two nephews, Delmatius and Hanniballianus, lasted only four months before being killed. The Empire was left in the hands of his three remaining sons. Constantine II was to rule Britain, Gaul and Spain. Constans took Africa, Italy and Central Europe, while Constantius controlled the East. Like most self-respecting brothers with too much power and something to quarrel about they fought. In 340 Constantine II was killed in a war with Constans. Constans was left in power in the West, while Constantius II remained in the East.

Constans soon had trouble with Britain, the irritatingly irrelevant repository for undesirables, and home to pretentious bumpkins (this was literally how Britons were regarded, even by Gauls). In or around the year 343, during the winter, he was obliged to sail to Britain to deal with some sort of problem. The spin put on this by the chronicler Julius Firmicus Maternus was that Constans was so heroic and virtuous he took no account of the seasons. Since only a fool, or someone with no choice, would undertake a sea-crossing to prosecute a campaign in mid-winter it must be that something critical had occurred in the unreliable island province. Libanius added to the image by stressing the foul weather Constans had to sail into, and that his arrival was a surprise. Libanius goes overboard by insisting that *if* Constans had been forced to do this by an island in revolt, then the compulsion would have degraded the impressiveness of his achievement. All he does is arouse our suspicions.

Somehow, everything Libanius and Maternus said about Constans sounds like nonsense. Constans evidently felt he had no option but to cross the Channel in the dead of winter to deal with something so important he was prepared to risk his own life and those of his assistants, as well as leave the rest of his domain to its own devices while he was in Britain. Why? We have no answer, but a very real possibility is the gathering religious storm of the newly-Christianised Empire. Diehard conservatives had little time for the new religion, and even less for the increasing legal restrictions on traditional pagan cults. Christianity in any case scarcely merited that single catch-all name at the time. Still evolving from its origins in Palestine three hundred years before, Christianity was in reality a thousand different sects, each of which had its own slightly different take on the meaning of holy scripture. Once Christianity was legitimised the question of which form of Christianity would be the official one was still far from settled. Most potent of all the controversies was the divinity of Christ. The Orthodox church had it that Christ was divine, like his Father. The Arians insisted that Christ was everything the Orthodox church said he was, except for the divine part. To the Arians Christ was a human being – an exceptional human being, but not a god. The Arians took their name from an Alexandrian priest called Arius who had died the year before Constantine I. In 325 Arius had been excommunicated, the usual punishment for dissenters from the official line.

The stage was set for a cataclysm that would echo across the Roman world for generations, and it started to split the Empire. Constans was an Orthodox Christian (and was the only one of Constantine's sons to be baptised, in 337), but Constantius II was an

Arian. He was also interested in imposing his brand of Christianity not just on other Christians, but also on pagans. In the earlier part of the fourth century, restrictions on pagan activity were limited but they rapidly increased after Constantine's death. It's unfortunate that we know so little about Christianity in Britain at the time. The so-called church at Silchester defies interpretation as anything other than a church, except for its superficially incongruous reversed orientation (it faces east, not west). But that is not much of an objection since pre-350 churches were far from common anywhere, and in fact this 'reversal' is found at others of that date, like St John in Lateran in Rome, and even St Peter's itself. Similarly, a lack of Christian finds merely reflects the fact that Christians of the age were thoroughly unlikely to leave religious equipage lying around, not least because they generally spurned valuables and those which they had were useful to them wherever they were.

The Christian silver treasure from Water Newton shows a curious mix of pagan and Christian traditions and probably belongs to the fourth century, though it was originally suggested it might have been as early as the third. Its nature suggests that it cannot be unique, but its rarity and date just go to show how extremely unlikely it is that such material would ever normally find itself deposited in a place where we might find it. Again, the mixture of traditions is really less odd than it appears to us. This was, after all, on the edge of an enormous Empire and it would not be surprising if in a place like Britain Christianity eased itself into Romano-British society by adopting familiar formats. In the Middle Ages, plenty of churches are known to have been built in places where far older pagan traditions had been well established. That Britain had bishops by the time Constans crossed the Channel, and Constantius II started throwing his weight around, is certain. In 314 three British bishops attended a Council at Arles, and in c.343 – the very year Constans came to Britain – the next generation of British bishops arrived at the Council of Sardica.

The Sardica event was arranged to deal with Athanasius by Constans and Constantius. Athanasius was a former Bishop of

Alexandria who had been deposed for his opposition to Arianism. Needless to say, the Eastern bishops refused to accept Athanasius' status on the synod and declined to attend. The Western bishops restored Athanasius who went back to Alexandria until he was deposed again in 356. In the meantime, just what sort of foothold Arianism had in Britain is unknown, but the Council of Sardica shows how highly charged the issue was. In the West, Orthodoxy was routine but it was not ubiquitous. Not only that, paganism did a remarkably good job of keeping going, especially in more remote locations. Britain is particularly conspicuous in its pagan revival of the fourth century, though it would be going far too far to suggest that it was an organised movement. Carausius seems to have spotted a hankering for ancient classical pagan imagery amongst the people who mattered in Britain in the 280s and based his propaganda campaign on that. If that was his plan, he was right since the mosaic floors in the flowering of Romano-British villa culture in the 300s show that the class of people who paid for and lived in the villas decorated their lives with images from ancient Roman pagan myth. This was not necessarily a contradiction of Christianity. Christians were perfectly capable of utilising pagan metaphors, not only to express moral religious issues, but also simply as representations of human life, fate and a sense of the aesthetic. But places like Maiden Castle, Lydney and Uley show that there was money, time and an interest available to be invested in operational pagan cults in fourth-century Britain.

So, Constans might have had wind of an Arian insurrection in Britain, or he might have uncovered a pagan plot. On the other hand, the reason for his risky journey across the sea might have had a more prosaic cause. During his account of a barbarian invasion of Britain in 367, the historian Ammianus Marcellinus made a retrospective reference to frontier forces in Britain he called the *Areani*. Ammianus said he had had cause to talk about them before in Britain in connection with Constans (that passage is lost). In 367 they proved treacherous, by having taken money from the frontier tribes they were supposed to be reporting on. Perhaps Constans had instituted these *Areani* in 343 after coming to deal with an incursion of barbarians in northern Britain. But this is no less speculative than a religious problem and, in any case, a military threat is frankly far less likely in the dead of winter than a plot more readily dreamed up in the towns in southern Britain.

Constans earned for himself a reputation as a thoroughly unpleasant character who was corrupt and decadent and who treated his soldiers in a contemptuous manner. Or so said the late-Roman historian Aurelius Victor. Considering the track record of his imperial predecessors Constans might have been a little more careful. Treating one's soldiers badly was, after all, a blatantly fatal error, and as usual there was always someone waiting for an opportunity to profit from the situation. This time it was Magnentius. Constans had compounded his ill-considered behaviour by promoting men to provincial governorships in return for bribes, rather than choosing well-qualified and experienced men of good judgement.

Magnentius reputedly had a British father but a Frankish mother and was born at *Samarobriva* (Amiens) in France, not so far from where Carausius had come. Appropriately for someone of such a background he served his military apprenticeship in a barbarian unit of Constantine I's army, though he seems before that to have served the emperor as a slave. He was said to be sharp-witted and very interested in reading, but also a coward who pretended to be brave to cover up this shortcoming. A man of 'immense size', he was high-handed in how he treated others, which is an intriguing defect, given that Constans was supposed to be very similar. Aurelius Victor said he had a 'savage personality' and attributed that to a barbarian origin (*de Caes* 41). But this probably also brought Magnentius the confidence and strength of character that allowed him to dominate those around him. Like so many rebels before him, Magnentius' skills and presence brought him promotion, at a time when the descendants of recent immigrants were playing an increasingly prominent role in imperial events. After Constantine's death he was elevated to the post of *comes rei militaris*, literally 'count of military affairs', and commanded prestige units of the army called *Ioviani* and *Herculiani*. In other words, he had risen from nowhere to become a senior officer in the Roman army that served the sons of Constantine in the 340s.

The coup took place in January 350 when Marcellinus, chief finance minister of Constans, held a sham birthday party for his son at *Augustodunum* (Autun) in Gaul. Along with Magnentius and others, he had hatched the plan when Constans was out hunting. Magnentius attended along with a number of other important men and, at an appropriate moment, disappeared as if to relieve himself. He returned dressed up in purple and was promptly acclaimed as the emperor. The army instantly declared for Magnentius and Constans had to make a hasty escape. Not hasty enough as it turned out. One of Magnentius' supporters caught him and killed him. That left only Constantius II as a legitimate emperor and like so many single emperors in the past, he found that controlling the Roman world on his own was far from straightforward.

The rebel regime staggered towards controlling the West, including Britain. Curiously, Magnentius managed to offend some of the upper classes in his territories by over-taxing them, though in reality it might be simply that they had expected reduced taxes in return for their support. On the other hand he was lenient about paganism, which was bound to outrage Constans and Constantius and at the same time extend his potential support amongst those who felt alienated by anti-pagan laws. Meanwhile, a nephew of Constantine I, called Nepotianus, declared himself emperor in Rome, but Marcellinus managed to have him and his family killed after only a month. In Pannonia, roughly in the middle of the Empire, the garrison dithered over whether to side with Magnentius or Constantius. Constantius' sister, Constantia, persuaded them to declare their own commander, Vetranio, emperor in support of Constantius. It was a vitally decisive move that bought Constantius time and a buffer zone while he consolidated control in the East before setting out to deal with Magnentius. Subsequently Vetranio would abdicate in favour of Constantius, in a rare instance of tactful deference.

After all these machinations, by the summer of 350 Magnentius controlled the Western Roman Empire, and had appointed his brother Magnus Decentius his Caesar, or junior imperial colleague. He was smart enough at this stage to realise the limit of his ambitions and tried to negotiate with Constantius by sending him envoys. Constantius imprisoned them, and then sent his own ambassador, a man called Philippus, on the pretext of offering a peace deal but who was actually supposed to gather intelligence about the Magnentian army. Although this was the plan, Philippus seems to have acted rather recklessly by haranguing the Magnentian forces for not staying loyal to the legitimate regime. So Magnentius had him arrested.

In 351 Constantius appointed his nephew Constantius Gallus as his own Caesar and put him in charge of the East, in order to make it possible for him to lead his army against Magnentius. With diplomacy in tatters, though neither side had conducted it very sensibly, war broke out and once again the Roman army was fighting itself. This time the consequences were catastrophic. With so much pressure on imperial frontiers, the Roman army could not afford the loss of men and equipment another civil war would involve.

The late Roman army was a very different beast from the one that had conquered and held the Roman world in the first and second centuries. The fourth-century army was based on mobile cavalry units, permanent frontier garrisons and a host of different units, many of which were little more than hired bands of barbarian mercenaries. Its strength and integrity always depended on maintaining loyalty and mobility. One of the problems with the late army system was the hierarchy of regional commands. In one sense this was efficient because it meant that blocks of the army were in the right place at the right time and properly led. On the other hand it also meant that loyalty was not necessarily directed at the emperor, institutionalising a problem that had occurred so many times before, for example when Postumus established the Gallic Empire. This was precisely what benefited Magnentius.

By spring 351 Magnentius had amassed a huge army, having hired various bands of German mercenaries, and based himself at Aquileia in Italy. He had more soldiers than Constantius and to begin with seized the initiative. Constantius was defeated on the north-eastern Italian border and forced to fall back. In spite of this setback Constantius offered to sue for a settlement with Magnentius, but Magnentius had become greedy. He rejected the offer and set off after Constantius.

The decision to chase after Constantius was disastrous. In September 351 at Mursa in Pannonia the two armies met in a battle that permanently compromised the Roman Empire's military defences due to the scale of the losses. The cavalry in Constantius' army defeated the Magnentian infantry, but it cost Constantius 30,000 men and Magnentius 24,000. It was readily painted as a crushing defeat for the rebel, but the vast losses speak for themselves and show that ultimately Constantius won simply because he had more men at his disposal. Nevertheless, Magnentius survived and fled back into Italy to lick his wounds and prepare for another campaign in 352. Constantius had the initiative now and he invaded Italy, forcing Magnentius to withdraw to Gaul. An imperial panegyric written for Constantius by a man called Julian claimed that Magnentius, 'the usurper', had been indulging himself by watching a horse race when the news came of the invasion. But it also went on to describe how Magnentius enjoyed having his enemies tortured, which was a routine part of contemporary spin. That sort of bad press provided a convenient justification for retaliatory action. More defeats for Magnentius followed, and after losing control of the Rhine he fell back further to Lyons. After a final defeat at *Mons Seleuci* in the summer of 353 Magnentius committed suicide.

Traditionally, Roman emperors were depicted on most denominations wearing a laurel wreath. The laurel wreath was also associated with sobering up after a pagan Bacchic bout of heavy drinking, an activity that provoked outrage by Christian writers like Jerome and Augustine. In fact, by the fourth century the normal imperial headdress for coinage was the diadem but Magnentius spurned both, except on a very few issues. Instead, the most abiding and striking image of Flavius Magnus Magnentius, leader of the coup of 350, is his bare-headed portrait on the obverse of his coins, and the Chi-Rho monogram on the reverse of some of his large bronze issues struck in 352-3. It was an important gesture that remained unparalleled in the history of Roman coinage. The legend surrounding the Chi-Rho commemorated imperial *Salus* (Health), and thus associated Christian *Salus* with the emperor's welfare.

Magnentius was a pagan but had realised the importance of exploiting Orthodox support in direct opposition to the Arianism of Constantius II. That alone was likely to provoke the wrath of Constantius, but he had also tolerated pagan worship, something that was just as unacceptable. Curiously his wife, Justina, would later actively support Arianism. After the death of Magnentius she became the second wife of the emperor Valentinian I (364-75), and as the mother of Valentinian II played a significant role in the events surrounded the rebellion of Magnus Maximus (see chapter 12).

A figure on the Hinton St Mary (Dorset) mosaic depicts a bare-headed man with a Chi-Rho. It has always been assumed that the figure portrayed is Christ, and certainly this writer has always accepted that, since the four male figures (one in each corner) have been very reasonably identified as the Four Evangelists. But given the Magnentian coinage and the explicit association of the Chi-Rho with a bare-headed emperor, it is equally possible that the pavement in fact represents Magnentius, or at any rate an ambivalent conflated image. The pavement is normally dated to anywhere between the 330s and 350s making this quite consistent with such a hypothesis. The Hinton mosaic portrait also has distinctly heavy jowls, and this is a characteristic feature of how Magnentius was depicted on his coins, and how historians described him.

The main argument against this conclusion is that the Hinton mosaic escaped destruction after the defeat of Magnentius and, as we shall see, the fall-out in Britain after 353 was very severe indeed. But it is also possible that the floor was deliberately ambiguous. After all, if the Magnentian coinage had had no legend naming the emperor, the Chi-Rho would almost certainly have led to the coin image's identification as Christ instead. The rest of the Magnentian coin series followed broadly contemporary themes, and were struck at a variety of western mints that marked out his territory: Trier, Lyons, Arles, Rome and Aquileia amongst others. He was 'liberator of the Romans', and his reign promised 'perpetual happiness'. There were the usual acknowledgements to the 'faithful army', so in these other respects the Magnentian regime was presented as another 'legitimate' rebel. One issue, struck at Rome, recorded his capture of the city and announced its 'renovation'. Coins and medallions struck at Aquileia include some showing him in consular robes, so it is possible this is where Magnentius may have been appointed consul for the first time – an important convention in imperial posturing.

Apart from Magnentius possibly having British ancestry there is little immediate suggestion of Britain playing a substantial role in the revolt, though it can scarcely have failed to provide him with troops. Coin hoards suggest that his money supplanted legitimate issues, and were readily accepted. In 348 Constans and Constantius had introduced a series of coins with the legend *Fel(icium) Temp(orum) Reparatio*, 'the restoration of happy times'. It was 1100 years since Rome had been founded, and the type was probably intended to commemorate that event. The Coleshill hoard, found in 1931, had coins dating right up to 353. Of its post-348 coins, nearly 700 were Magnentian but only 532 were of Constantius and Constans. Of those 'legitimate' 532 coins nearly half were in the name of Constans, who had died in 350. Since coins of the two brothers circulated in roughly equal numbers everywhere that means most of the 'legitimate' coins probably reached Britain by 350. In other words, once Magnentius was in power his coinage took over because 'legitimate' supplies were interrupted. The Wokingham (Berks) hoard of 1970 shows the same pattern. Even hoards ending at a slightly later date, like the Cobham (Kent) hoard of 1883, exhibit a similar bias. Of 836 coins, 430 were of Magnentius and Decentius, with the rest being made up of 256 Constans, 98 Constantius II, 1 Constantine I, and then 51 of Constantius Gallus. In each of these instances the coins of Constantius II clearly could belong to the revolt period, but the greater numbers of Constans' coins, and thus obviously of 350 or earlier, suggest the reverse. The hoards of this date form a distinct group and were abandoned, probably not because their owners were implicated in the revolt, but for the simple reason that Magnentian coinage was demonetised.

Magnentian coinage was just as susceptible as legitimate coinage to the prolific copying which so characterises the coins finds of the period, and which was responsible for producing the majority of coins found as singletons in fieldwalking and excavations. The Bath spring, which contained more than 12,500 coins from across the whole period, produced 159 Magnentian coins, of which 84 were contemporary forgeries. This alone emphasises that Magnentius was considered wholly acceptable amongst the coin-using Romano-British public.

Constantius II knew, or believed, that in Britain Magnentius had enjoyed popular support. What mattered especially was the extent to which the curial class – landowners, councillors and the like – had taken him to their hearts. A Spanish imperial *notarius* (secretary) called Paul was sent by Constantius to Britain to flush out any Magnentian military supporters. Paul was so ruthless that it is now impossible to work out to what extent he was dealing with real, or imagined, Magnentian supporters. He initiated a campaign of terror that got off to an excellent start because there was initially no resistance, apparently because the victims were powerless to do anything about it. Nevertheless, entirely innocent men and landowners were accused of supporting Magnentius. Fortunes were requisitioned, freemen incarcerated and put in chains, and others murdered. In spite of attempts to clear innocent men by Flavius Martinus, then vicar of Britain and governing the provinces of Britain in place of the prefects, Paul continued to imprison anyone he fancied. This helped explain why Paul was known as *Catena*, 'the Chain', thanks to his ability to complicate anything.

Eventually Paul threatened to imprison Martinus who promptly rushed Paul and tried to kill him with a sword. It was a rash act, not least because Martinus had a weak hand and lacked the strength to strike a mortal blow – except, that is, on himself, since having failed to assassinate Paul he committed suicide with the same sword then and there. We simply do not know what was really going on. Perhaps Paul had been told to operate his terror campaign as a way of seizing wealth and land for the state. Or, perhaps the Magnentian revolt was used as an excuse to intimidate Orthodox Christians, and pagans who had thought they could openly worship ancient cults in Britain. Certainly, by 360 Constantius II had succeeded in imposing Arianism across the Roman world, and at the same time made Christianity not only the premier but the only legitimate religion. In any case, Paul's behaviour was entirely appropriate to Constantius II, whose suspicion and distrust of any potential threat to his power bordered on the paranoid. With Martinus dead, Paul then left Britain with a phalanx of prisoners whom he delivered to Constantius. They were then variously punished. Some were forced into exile, others were denounced as outlaws, and the rest were executed.

Even the coinage shows that direct measures were taken to suppress that most visible manifestation of the rebel. Magnentian coins might have dominated coins circulating and hoarded in Britain between 350-3, but in the years following the revolt hoards rarely include any at all, showing that they fell out of circulation almost immediately. The Manchester hoard of 1852 had more than 1,660 coins covering the fourth century right up to the reign of Valentinian I. Not a single coin of Magnentius or Decentius was included. The sudden shortfall in supply was made good by a colossal bout of copying of Constantius' issues, mainly the *Fel Temp Reparatio* type. The Bath spring produced 357 coins belonging to 353-60, of which 298 were copies.

A curious side-show took place around this time, or rather, it might have. Some of the coin hoards found buried after 353 include occasional scrappy examples of an emperor who seems to have called himself after that great adventurer of more than sixty years before: Carausius. Known now to historians and archaeologists as 'Carausius II', this individual goes without mention in ancient chronicles and would be undatable were it not for the hoards, and

his habit of using copies of *Fel Temp Reparatio* coins as 'blanks' on
which to strike his legends. These copies of official coins struck 348-
50 were produced in abundance in the Britain of the late 350s to
make good a lack of legitimate supplies, and normally bear the name
of Constantius II. The very few that mention this mysterious
Carausius use legends in the dative case, thus *Domino Carausio*, 'to
the Lord Carausius', while an even smaller number seem to mention
an even more shadowy figure called Cenceris. So, there is not incon-
siderable doubt whether either existed. The so-called Carausius II
might be just a retrospective gesture to the original Carausius, and
perhaps represented an indulgence by a small group of protestors.
Since even Ammianus Marcellinus makes not even a hint that there
might have been another rebellion in 350s Britain the position
remains a total mystery.

The Magnentian revolt clearly had a devastating effect on some of
Britain's upper classes. That Paul even had a pretext for throwing his
weight around suggests that Magnentius must have enjoyed significant influential support, though it is now impossible to know how
much. Likewise, we can only guess that perhaps Magnentius had
managed to associate himself with those in Britain who resented the
murder of Constantine II in 340 and who still blamed Constans for
the quarrel. In this context it is simple enough to speculate that
certain villas, which show abandonment around this time, might
have belonged to Paul's victims, but the connection is impossible to
prove. Gadebridge Park (Herts) was a long-term villa site and grew
into a substantial complex of wings and outbuildings by the early
fourth century. By 360 it had been demolished and became
farmland. This is premature in villa history, since for the most part
such great villas in Britain did not really enter that widespread phase
of terminal decline until the 380s and 390s. If we take the political
upheavals of England's Commonwealth in the 1650s as a model, we
can see there the destruction of many great houses as lands and

buildings belonging to the exiled king Charles II's supporters were confiscated. Many fell into ruin and were demolished, such as Theobalds (also in Herts). William Cecil originally acquired Theobalds in 1564. Subsequently he built a hugely enlarged and elaborate house, but after the Civil War by 1650 it had been demolished. Just two arches survive today, and like Gadebridge, which is not so far away, it became and remained open land.

Associating Gadebridge's demise with Paul is an attractive idea. However, in the absence of specific records, there are many other possible reasons – some villa estates were still growing and there is no reason why Gadebridge Park need not have been demolished in the process of acquisition and estate aggrandisement. Ironically it was Magnentius who was remembered for alienating some of his own supporters by excessive taxation. The barbarian invasion of 367 was just one more event that could have easily caused fatal commercial damage to certain wealthy people. In any case archaeology is just not precise enough to link any one site to abandonment at a tightly-dated time. Gadebridge's abandonment could have occurred at any time in a decade or more after Paul's pogrom. Nevertheless it is likely that a number of major villa estates suffered appropriation at this time, simply because the kind of people who are likely to have owned them would have been in the positions of administrative and military responsibility that would have attracted Paul's attention. But a requisitioned villa estate that was handed on to a supporter of Constantius II would be very unlikely to produce any archaeological evidence that demonstrated a change of ownership, and certainly not allegiance.

Constantius II was an uncompromising Christian, and an Arian at that. His reign was marked by a radical level of intolerance, expressed in temple closures, seizures of temple plate and the outlawing of pagan worship. Magnentius offended Constantius in every religious sense. He had presented a very dangerous threat to the Empire's survival, and had survived for more than three years. Perhaps Constantius began to realise that it was impossible for him actively to suppress undesirable religions everywhere, especially in the more remote West. This might explain the promotion of an obscure cousin of his called Flavius Julius Claudianus. Known to history as the emperor Julian II, this man was married to Constantius' sister Helena and elevated to the post of Caesar in 355 and placed in charge of Gaul. He was learned and a proponent of traditional paganism, which he preferred to the internecine theological and liturgical warfare conducted by Christian factions. Constantius cannot have overlooked this and perhaps thought that Julian would be the acceptable face of his regime in the West.

Julian was in any case a practical man too. He fought the barbarians on the German frontier and had a special fleet built to import grain from Britain to support his frontier forces. It illustrates perfectly that Britain, however derided, was a vital component in imperial security. Relatively immune to the worst barbarian excesses, its economy was of vital strategic significance. But it was of little consequence to the Britons. In 360 the north was overrun by Scots and Picts. Worn down by the problems of recent years 'fear engulfed the provinces [of Britain]' (Ammianus, xx.1.1). Julian could not even leave the continent, fearing that renewed attacks by the Alamanni would take advantage of his absence. Britain was now to find itself steadily pushed aside and even further down the list of imperial priorities.

12

Ill-Weaved Ambition
MAGNUS MAXIMUS

———◆◇◆———

In the 380s, a generation after the end of Magnentius, the Roman Empire was struggling to stay together. Britain was on the margin in every sense of the word, and sustaining her in the Empire became harder and harder. Dissatisfaction combined with military ambition was a disastrous combination, and the last thirty of years of Roman Britain would see catastrophic revolts.

———◆◇◆———

Between 364 and 378 the house of Valentinian brought a certain amount of centralised stability. But Valentinian I, who ruled the West, died in 375 and in 378 Valens, ruler of the East, was killed in a major battle at Hadrianopolis in Thrace while trying to expel Visigoths. In fact this had not been in response to a conventional incursion. The Visigoths, pushed from their own lands by the Vandals, asked Valens in 376 for the right to enter the Empire and settle in Moesia and Thrace. Valens allowed them in, but overlooked the hostility of locals, who reacted so badly that they provoked a rebellion by the immigrants. Remarkably the dynasty, for the moment, remained intact. In the West, Valentinian's son Gratian, now about twenty, had succeeded his father in 375 and on the death of his uncle Valens in 378 he took over the East as well. Wisely, he placed it under the government of his general Theodosius the Elder. In theory Gratian shared his rule with his younger brother Valentinian II, but the latter was only seven years old.

As a youth, Gratian depended on his ministers, in particular Ausonius. Gratian himself grew into a competent warrior, but he had a reputation for being too easily distracted by the chance to play the fool and engage in trivial pursuits. Ausonius was not unusual for his age in admiring the ideals of the pagan past. He modelled himself as a writer on poets like Virgil, and accommodated those with pagan sympathies. As a matter of passing interest, it is clear from some of his poetry that he regarded Britons, by definition, as coarse, bad, and foolish. This probably reflects an attitude shared by most of his sophisticated contemporaries in the north-west: Britain was a boorish province filled with backward yokels. That meant Britain was a low priority in every respect.

When he became emperor in 378 Gratian issued an edict of religious tolerance in a spirit of accommodation towards the fracturing components of the Christian church. However, he was persuaded by the pope, Damasus I, to recognize Rome as the primary see and to help bring all bishops, whether they liked it or not, under papal jurisdiction. The event is of itself an important reminder to us of how relatively ill-defined the church's hierarchy still was. The issue of the church in Rome would return under the revolt of Maximus.

Gratian based himself at Trier to be close to the centre of operations on the German frontier. He had no choice, but it had alarming consequences. He was unable to come to Valens' help in 378, and in 383 was involved in Raetia in preparations for a new war against the Alamanni. He also had to buy the support of Alan mercenaries with special favours. He gave them bounties, and placed them in positions of the highest responsibility. This was not necessarily foolish since in owing their elevation to him, he could count on their loyalty – in theory. But it gave the rest of his troops a grievance and he was far away from the centre of the Western Empire. It was while Gratian was preparing to tackle the Alamanni once more that news was brought to him of a revolt in Britain. The soldiers there, who took particular exception to being marginalised in the queue for handing out favours, had declared a general called Magnus Maximus emperor.

Magnus Maximus was a Spaniard. Perhaps that helped provoke his ambition, since Spain was where Trajan and Hadrian – two of the all-time greatest emperors – had come from. His name, in translation, seems ludicrously pretentious. It means, 'The Great, the Greatest'. In fact 'Magnus' and 'Maximus' were quite common names, but having both seems rather over-egging the pudding. It is intriguing how many usurpers had thoroughly appropriate names to match their ambitions. There must have been a certain amount of retrospective amendment by usurpers themselves, their adherents, or the chroniclers, unless the usurper's natural name attracted attention. Constantine III (see chapter 13) was said to have been promoted purely because his name recalled that of Constantine I.

Either way, Magnus Maximus was believed by the historian Orosius to have been a man whose qualities of leadership and soldiery would have entitled him to the highest honours – if he had not allowed himself to become an imperial usurper (vii.34.9). That sounds like an astute judgement, but it recalled closely the observation made by Tacitus of the emperor Galba (68-9), when he said that had Galba not become emperor no one would have doubted his ability to rule (H i.49). Late Roman history and literature often lost the plot in the desire to emulate the works of a greater age, which makes it difficult to know where the literary style ends and truth begins. While Orosius was trying to be Tacitus, Gratian's tutor Ausonius was doing his level best to be Virgil and Pliny the Younger.

Magnus Maximus dreamt up ideas above his station during the aftermath of the barbarian invasion of Britain in 367. He served alongside Theodosius the Elder, sent to Britain to resolve the chaos and refortify the cities of Britain and its military bases. Theodosius' son, Theodosius the Younger, was the man selected by Gratian to serve as emperor in the East after the battle of Hadrianopolis. This seems to have annoyed Maximus, who evidently thought it was unacceptable that the son of his compatriot was favoured over himself. In fact there is some confusion in the sources. Zosimus, the chronicler of this event, seems to have assumed that the two Theodosii were one and the same, and believed that Maximus was annoyed by the promotion of his colleague to the position of emperor. That makes little practical difference since either way Maximus was not an emperor, and he decided to rectify that administrative oversight.

In Britain of course, the same pattern was repeating itself. Theodosius the Younger might have been able to benefit from his father's post-367 reputation in Britain, but he now ruled in the East as Theodosius I. Maximus was on the spot in Britain and must have continued to enjoy loyalty and support amongst troops, renowned for their insubordination to imperial control and their inclination to rage. Maximus took advantage of this and ran a campaign to put about his grievances as well as to circulate damaging reports about Gratian. It seems to have been easy for him to create a climate in which a rebellion broke out, and he was appointed emperor by the British garrison.

This was an important sequence of events but it is an interesting question whether Maximus was the 'victim' of his troops' regard or whether he had orchestrated his rise to power. Orosius thought that Maximus was virtually coerced into power, but Zosimus saw him as a much more willing participant. Certainly, what happened allowed the troops the vanity of having made the choice, though in reality they had probably been manipulated by the usual spin – though this might not actually have come from Maximus himself. We tend only to hear about troops and usurpers, and not the silent cabal of back-room officers, politicians and fixers who helped coordinate and stage-manage rebellions. But the army in Britain had a reputation. Zosimus thought them easily the most ill-disciplined and they might perhaps have been inclined to try and live up to that image.

The army of Britain in the 380s is only really known to us in a formal sense from the cryptic, incomplete and rambling *Notitia Dignitatum*. This 'Compendium of the Great Offices of State' was compiled in the fifth century from what seems to have been any records to hand, regardless of whether they were out of date or not. Most seem to belong to after 368 but not all. So, the information is inherently unreliable and really records a paper army. We have truly no idea about which units were in an operational state and which were simply grandiose labels from times gone by applied to skeleton garrisons in semi-derelict outposts. It is as potentially misleading as a list of British army regiments, gathered from random dates in the twentieth century – literally.

It is unfortunate that archaeology, particularly on forts along Hadrian's Wall, has produced more ambiguity rather than certainty in how we understand the army used by Magnentius and Magnus Maximus. Barrack blocks at Housesteads were altered by the early fourth century. In their original Hadrianic form the barracks were built as rectangular blocks with individual rooms separated by a single wall between each. By the very early fourth century these had been rebuilt in 'chalet' style, where a pair of walls separated by a very thin gap divided each 'chalet' from the next one along. This is a significant structural change but it tells us absolutely nothing about whether the people living in them were different. That the fort *vicus* had largely fallen into disuse under Constantine I might suggest that military families had moved into the fort and shared quarters with the troops. But even the excavator of the fort, James Crow, recognised that distinguishing sexes based on artefacts found in the barracks was nigh-on impossible. What it did suggest to him was that the barracks were maintained, and that means that the usurpers of the fourth century almost certainly had a well-established Wall garrison to draw on for their rebellions. Unfortunately this sort of evidence is limited in its availability. The coastal forts like Richborough and Pevensey have produced virtually no traces of structures, let alone definably military artefacts, leaving the information about units in the *Notitia Dignitatum* as little more than speculative theory.

Back in the second century, the Roman army was divided between citizen legionaries, and the auxiliaries. All had nominal bases, with auxiliaries bearing the brunt of frontier and battle duties, and all were liable to piecemeal and individual movement within and between provinces on a daily, weekly or monthly basis. In other words there was a static foundation to the system on paper, though in reality virtually no unit was ever all in one place together. Britain had three legions, based in their fortresses at York, Chester and Caerleon, and several dozen auxiliary units. If war broke out, vexillations from other legions could be sent across the Channel to help out, and at other times the British forces supplied legionary vexillations and auxiliary units to continental wars. The fluctuations were continuous.

In the fourth century the emperor controlled a mobile field army, the *comitatenses*. The word means literally the 'accompanying body' and is best translated as something like the 'imperial troop'. Appropriately its divisions were normally commanded by a *comes*, which means 'companion' and in this context an 'imperial companion'. So, in Britain today we might call it the Household Cavalry. Roman Britain did not normally benefit from the permanent presence of this wing of the army though the *Notitia* says that six of its cavalry wings and three of its infantry units were in Britain. The field army was primarily utilised on the continent as a crack response to border incursions along the Rhine and Danube. Instead, Britain depended more on two garrison bodies classified as *limitanei*. This means literally 'those of the frontier' and derives from the word *limes*, 'frontier'. A *dux* (duke) at York controlled the *limitaneus* army of the north, including Hadrian's Wall, and a *comes* (count) ran the other along the forts of the Saxon Shore on the south and east coasts. Most of the unit names listed in the *Notitia* hark back to the auxiliary forces of centuries before. It is a pity that we do not know how or in what capacity Magnus Maximus served in Britain other than that it was alongside count Theodosius. He may have become the *dux* at York or was perhaps left in a higher tier of control over the provinces of Britain. He evidently commanded massive, and decisive, prestige.

In 383 Magnus Maximus moved swiftly, and as such he marked himself out as entirely different from Postumus and Carausius. Maximus organised his army the moment he had been awarded with the imperial trappings and left Britain for the Rhine. He knew that capturing the loyalty of the Rhine garrison would be a key move, and he must have been fully aware that Gratian's favouritism towards the Alan mercenaries had dealt him the upper hand. Gratian and Maximus met in battle, but Gratian was horrified to see that his own forces melted away with shameless speed. He fled south towards Italy and reached the Danube at Belgrade before a cavalry commander called Andragathius, sent by Maximus, caught up with him.

Gratian was killed on 15 August 383 and Magnus Maximus was only left with the immediate problem of the twelve-year-old Valentinian II. Valentinian II was obviously too young to have played any part in the government of the West. But he presented Maximus with a critical obstacle. Maximus was perfectly well aware that Theodosius in the East was scarcely likely to tolerate his rebellion. If he did away with Valentinian II, the wrath of Theodosius was likely to be measurably worse. So, he took a risk and bought time by making a treaty with Justina, the mother of the boy emperor, in 383. Maximus would control all the West, except Italy where Valentinian II would be left in nominal power. For the moment, even Theodosius accepted the situation.

The emperor Theodosius I was in every sense the equal of his father, the *comes* who had operated so brilliantly in Britain after 367. Gratian had wisely recognised this in making him emperor in the East in 379. Theodosius immediately focused his attention on the eastern frontiers and the Goth invasions. The combination of this distraction, and the deal with Valentinian II, seems to have achieved what Maximus wanted. He had the time he needed to establish his regime without interference or the need to mount an immediate defence of his domain.

The coinage of the reign is thoroughly conventional. Maximus struck coins at Trier, Lyons, Arles, Milan and Aquileia in the West. Legends describe him as 'restorer of the republic', and others recorded the 'heroic army', 'the Hope of the Romans', and 'Victory of the Emperors'. He might have struck some gold at London but that is based on a mintmark AVG found on some of his gold. It might refer to *Augustodunum* in Gaul or London, if London had retained the new name *Augusta* believed by some authorities to have been given it after 367. It certainly does not apply to any of the bronze or silver, so Maximus evidently had little or no desire to promote himself within Britain as Carausius had. Coinage struck after 379 and found in Britain declines steadily as a site find, because a reduction in supply meant initially that what was left was looked after, and also because its actual use declined. That the latter occurred is evident from the lack of contemporary copying that had always taken place at earlier times to make good supply shortfalls (for example under Magnentius, see chapter 11).

The use of coinage marks out Maximus as the usual breed of self-regarding opportunist. He exploited Britain's garrison for his own ends, and the minute he was in power he left and never returned. Much later Gildas, that notoriously unreliable 'Dark Age' chronicler, castigated Maximus for denuding Britain of vitally needed troops. The truth is that we know little or nothing about the extent to which Britain's garrison was reduced. The archaeology of the period has made it clear that distinguishing civilian and military occupation becomes very difficult, though a key factor seems to have been the decline of civilian extra-mural settlements around forts. Military bases therefore seem to have reduced in size with a mixture of military and civilian elements moving within the walls. Many exhibit serious physical degradation in the last few decades of the fourth century, with derelict gates, patched-up walls, and semi-ruinous internal buildings. The *Notitia Dignitatum* says that *II Augusta* was based by this time at Richborough, a fraction of the size of its old base at Caerleon (which is unmentioned). Therefore it must either have been a shadow of its former self or was spread out amongst several different places. Magnus Maximus must have played a part in the decay of the British garrison, but it may only have been a part in a longer sequence of decay, characterised by piecemeal desertion, lack of pay and administrative support. If, for example, Magnus Maximus failed to organise pay for the troops left behind in Britain, some of the decay may have been caused by individuals drifting away during the years of his reign, in addition to those who went to fight with him.

Maximus knew that so long as Valentinian II was alive he was always publicly an illegitimate ruler, who was no more than a pretender to the imperial throne. His rule would of course always be a legal fiction, even if he got rid of Valentinian, but under the rules of the time, being in sole charge made it legal in consequence of the fact. He had installed his son, Flavius Victor, as his Caesar in 387 in an effort to create the beginnings of a dynasty. It was the usual poisoned chalice. Taking advantage of silence from Theodosius, Maximus dreamed up a pretext to oust Valentinian. He decided to accuse Valentinian of maltreating the church in Italy.

Magnus Maximus was, unlike Gratian in 378, no religious neutral. By asserting himself as a supporter of Orthodox Christianity he made sure both secular and ecclesiastical control in the West was his. Priscillian was the leader of a heretic group in Spain. Their practices included avoiding church during Lent, and fasting on Sundays. True to the dogmatic Christian bigotry of the age, such apparently innocuous idiosyncrasies were enough to provoke a war. Despite attempts to crush the heresy, Priscillian was made bishop of Avila around 380, but the next year his enemies had him exiled by the pope. In 381, the exile was overturned in the civil courts and Priscillian returned to Spain where his movement grew in strength.

Knowing that the continued success of his regime would depend on support from the Orthodox Church in the West, Maximus had Priscillian tried at Bordeaux by a synod of bishops. Priscillian rejected this and set off to plead with Maximus in person in 385. Maximus set a precedent by being the first to order execution for heresy. Priscillian was instantly treated as a martyr by his followers, though the heresy remained underground until after the year in which Maximus fell. It is worth emphasising how radical this was in a world where religious tolerance had been so advanced in earlier years. The Priscillianists were not accused of anything extreme like child sacrifice, merely liturgical differences which in their trial were described as magic. Had it not been for the intervention of St Martin of Tours the occasion would have led to a widespread persecution of anyone suspected of being a Priscillianist.

In fact, Maximus nearly lost the support he sought. The pope, then Siricius (384-99), criticised Maximus for his treatment of Priscillian, and excommunicated the bishops responsible for passing the sentence of death, recognizing it to be a terrible precedent. This was in spite of the fact that Siricius disapproved of Priscillianism, but had the wit to appreciate the destructive polarisation of stances that the politicisation of religious differences could cause.

In Italy, the conflict between the Arians and the Orthodox Church now became an issue. There was a remarkable link with the revolt of Magnentius (see chapter 11). Justina, the wife of Magnentius, was afterwards Valentinian I's second wife and had borne him Valentinian II. She was the driving force behind her son's rule. Despite her first husband's pagan inclinations and political sympathies with the Orthodox Church, Justina was an Arian. She obliged her son to pass a law making Arianism a legal faith, and insisted that Arians be given a church for their use in Milan. She was thwarted by the bishop of Milan, Ambrose. Ambrose never hesitated to use his episcopal status, rather than any legal entitlement, to interfere in civil and religious disputes, but it did not stop Maximus from capitalising on the occasion.

The Arian incident provided Magnus Maximus with a handy pretext to tear up his deal with Valentinian II and topple the irritating obstruction to his legitimacy. It was a huge gamble. He announced that he was off to protect the interests of the Church from the abuses being heaped on it at Valentinian's behest. He organised an army made up of Britons, Gauls and 'Celts', though it is not clear whether these were forces he already had, or whether he took more troops from the western provinces and thereby denuded Britain's defences even further.

The army entered Italy. Maximus left Flavius Victor to control Gaul, and holed himself up at Aquileia, strategically located at the north end of the Adriatic and almost exactly at the mid-point between the Western and Eastern halves of the Empire. He sent Andragathius south at the head of his army to enter Italy, which he did after securing all the routes into the peninsula to protect his rear Theodosius. Those familiar with the history of the Second World War will recall Hitler's occasional inclinations to make what seem now, and to his less-toady advisors then, extraordinarily stupid decisions that helped cost him the war. Perhaps Andragathius felt he had over-stretched his forces because now he unexpectedly decided to remove the garrisons he had set up in the Alpine passes, while leading a naval force against Valentinian's supporters.

It can only be assumed that Andragathius had no idea Theodosius was on his way, or perhaps had been quietly bought off. We do not know, but abandoning the positions left the way wide open. Theodosius laid siege to Aquileia, and in the Battle of Poetovio defeated Maximus' army. Maximus seems to have tried to make a run for it, but he was caught a few miles away. In a process of ritual humiliation, his imperial clothing was torn off him and he was executed. In Gaul, Valentinian's *magister militum*, a Frank called Arbogastes, killed Flavius Victor. Arbogastes would go on to play a major role in imperial events yet to come, setting up another rival regime in the West.

The revolt of Magnus Maximus was destroyed in 388. What was left of the British component of his army was said to have settled in Armorica, and never returned. Despite his moralising unreliability Gildas painted a graphically memorable picture of Britain in the aftermath of the rebellion. Deprived of her garrison, Britain was 'groaning in a state of shock', only to be overrun by Scots and Picts. Rome responded to pleas and a 'legion' was sent to drive the barbarians back. That the troops were said to have advised the Britons to build a wall to keep the raiders out shows just how unreliable Gildas could be. This was clearly a confused attempt to explain the Antonine Wall, by then some 250 years old, or perhaps the Vallum ditch and rampart system behind Hadrian's Wall. But the account may preserve a sense of the state of disorder that prevailed in the aftermath of the rebellion.

Roman Britain had little more than a generation left to run. Her cities were shadows of their former selves. Public buildings scarcely existed in their original form. Many of the basilicas were semi-derelict, or had been adapted to house industry. The theatres, traditionally linked to temples for pagan festivals, were disused. The greatest of the rural villas were just passing through the last few years of their zenith. Apart from remote rural temples, paganism had retreated into the shadows. Around this time, or not long afterwards, the Faunus sect plate was buried at Thetford. Linked to an ancient Latin pagan deity, nothing is known of the sect other than that somewhere a wealthy secret cell preserved something of the old Roman world. Few of the villas were still being improved. Instead they were just beginning to decay or at least stagnate. At Lullingstone the house church functioned. In the north the forts were disintegrating as units increasingly became semi-autonomous bands, controlling their areas like gangs.

For some strange reason, Magnus Maximus was not forgotten. It is usually said that Welsh traditional lists of kings preserve him in the name Macsen Wledig, and he certainly features in several Dark Age dynastic genealogies including the rulers of Galloway. This kind of linkage was a useful component in legitimising a line of rulers, and really no different from how Julius Caesar was happy to see himself as descended from Iulus, the son of Aeneas, and therefore ultimately from Venus. Augustus, his nephew and first emperor of Rome, perpetuated the myth by encouraging the popularisation of Virgil's *Aeneid*. Similarly, the Magnus Maximus tradition was just as fictionalised. Despite being a murderous usurper who ripped off Britain by taking her garrison to support his bid for power, he was immortalised as a folklore hero with a British wife, whose rebellion was converted into a quasi-nationalist revolt that set out to throw off the tyrannical rule of Rome. Other chroniclers were less inclined to such nonsense fantasies. Bede, writing in the eighth century, repeated the basic story from Roman historians like Orosius.

Destroying Maximus brought the West no peace. Arbogastes killed Valentinian II in 392, and promoted a learned palace official called Eugenius to act as his puppet ruler. In 394 Theodosius returned to Italy to demolish this new challenge to his power, which also took on a politico-religious tone when Eugenius started offering concessions to pagans. This gesture made Eugenius suddenly look attractive to the established pagan aristocracy in Rome, and it amounted to a direct challenge to Theodosius who in 391 had passed laws finally outlawing any pagan activity. Eugenius was executed, and Arbogastes committed suicide, but only a few months later in January 395 Theodosius died of dropsy at Milan.

13

End of Days

CONSTANTINE III

Romanus orbis ruit ('The Roman world is falling into ruin'), wrote St Jerome in 396 (*Letters* lx.16). In fact it had a while to go yet, but the omens were bad and he had good reason for his pessimism. In Britain the end was a good deal nearer. The last great adventurer from Roman Britain, Constantine III, presided over a short and violent reign. He saw the official end of Roman Britain and marked out the shape of things to come. The sources that provide us with the events of the rebellion are confused and very incomplete when it comes to details of motive and faction. What we do know is that the period was racked by the consequences not only of usurpation, but also the practice of powerful generals and statesmen ruling through emperors.

Constantine III started his reign as a usurper but changed his position to try and pose as a legitimate associate emperor of the regime of Honorius. This was typical of the rebellions of the age. They were never cast in a new form, with a new name. They were always Roman emperors, and posed in conventional ways with conventional titles. When Constantine failed to win supreme power as a Roman emperor in his own right, the logical step was to integrate himself with the existing regime. To begin with Honorius accepted this, and used it as a pretext to buy time. Constantine III led his revolt from Britain, but he was not unique in his ambitions. The disorder of the age in the face of barbarian invasions, influential barbarian military leaders, and the weakness of the legitimate regime meant that various other adventurers and puppets appeared on the stage in the Western Empire. The rebellion, like all the others, fell apart for a variety of reasons. In that sense it was not much worse off than the legitimate regime. While the centre of the world was falling to pieces, the final act in Roman Britain's drama was taking place. By the time it was over, Roman Britain had been cast off into the sea from which she had come, though there was room for one last curtain call.

In 383 Theodosius I made his eldest son Arcadius joint emperor with himself, although Arcadius was then just six years old. The following year Honorius was born and he was honoured in the same way in 394. When Theodosius died the following year Arcadius inherited the East, and Honorius the West. The tradition was well-established, and by making them joint emperors Theodosius was only doing what Constantine I had done many years before. However, Constantine's sons were adults, and had at least some of the skills needed to rule their domains, although they abused that by squabbling.

Arcadius and Honorius were too young to live up to their positions. Neither had any real calibre and were pathetic heirs to their father's, and grandfather's, tradition. So it was inevitable that other people would hold the real power. It was ironic that in the aftermath of the revolt of Magnus Maximus, Theodosius had gone after Arbogastes, the Frankish soldier who had tried to rule through his puppet emperor Eugenius, since Honorius was left wholly under the control of a Vandal general called Stilicho. Stilicho controlled almost the entire Roman army, and cemented his ties by marrying a niece of Theodosius. In turn Honorius even married Stilicho's daughter. It was an interesting change in style. In the third century,

Stilicho would simply have usurped Honorius and attempted to become emperor in his own right. In the fourth century power politics was sometimes more subtly conducted. Stilicho inveigled himself into the ruling dynasty to rule through it, not in spite of it.

It was the historian Gildas who blamed Magnus Maximus for permanently compromising Britain's security by selfishly appropriating her troops for his own futile ends. There is bound to have been some truth in this, not that Gildas usually troubled himself with relying on facts. On the whole he preferred moral judgements, and interpreted bad events as evidence of divine wrath. Stilicho seems to have paid some attention to Britain's troubles. By 400 Claudian was able to compose a panegyric on Stilicho's term as a consul, and referred to how he had come to Britain's aid against an invasion of the Scotti from Ireland, and had improved security against the Picts and the Saxons. In 402 Stilicho expected the compliment to be returned. A 'legion' installed on the northern frontier was summoned to Gaul to take part in the war against the Goths. The reinforcements made no permanent difference and the barbarian wars on the continent grew steadily in intensity.

In 406 a barbarian confederation led by the Vandals attacked Gaul, reputedly on the last day of December. It is not clear whether they were bent on conquest, raiding, or were simply fleeing from the Huns behind them. They seem to have incurred little or no resistance as they crossed the Rhine. One of the many mysteries surrounding the event is that Stilicho appears to have done nothing about it, unless the date is wrong. One suggestion is that the Vandal crossing took place a year before, during a time that Stilicho was fighting a Gothic army in Italy. Not unnaturally, the security of Honorius would have been his priority until he secured a victory in August 406. Either way, the occasion brought home to the Britons the precariousness of their situation. With the Western Empire on the brink of terminal collapse, a climate of fear took over which benefited those who fancied themselves as emperors.

Taking advantage of, or reacting to, the general mood of crisis, a sudden rush of pretenders appeared in Britain. The provincial

5 The Western Empire in the late fourth century. Province names are in their ancient form, but for clarity towns are given by their modern names

government of Britain resembled a modern political party indulging in rapid changes of leadership in a desperate attempt to find someone capable of steering the ship. We know almost nothing about the first two except that their elevation took place before Honorius started his seventh consulship, which began on 1 January 407. This places the risings not later than the latter part of 406. A man called Marcus was appointed emperor by the British garrison. Why they did this is a mystery since he was said by the historian Zosimus to have turned out not to be 'in harmony' with them. That meant executing Marcus and installing a substitute, this time called Gratian, who was possibly a magistrate and was said to have been a Briton. Gratian was awarded the full trappings of an emperor but the garrison took against him as well and killed him after a perfunctory reign of four months. Neither struck coinage and we know nothing else about either of them – even whether they were civilian puppets or soldiers.

Perhaps the troops were after an adventurer, because their next candidate seems to have been far more popular. It was, after all, around twenty years since the rebellion of Magnus Maximus, long enough for a whole new generation of troops to grow up and daydream on the bleak frontier; and dreamers of the day are dangerous men. It was also long enough for the legends about Maximus, which circulated for centuries afterwards, to have started evolving in popular lore. The rebellion might have been more calculated than just a terrified response to the possibility of more invasions. Stilicho was focused on the East, and if Britain revolted – well, that might have been a risk he was prepared to take. If so, he miscalculated the way things were to go. Having the right name can make all the difference and an ordinary soldier called Constantine emerged into the spotlight to be declared emperor in Britain early in 407. Constantine I, it will be remembered, had been declared emperor in York almost exactly a century before, and his son Constantine II was placed in charge of Britain and Gaul on his father's death. Just to reinforce the credentials, his full name was Flavius Claudius Constantinus, which conveniently echoed great imperial dynasties of four centuries before. This helps explain why it was that an ordinary soldier was created emperor, rather than a general, though this may have just been a device used to denigrate his memory. To put it another way, it was as if a modern British private named Henry V Tudor Windsor was plucked from the ranks to become a usurper. Crass and simplistic it might seem, the name was thought by the historian Orosius to have been the defining spin in why the new Constantine was chosen (vii.40). Sozomen, writing in 439 (and using an earlier source called Olympiodorus), says that a number of other people with the same name were chosen to join 'the tyranny' (ix.11).

Constantine III, as he is known to history, moved quickly, which suggests his intentions were already known to the troops or that they made it clear what they wanted. It just might be a mistake though to attribute too much of the strategy to Constantine. There is a very real possibility that he was initially promoted as a convenient figurehead with the right name and looks by a cabal of generals who had a more sophisticated game-plan in mind. This might explain some of the problems that occurred later in the rebellion. For the moment Constantine put two of his associates, Justinian and Neviogastes, in charge of what are called the 'Celtic forces' in Britain. This presumably means the long-term resident frontier troops whose family and social ties had long been local to the forts where they were based. These two men seem to have led the army as it crossed into Gaul. Constantine then left Britain himself and made for Boulogne. Here he negotiated with the garrison in Gaul and Germany and seems to have won their support quickly and decisively. This was critical, and if Stilicho had made any sort of risk assessment, this unfortunate development would not have been part of it. The loss of the Rhine garrisons to a usurper was unacceptable, and followed the fall of the frontier to barbarian incursions in 406. The collapse of the frontier was thanks to derelict morale, and the impotence of an inadequate garrison faced by a motivated and mobile force of invaders. Honorius had no prestige, and Stilicho's favouritism of barbarian troops had alienated the mainstream forces. Why would they bother to stay loyal?

There is some evidence for Constantine III at least helping to hold back the barbarians. Although the Vandal invasion of 405 or 406 had occasioned great fear, a letter by St Jerome referring to the event suggests that by mid-409 the Vandals had still not really moved much beyond northern and central Gaul (*Letters* cxxiii.16), though they entered Spain by the end of the year. Jerome trots out a list of miseries suffered by the Gauls, including the massacre of a church congregation during the destruction of *Moguntiacum* (Mainz). He talks about the desolation that had spread into *Gallia Aquitania*, *Lugdunensis* and *Narbonensis*, but only specifies cities that had actually fallen in the north. Not that that was really much to be pleased about. Toulouse, Jerome said, had so far escaped, but everywhere so far spared by the sword had been afflicted with famine as a result of the war and destruction. Even so, it was perhaps the presence of Constantine III on the continent that had helped slow things up. Jerome wrote in Bethlehem so his information was probably slightly out of date, but it provides a vivid image of the state the West was in. Looking for a usurper to do the emperor's job is easy to understand.

Constantine's power depended on his troops, and this explains why although his output of coinage was limited, he still produced gold and silver. He made no attempt at all to compensate for the collapse in official supplies of bronze to Britain. This means that he was unconcerned about promulgating his image there, and also had no concern about reversing the gradual deterioration of a cash-based economy in Britain where supplies of official bronze coins had almost ended and were not being made good by local copies. Constantine III's coins only refer to Victory, with the legend *Victoria Aug(usti)*, and are sometimes quite crude in style. However, some of the legends pour a little light on his aspirations since they multiply the *g* to denote more than one ruler. Those with the suffix *Augggg* show that Constantine III was trying to pose as the fourth member of the imperial partnership held by Honorius in the West, and Arcadius and Theodosius II in the East. The death of Arcadius in May 408 was followed by conversion of the legend to *Auggg*.

The coins were eventually all struck at Trier, Arles, Lyons and Milan, reflecting Constantine's power-base. The issues revived the Gaulish mints, which had last been used more than a decade before. Lyons was the first to be reactivated, and marks the direction in which the usurper's campaign took to begin with. The new coins reached Britain in extremely small numbers, probably in private stashes of bullion. The Hoxne (Suffolk) hoard, which contained

14,865 gold and silver coins of the fourth and early fifth centuries (as well as various artefacts made of silver and gold), ended with two silver coins of Constantine III, struck at Lyons around 407-8. We know absolutely nothing about the owner of the hoard. It might have been private wealth of one or more families, buried to protect it either from the usual dangers or to prevent it being requisitioned by the authorities (such as existed at the time) to use as bribes for barbarians. Equally, it might have been bullion already requisitioned or paid as tax, which was buried by the officials responsible for its safekeeping. Another hoard, with a similar spread of coins, was found nearby at Eye in 1780. The Ballinrees Hoard found in Ulster was undoubtedly a collection of coins, ingots and fragmentary vessels, owned by someone whose sole interest was its value as bullion. It is very plausibly interpreted as bribe money paid to a would-be raider to keep away, or possibly as material stolen from Britain. The coins were all silver, and ended with a single identifiable one of Constantine III.

The rarity of his coin in Britain is easily explained, for Constantine III's gold is not especially rare on the continent. It was surely used to pay the troops he was using to hold Gaul and spread his power in the West. Constantine took over the city of *Valentia* (Valence), and seems to have been joined by Justinian. This must mean that more troops had left Britain, and together with the continental forces Constantine used his army to hold all of Gaul down to the Alps. It seems that the Constantinian army set about helping themselves to loot from across the province. Stilicho sent an army under the general Sarus to force Justinian to a battle, which he did. Sarus destroyed Justinian's forces and captured the booty the rebel army had been holding onto. Sarus then laid siege to *Valentia*. Neviogastes realised the game was probably up and, as has always been typical of military opportunists, he tried to change sides once more. He had talks with Sarus in the hope that he could protect himself that way. The negotiations looked promising, but Sarus had no intention of accommodating a rebel general and had Neviogastes killed on the spot.

Despite this reverse, Constantine remained in power and found at this point that his prospects suddenly started to look a good deal better. The Lyons coins of 407-8 were joined by issues struck at Trier and Arles in 408. So, within a year of seizing power Constantine had spread his control south and east across Gaul. Constantine III promoted his eldest son to the status of Caesar, an essential device to broaden the new regime's power. This took place after Arles fell to the usurper. Constantine renamed his sons Constans and Julian, just to reinforce the propaganda value of his own name. Constantine III was clearly out to found a retro-dynasty. In this, it seems, he found plenty of support in Gaul. Not only was this where he based himself, but later events would reinforce this impression. Constantine took advantage of this by choosing prominent Gallo-Romans to help his administration, though it is possible they were given no choice. In 408 his praetorian prefect was a Gaul called Apollinaris, and his 'Head of Offices' Decimus Rusticus. Constantine also appointed new generals: a Frank called Ediovinchus, and a Briton called Gerontius. Sarus knew that both these men were first-class and successful soldiers so he decided to retreat in haste. He was not hasty enough, and soon had the Constantinian forces on his tail, obliging him to use the loot he had captured to bribe himself out of trouble and over the Alps into the safety of Italy.

With Gaul now relatively secure, Constantine took control of the Alps and sent Constans with Gerontius into Spain in 408 to confront supporters of the legitimate regime. They met resistance and it was not until two battles later that Gerontius was left in control of Spain, along with Constans' own family, while Constans returned to his father at Arles. Part of the price had been murdering members of the family of Honorius, and Honorius had yet to find out. It will be obvious that while Constantine might have started off in Britain, and been dependent initially on British troops, Britain had played no part in the revolt thereafter. But it is quite conceivable that, had he been successful in consolidating his power, Constantine might have secured for Britain a place in a north-western imperial domain that looked after itself.

At this time a sense of complacency seems to have pervaded the regime. Constantine was said by some to be indulging in gluttony and drunkenness, though he was not the first usurper to be described this way. Indeed, there is no record that he ever actually led an army during his revolt despite a reputation for being a disciplinarian. This is an important reminder of how he had come to power, and that perhaps he was more of a figurehead than a genuinely effective leader. But he seemed to be secure in his power base at Arles, especially after Stilicho's execution by Honorius in the late summer of 408. Perhaps Constantine started reading history books and realised what usually happened to people like him, because now he decided to change tack altogether.

Constantine wrote to Honorius and apologised for assuming the name and position of an emperor. He said it was because the soldiers had made him do it. Honorius decided to accept the status quo because he could not afford to spare soldiers to take on Constantine's army, and fearing for his family in Spain accepted him as an emperor, though he had no idea what had happened to them. Right now, the prospect of Alaric and the Ostrogoths marching on Rome was preying on his troubled mind. The death of Stilicho in August 408 left him with a vacuum in his military command. So, at the beginning of 409 Constantine III and Honorius served as joint consuls.

In 409 Gerontius rebelled in Spain against Constantine III, and soon after placed his own candidate on the throne, a man called Maximus, and even started striking silver coins in his name at *Barcino* (Barcelona). We do not know why he did this. He may have resented Constantine's overtures to Honorius, or he may initially have seen himself as a potential alternative ally to the court of Honorius and only elevated Maximus out of frustration when nothing happened in his favour. The other possibility is that Gerontius was one of the generals who had promoted Constantine into his position as usurper, and who found his nominee acting rather too much on his own initiative. Gerontius had another problem. If Constantine was making up with Honorius, then it was possible that Constantine might decide to blame Gerontius for the murder of the emperor's Spanish kinsmen.

Gerontius seems to have had the support of the Vandals and their associates. The barbarians began to move down through Gaul and invaded Spain by mid-October of the year 409.

Britain was said at this time to have expelled any imperial officials and taken charge of its own defences. The model for this is probably what went on to happen in Gaul during the fifth century. Here, wealthy and influential men organised retainers and other local people into what might best be called self-help bands of amateur soldiers, making good the lack of imperial leadership and resources. After all, if it was true that the revolt of Constantine III had been supported in a hope that he would keep the barbarians under control, he had in the end patently failed to do this in spite of the indirect evidence from Jerome that he had initially slowed their advance. Honorius was already as good as irrelevant, and Constantine was no longer able to control his own lieutenants.

Through an envoy, Constantine III admitted to Honorius that some of the latter's family had been killed in Spain but promised that he would now use his army to help protect Italy from barbarian attack. Constantine III was desperately trying to buy himself a place in the 'legitimate' imperial college. Either way, Britain's garrison was doing very little to save the province from which it had been taken, which might have diminished support for him in Britain, though as it would turn out the initial support for him was a fatal blow as far as Honorius was concerned. But in 410 Honorius reversed his policy of tolerating usurpers, and Gerontius was on the move because he felt he had no choice, or perhaps had been encouraged by Honorius. Either way, Constantine III found himself under assault from two directions. Honorius despatched an army with instructions to defeat Constantine III at all costs. Meanwhile, Gerontius marched into Gaul from Spain and murdered Constantine III's son Constans at Vienne.

Gerontius was out of control, and Constantine had lost his son and co-emperor. Constantine was still nearby at Arles, where the Honorian arm besieged him. It took a while, but in 411 Arles fell. Constantine was captured and executed in September, along with his younger son. As a reminder to others, Constantine's head was displayed in public. Gerontius was wrong-footed by the decision of the bulk of his troops spontaneously to join the Honorian army. With his own soldiers besieging his headquarters, Gerontius did not take the chance to escape with his servants. Instead he hung back, killed his wife at her request, and committed suicide.

With the rebels removed as an immediate problem, Honorius moved to limit his liabilities, though of course his personal prestige was enhanced by how things had turned out. It is interesting that in the same year Constantine III fell, a Gaulish usurper called Jovinus jumped in to fill the gap. Like most imperial figureheads of the period, legitimate or otherwise, he had barbarian backers. But Jovinus was his own man, and his status as a Gallo-Roman aristocrat suggests that the broader upper echelons of Gaulish society had little time for an impotent emperor like Honorius, and were likely to have played a major part in Constantine III's rebellion.

Honorius had already recognised that he could no longer support Britain and was said in 410 to have instructed the regional govern-ments of Britain to look after their own defences. In the same year Rome fell to Alaric's Goths and the Roman world was never the same again. Jovinus negotiated with the Goths, but by 413 the Goths had allied themselves with Honorius. Jovinus was captured and executed. And so it went on. Constantine III might have survived to create a kind of late Gallic Empire in which Britain, Gaul and Spain were managed as a regional unit. But when Gerontius betrayed him the chance was lost. His legacy was to have removed much of Britain's garrison, and as a result Britain was left exposed and with no alternative but to fall back on her own resources.

14

Abominable and Noxious Teaching

PELAGIUS

The seventeenth-century French theological historian Louis du Pin
said Pelagius 'was not learned, but he was a man of good sense'. Back
in the eighth century to the diehard orthodox historian Bede,
Pelagius was responsible for 'abominable and noxious teaching'.
Pelagius was a rebel against Rome in the sense that he led a religious
movement to challenge the religious orthodoxy of the Roman
world, an orthodoxy then being utilised to hold what was left of the
Empire together. Pelagius' name came from the Greek *pelagos*
('ocean') and meant something like 'of the sea'. Having a Greek
name was a mark of social and intellectual aspiration, and it had
become common to adopt them across the Roman world.
Unfortunately this means it tells us nothing reliable about his
parentage, even if he had been born in Britain, especially as we do
not know what the rest of his name was.

Pelagius was one of many religious leaders in the early Christian
church who had his own specific interpretation of Holy Scripture.
Unlike pagan religion, which would usually have recognised any
idiosyncratic sect as a variant or another cult and left it at that,

Christianity was formulating itself into a more totalitarian brand of cult. Once it had become politicised as the religion of the state, Christianity could not be allowed to manifest itself in infinite variations. One of the inherent problems with this is that any protagonist of a variant form tended to treat other types of Christianity as demonic, and unacceptable. The problem of Arianism had already split the Empire in two, and it challenged Christianity's future and the stability of the Empire.

It is sometime said that when Roman rule ended in Britain, Christianity disappeared too. In fact, the truth is that evidence for almost everything disappears after 410, and religion of any form is another part of that vacuum. Paradoxically, Christianity is one of the few aspects of Roman Britain that does survive in the record. The Pelagian heresy enjoyed such popularity in Britain a generation after Honorius told the cities of Britain to take of their own defences that a plea for help had to be sent to the church in Gaul. The record of the event paints a remarkable picture of Christianity's survival in the Britain of the early decades of the fifth century, and it forms one of the few windows we have on that mysterious period.

As a Briton, Pelagius played a special part in Roman history simply by being a major player on the world stage. No other individual Briton is recorded as having so great an impact in antiquity beyond Britain's shores. Pelagius left a legacy that lasted for generations after his death because what he taught provoked a firestorm of religious controversy that echoed down the fifth century, while the Britain he had come from gradually retreated into remote obscurity. But the popularity of his teachings in Britain helped maintain links with the continental church, and the records of those sent to Britain to help wipe out the heresy have contributed important information about society in post-Roman Britain.

Pelagius was born in Britain. Some versions of his life mention Ireland as a possible birthplace, but in his own time he was usually described as a Briton. He was said by St Augustine, his sworn enemy, to have been a monk. We know little or nothing about his childhood or youth but he reached Rome around the end of the fourth century, where he started to publish his religious teachings in a book called *de Natura*. This is said to have occurred before the fall of Rome in 410. This must mean that he was born around the 350s or 360s, and therefore grew up in the time of Valentinian and Theodosius. By his middle years he was able to witness the dereliction of imperial power and the succession of usurpers that propelled Britain's garrison into continental wars and left her woefully unable to confront the threats to her security from barbarian incursions. Exactly where he was by then is unknown. He may have reached Rome by the 380s, since the Christian teacher Jerome, who was there at the time, seems to have known him.

The relative social isolation of Britain must have helped Pelagius evolve his own ideas about Christianity, though in fact he may have been just one of many such people. One of the most burning issues in theological debate at the time was the question of how much power men and women had over their own salvation. In other words, what could human beings do to enter Heaven, or was it already predetermined by God? St Augustine had written, in his widely disseminated *Confessions*, that God was able to command what he wanted. It was derived from the belief that men were sinful from the outset, connected to the concept of 'original sin' established in the Garden of Eden. As far as Pelagius was concerned, this was a statement that any individual was predestined to enter Heaven – or not, as the case may be – and that God had decided who. Pelagius thought this absurd. It was not unnatural that he did so, because the pagan world had been based on the assumption that each and every person could affect his or her own destiny by interceding with a god.

By publishing his work in *de Natura* ('on Nature'), Pelagius provoked a public debate. Augustine replied with *de Natura et Gratia* ('on Nature and Grace'). Pelagius attracted support from wealthy and educated young men, attracted by what Augustine called the *nefarius error* ('wicked mistake') of rejecting God's grace. Today that concept is not well known, but Augustine defined it as a gift of God's mercy that made men good enough to enter Heaven. In other words, it was not enough to do good things, but God's grace was needed as well. It is immediately obvious that this contained an element of selection; since God knew everything he must know who would be chosen this way. So, if one was not chosen to be one of the 'elect', there was nothing to be done about it. To Pelagius this amounted to a cheat, and since God did not cheat people it could not be true. Paradoxically, as a young man Augustine had made much of free will, but later found in Paul's *Letter to the Romans* the evidence for an elect few, 'selected by the grace of God' (xi.5). From Augustine's perspective, Paul's statement demonstrated that grace came first, 'good works' second, and no amount of good works could compensate for not being one of the 'elect'.

Pelagius did not dispute the idea of God's grace, but he interpreted it as a straightforward universal gift of free will: the choice to do good, and earn a place in Heaven, or the choice not to. He published this in his *Commentary* on Paul's letters. Augustine considered that an unconscionable level of arrogance exhibited by a man before God, and believed that Pelagius was refuting the belief that all gifts came from God, and encouraging people to glory in themselves rather than Christ.

Pelagius also challenged the idea that Christ was the only person who had never committed a sin. He pointed out that in the Bible the sins of Adam, Eve and Cain are all specified, but there was nothing about Abel committing any sin. As only four people existed at the time, it must be that Abel had done nothing wrong. Therefore the possibility existed that other people were sinless, and that included 'original sin'. Augustine of course subscribed to the orthodox view that Christ 'alone in mortal flesh was without sin'. Pelagius also believed that the consequences of an early sinful life could be overturned in later life by using the gift of free will to mend one's ways. Being inherently sinful and needing baptism to cleanse the soul of original sin was a test of orthodoxy so far as Augustine was concerned, and he could not accept a theory that not everyone might need it. Needing baptism would be, quite literally, the distinguishing factor between Christ and all other men, and Augustine seems to have been instrumental in making baptism a test of faith.

It would be wrong to believe that Pelagius was a 'wrecker', though Augustine thought that was exactly what his enemy amounted to. Pelagianism focused on the freedom of human beings to choose, and influence, their own destiny, but this was not done out of a reactionary desire to cast Christianity in a pagan mould. Rather, Pelagius was trying to reform Christianity by expanding its inclusiveness. His brand of Christianity allowed everyone the chance to recover his soul and find a path to Heaven. Pelagius thought the Augustan concept – that God had included in creation men incapable of fulfilling his requirements – absurd. In this sense, his attitude directly inherited the classical idea of self-determination, while Augustine played a material part in creating the idea that human beings were powerless against the power of God. While Pelagius looked back to the classical world, Augustine anticipated the 'victim' status of the medieval Christian.

Today it seems slightly strange that this could have provoked an international crisis, since it is the kind of pedantic dispute that would normally run its course in the obscurity of an academic journal. But at the time, it really was a compelling issue and as adherents of the different points of view gathered round the opposed camps a political crisis evolved. Pelagius was by now on the move, spreading his word across North Africa and the East by 409. The two men sustained a torrent of hate mail, and the machinery of the Church was put into operation to tackle the Pelagians in synods and councils. Augustine's campaign to vilify Pelagius was given added momentum by Jerome, who joined in the attack. The effect on the Pelagian cause by its creator being a Briton should not be underestimated. Britons were not held in high social, intellectual, aesthetic or political regard. That someone of such consummate inferiority had sought to challenge sophisticated Mediterranean minds contributed to the apoplectic bile fired off at Pelagius. Not that being sophisticated meant necessarily constructing sophisticated arguments. Pelagius was described on more than one occasion as being fairly well rounded, which Jerome attributed to an excess of eating Irish porridge with a detrimental effect on Pelagius' ability to remember things. Insulting Pelagius for his size became a popular theme, with ever more baroque descriptions like those composed by Orosius, which turned him into a blubber-laden behemoth whose days were spent gorging and bathing.

Such honed liturgical objections to Pelagianism did it little immediate harm. Pelagius was not a pretentious barbarian, or an oaf posing as a philosopher. He was educated up to a point, and was well received in many places that he travelled, along with his chief supporter and fellow Briton, Caelestius (whose name, incidentally, linked him to the pagan goddess of the Heavens, Caelestis). Although less conspicuous in the record we have, Caelestius might have had rather more to do with the high profile of Pelagianism than at first appears. Both Jerome and Augustine acknowledged his intellectual skills. Either way, Pelagianism was popping up all over the Empire, no doubt reflecting the long-established pagan tradition of religious self-help. Pelagius enjoyed support from powerful and influential families in Rome, and he was quite willing to answer the synods and councils with guarantees of his faith. Britain might have been remote, and Britons often ill-thought of, but in that cosmopolitan world of late antiquity plenty of wealthy families owned estates scattered throughout the Roman Empire. Pelagius could easily have made influential contacts in Britain and travelled to the Continent on the back of some of them.

In the face of this Augustine had to find more effective methods, so as Bishop of Hippo (since 396), he brought all his influence to bear in order to spread the word that the Pelagians were a direct challenge to political and social stability. In an extraordinary twist he even orchestrated the provision of eighty fine cavalry horses amongst army officers to persuade them to break up Pelagian groups. Even though Britain was no longer a part of the Empire it, too, was targeted by the forces of Augustinian orthodoxy.

In 418 Pelagius was banished from Rome and denounced as a heretic. It had been far from straightforward and Augustine had to bring all his influence to bear. In 417 Pope Innocent I had excommunicated Pelagius and Caelestius. This delighted Augustine, but within a few weeks Innocent was dead. His successor, Zosimus (417-18), was rather more accommodating and told the Augustine camp that the Pelagians had demonstrated to his satisfaction that they were not heretics. Augustine and his supporters weighed in with everything they could muster, including appealing to Honorius, and forced Zosimus to back down and reiterate the excommunication. They secured a declaration by Honorius that Pelagius and his supporters were heretics, which left Zosimus with no choice but to join in with the condemnation of Pelagians.

The banishment from Rome in 418 is the last we hear of Pelagius the man, but it was by no means the end of the heresy. By 429, when we first hear about Pelagianism in Britain, it had already taken a serious hold. Perhaps Pelagius had gone home, and was personally responsible. There may have been some regional loyalty, but it is more likely that Pelagius was promulgating an underlying attitude of mind that the resilient underground paganism found appealing, especially in Britain, whether he was there or not. Augustine could easily have been seen to be arguing that if Britain fell, or was deemed unworthy, it was because God had predetermined that and so therefore there was nothing to be done. Falling to barbarians proved Britain's lack of worth in the eyes of God. Pelagianism though offered the exact opposite: the chance to examine past actions, and change one's ways to earn a righteous future. With the barbarian threat knocking on Britain's door, and a history of reckless usurpers, Britain must have found Pelagianism altogether more promising. However, we have no evidence that it was consciously adopted as a response, and nor do we have any idea that it might have contributed to the ideology (or lack of) behind the revolt of Constantine III.

In 429 news reached the church in Gaul that Pelagianism was rife in Britain, and the orthodox church was under threat. What is impossible to verify is whether it had just arrived, or whether it had been quietly circulating for the past twenty years or more. Writing three centuries later, Bede reported that Agricola, son of a Pelagian bishop called Severianus, had brought it over. Together with Fastidius, said to have been a British bishop, Agricola worked to promote Pelagianism in Britain. Bede conceded that Pelagianism had such 'plausible arguments' it had proved impossible for the Britons to reject it, a neat spin that absolved his predecessors from guilt. Either way, the Gaulish bishops met in 429 and decided that two of their number, Germanus of Auxerre and Lupus of Troyes, be sent across the Channel to sort things out. Some sort of public gathering appears to have been organised so that the two sides could battle it out with words in front of a vast audience drawn from the public of all ages. The Pelagians were said to have decked themselves out with ostentatious vestments and decoration to much admiration from their acolytes. Of course this is perhaps just a metaphorical way of drawing attention to the Pelagian glorification of the self, or so it was interpreted.

The account is, of course, thoroughly biased, so the event is reported to have begun with the Pelagian case. Germanus and Lupus then leapt in with their speeches, bursting with snappy scriptural references and other convincing arguments. For good measure they threw in a miracle, and then the two visited the shrine of St Alban, which some now take as good evidence that the whole public debate had taken place nearby. It was also a calculated swipe at the Pelagians who opposed the edification of saints in this manner. They had various adventures that only went to demonstrate their superior brand of Christianity. Germanus, for example, was left unscathed in a fire that burnt down buildings around him. He was resting after a fall. Needless to say he experienced a miraculous recovery after curing various other disciples who came to see him. Just to reinforce his impact, Germanus led an army against a force of Picts and Saxons, and routed the lot. The two bishops then returned to the continent after a tour-de-force display of early Christian superhero activity. In 446 Germanus was recalled since, despite his efforts, the Britons had reverted to Pelagianism. Evidently, the previous trip had failed to have a lasting impact, though he escapes any criticism for that. Accompanied by a bishop called Severus this time, Germanus had an easier trip because he seems to have avoided fires, falls, and battles. Instead he worked miracles and preached with the result that the Pelagians were handed over to him so that they could be banished to Gaul.

That was not the end of Pelagianism. The heresy had to be condemned again by a council in Orange in Gaul in 529, but it was still around in the late sixth century before it finally disappeared. Later, the historian Bede would recount these events, showing that the episode had left powerful memories in Britain as it had elsewhere. But like so many of Britain's later rebels, Pelagius played out his own final act beyond Britain. He is an important figure because his British birth and international significance were a unique combination for the age. A number of writings, alleged to be his, survive and that makes him exceptional too for someone born in Britain during the period of Roman rule. But, in the end, Augustine's way won. The Pelagian idea of individual self-determination was as anachronistic as Carausian yearnings for ancient classical themes.

Pelagius had tried to cast Christianity in a mould that the traditional Roman world would better understand. It is ironic that he came from Britain, since this was the very place that originally seemed so organically segregated from the essence of the classical mindset. Yet, it was Britain in the fourth century that was characterised by a villa-owning élite, which surrounded itself with the iconography of pagan culture even if many of them were nominally Christians. This is a fundamental concept that we often struggle with since we have inherited a long-term ancient Christian tradition that sought to suppress pagan roots. In late antiquity this was often not the way, especially amongst the educated upper classes. For them, Christianity was easily perceived within the metaphor of classical myth and imagery. In this context, Pelagius found a ready public. The Pelagians in Britain had tried to define Christianity within pagan perceptions, but Britain was characteristically out of step with the world beyond. The rest of the Roman world was already steadily moving into a new kind of mindset, where self-determination was giving way to the passive impotence of human beings before the all-powerful and predetermined grace of St Augustine's God. The world had moved on, and from now on the Britons had nothing Roman to rebel against. Instead they clung to what was left until like Bede they, and the immigrant arrivals like the Saxons, could only marvel at the work of giants crumbling across Britain's landscape.

15

Patriots and Tyrants

In 1787 Thomas Jefferson, one of the leaders of the American Revolution, and later third president of the United States, wrote a letter in which he said that 'the blood of patriots and tyrants' was essential to the nourishment of the 'tree of liberty'. But what did he mean by patriots and tyrants? For patriot, read the leaders of the Revolution, and for tyrant read George III. George III and his government, naturally under the circumstances, took an entirely different view. Had the American Revolution collapsed, then Washington, Jefferson and all the others would have been consigned to history as the leaders of a futile revolt. But Jefferson also said that year, 'a little rebellion now and then is a good thing'. As someone who had won power through successful rebellion he was bound to think that. But even in a more general sense he had a point. Even unsuccessful rebellions can contribute something to the ruling state by provoking a reassertion of power, sometimes for the good because the redefinition can be made in a more humane and tolerant fashion. After all, Classicianus was made procurator of Britain following the Boudican Revolt for that very reason.

So, what do we mean by a 'rebel', and what did the Romans mean? Today we argue over what constitutes a terrorist and what makes a freedom fighter. Some of today's legitimate (and even celebrated) politicians were once 'terrorists'. Carausius was damned by Rome as a pirate and a criminal but in many other senses he was the ultimate patriot – and certainly in his own eyes. He, like Postumus, Magnentius and others, thought that by defining himself as the arbiter of Roman power and identity he was buying into a winning streak. In marketing terms, 'Rome' was the best power brand there was. The Roman Empire was the total package, because it defined power, its possession, expression and manifestation in every conceivable aspect. Coinage, statuary, military power, and architecture, were all harnessed to this one end. Even the tribal leaders of the first century AD had found this, before the Roman invasion, when they Latinised and classicised their images on coins. Conversely, Constantine I, had he been defeated in his own bid for power twenty years later, would have been remembered as just another usurper. Elevated to the purple in York he had effectively usurped his place in the imperial college and had to fight to win control of the whole Empire. Constantine even took the radical step of legitimising a new religion to help him do it. He won and thus became truly 'legitimate', backed by both the force of arms and his god. The fourth-century Roman world was rebranded in a Constantinian mould. That was the reward for victory as it had been for Vespasian in 69 and Septimius Severus in 197.

It was exclusion that drove revolt in Britain. In her earliest years as a Roman province, Britain's most influential personalities mobilised whole communities to throw off the power of an invading force. But Caratacus and Boudica had misjudged the age, their people and the enemy. Sensing their own exclusion from the new system being imposed on them, they challenged it head-on and forced a stark choice on themselves and their people. Caratacus was obliged to retreat to remoter territory to find the support he needed for his resistance. Although the Boudican Revolt was in every sense a cataclysm, and the resistance Boudica drew into her ranks a physical and metaphorical force that nearly destroyed the nascent province, the rebellion fell apart in an instant once Boudica was dead and winter was upon the rebels. Southern Britain never again attempted to rise up against the Romans behind a tribal leader.

In the later Empire, Britain was part of the Roman world but was never fully accepted. This theme is as apparent in the story of Caratacus as it is in that of Pelagius. No Briton is recorded as having become a senator, and there is a disproportionate absence of Britons from the epigraphic record in Britain and elsewhere. This suggests that Britons were marginalized from full participation in the upper tiers of provincial Roman society from the outset, and that it remained that way. Claudius had awarded full Roman citizenship to the aristocracy in part of Gaul in 48, and this was partially extended by Galba in 69. Tacitus pointed out that the areas of Gaul excluded from this special grant were equally irritated, whether they totted up how they had lost out from their own land confiscations or by how much their neighbours had gained (*Annals* xi.23; *Histories* i.8). It is easy to see why Britain should have felt the same or worse, and thereby sustained a perpetual and dangerous sense of grievance. Likening provincial status with enslavement to the Empire, Tacitus used the speech of the Caledonian leader Calgacus in 84 as a means to describe how Britain's recent conquest and thus enslavement to Rome made her a *ludibrio*, 'mockery', even to her fellow provincial 'slaves'. In their rock-bottom status in the provincial pecking order, Britons were thus disposable labour used to build roads, and were flung aside when exhausted or no longer required (*Agricola* 31.1-2).

While Britain will have experienced the effects of universal citizenship granted in 212 by Caracalla, this does not affect the point that Britain's indigenous élite scarcely experienced any of the special treatment afforded certain other provincial communities, and that the rest of the population were often regarded with a special disdain by almost everyone who lived on the continent. This alienation must have lain as much behind Pelagius as it did Carausius, Magnentius and Postumus. On the face of it, the role of Gaul in the revolt of Postumus might seem a contradiction of this, but in reality he probably only enjoyed significant support in northern Gaul which was to some extent as marginalized as Britain. When it came to Carausius he held on to a coastal strip of Gaul only briefly before losing it entirely.

The difference of course between early exclusion, and later exclusion, is the fact that those who supported Boudica and Caratacus wanted separation from the Empire, while those who supported Carausius, Magnentius and the like had come to accept being part of the Roman world, but who were denied full inclusion. The individual leaders themselves, like Clodius Albinus, felt their right to rule had been denied by the system or by rivals. It might seem curious to link Boudica with a rebellious British governor 140 years later, but both felt entitled to power. Even Pelagius rose up only to find that the new Roman order, in the form of Christianity expounded by Augustine, excluded him and denounced him as a lesser being in the derogatory racist terms of the age that classified Britons as steerage passengers being carried by the Roman Empire.

Exclusion seems to have played a consistent part in rebellion, at whatever level, but it seems to have been a peculiarly conspicuous feature of Roman Britain. Empires can never exist in a static form. Instead they feed on a diet of expansion and inclusion. This was how Rome worked. When she, or her representatives in the form of governors and soldiers, failed to match conquest with inclusion, then tensions arose. People like Caratacus, Boudica and Venutius could see no future for themselves within the imperial system. In one sense, why would they? After all, they had neither invited nor solicited the Roman conquest. But it is also true that aspects of the Roman approach were deeply flawed. A more cynical, but sympathetic, policy of subtle and patient exploitation might have gradually dissolved the tensions and evaded armed rebellion. Togidubnus is the critical case in point. He evaded exclusion for himself and his people by taking advantage of the conditional status of client king. Perhaps he humiliated himself and them in doing so. But he lived and died in peace, and so did they.

Being marginalised also meant that very few recorded Britons of substance or influence were the beneficiary of imperial favour or patronage. Togidubnus is the exception that proves the rule. Patronage was of particular importance in the late Empire, which conspicuously relied upon the interweaving of dependence in this way. In this context a rebellion led by a regional military commander was bound to harness support from influential members of Britain's cantons and her military units. This was the chance, perhaps the only chance, ambitious civilians had to rise to positions of significance, albeit in a breakaway regime. Exiled opponents to the legitimate Empire might see opportunities to pursue their grievances by joining forces with men like Magnentius and Magnus Maximus. Ordinary soldiers were transformed overnight from dozy frontier idlers in ramshackle forts, with nothing to do except fend off barbarians, into the vanguard of a glorious cause. However, such rebellions only retain and enhance their strength while they have momentum. One need only consider the way in which the 1745 Jacobite Rebellion gathered a head of steam when Charles Stuart, the Young Pretender, defeated the English at Prestonpans but lost it within days when he failed to gather new supporters on his march through England, and as his own troops started to melt away.

This is a key issue, and it affected Boudica as much as it did Carausius or Constantine III. The ideological basis of a rebellion is not necessarily the motivation for many of the participants. The Boudican Revolt is characteristically presented as a popular uprising, driven by a common experience of exploitation and brutality. In reality, Boudica's hordes were as keen on burning and robbing the Roman towns as they were on expelling the invaders. Indeed, many of them may have been keener on rape and pillage than worrying too deeply about the battle for 'liberty', especially as none of them seemed to have burned a torch for her once she was gone. Carausius might have had a keen vision of restoring Rome, but doubtless many of his 'supporters' had an interest in the regime only so long as it was winning, and could benefit them. Under Constantine I, being a Christian was an essential qualification to promotion and many people would have been baptised for that purpose.

Perhaps the most remarkable aspect of separatist regimes like the Gallic Empire is how they anticipated the post-Roman kingdoms of Europe, like the Holy Roman Empire, though by and large these latter regimes rose to the east of the Rhine. Each attempted to dress itself up in the psychological, literary and military imagery of Rome, but did so in a place other than Rome. The ruler buried at Sutton Hoo, probably Raedwald of the East Angles who died in 626, went to meet his maker furnished with an eclectic collection of his own military equipage together with Roman and Byzantine silver plate originating variously in the fourth, fifth and sixth centuries. Even his helmet harked back to those worn by the Roman army in the fourth century. Part of the reason is that Rome had evolved into a compelling abstract concept of imperial power from the moment the civil war of 68-9 erupted. It was then that it became clear that a 'Roman' emperor could be established in a place other than Rome herself, as Tacitus memorably noted (*Histories* i.4). But it was not until Postumus arrived on the scene in 259 that a renegade made no attempt to make Rome his seat of power. His 'Rome' was Cologne, and in 286 the Rome of Carausius was London.

Britain's role in rebellion is explained partly by the pattern of exclusion, whether social or economic, but there was also the question of resources. One of the intriguing features of this wayward province was the manner in which it was ignored, unless it was causing trouble. However, relatively vast resources were poured into Britain. Delegation was fundamental to the Roman system, but at this distance from the centre of the world perhaps an element of lawless frontier life crept in and went unnoticed by the administration until it was too late. Tacitus attributed the relative indifference of the British legions to the civil war in 69 to their remoteness *Oceano divisiae*, 'separated by the sea', and that they had learned to focus their aggression on barbarian enemies. It suggests that no one seriously considered Britain would become a danger, either because of a failure to control the population or because the soldiers would mount their own rebellion (*Histories* i.9).

Boudica rose, so it was said, because of the unspeakable maltreatment she and her people were subjected to by the Roman authorities. The Roman world had provided Britain with a huge number of troops, which meant that if they abused their position there were enough of them to do real damage to relations with the Britons. On the other hand, at least their misbehaviour was safely located across the English Channel. Had Britain been lost it would have been a less catastrophic amputation than, say, the loss of Greece or Spain. The support to Cartimandua simply helped provoke a catastrophic split in

Brigantian hierarchy. Clodius Albinus had enough of an army to mount an attack on the Empire itself when his ambition got the better of him. Postumus and Carausius both rose to power because of the military resources they had at their disposal – they needed them to do the job they were commissioned for, but they were also in a position to use them to their own advantage without being challenged until it was too late. The same applied to the adventurers of the fourth century.

Despite the division of commands, first instituted under Septimius Severus and then elaborated by Diocletian, Britain seems to have remained both excluded from the Empire and a repository of resources for rebellion. In the last 150 years of Roman Britain, the island province became home to a succession of ambitious men who cast themselves in a mould that would have made Boudica turn in her unknown grave. Carausius was the finest exponent of the lot, but all of them manufactured proxy Roman Empires and masqueraded with the grand conceit that they were the inheritors of the world of Augustus Caesar. It is astonishing that Carausius could indulge himself in this way, but it was a consequence of the greatest image of power ever created in human history. So, it should be no less of a surprise that Carausius, Magnentius, Magnus Maximus and Constantine III should all have been inclined to romance themselves as Roman emperors. The fear that Rome's declining power provoked should never be underestimated either. Jerome (see chapter 13) was not the only one who recorded the growing insecurity of his time. The rebellious regimes of men like Constantine III were based on opportunism, but there was also an underlying desire to try and turn back the clock and restore what by then seemed the enviable stability of the past. Today, many people oppose the actions of the United States, but there are many others who sense the prospect of uncontrolled disorder if the world's last superpower was denied its self-appointed role as the world's policeman.

Those later rebels against Rome challenged the Empire because that was what they wanted to be, and because they had the resources and pretext to do so. They could not conceive of there being no Empire, only that their versions would be better. But there only ever was one Roman Empire and ever since she fell, there has been an endless queue of pretenders to her tradition. Carausius renewed the Roman world's veneration for its past, but in hijacking those traditions he left the Empire no choice but to seize back its identity. Even Boudica and Calgacus were symbols to the Romans of how they wished to see themselves and enhanced their sense of what their rulers should be. Boudica and Calgacus were utilised as literary devices to that end – and this is almost the only medium through which they have come down to us as historical personalities. They were Rome's wake-up calls. It was a mark of Rome's political sophistication that there was such a clear sense of her paradox: winning such great power had been built on a foundation of spirited nationhood, leadership, bravery and immunity to indulgence, but the very success had sent the Roman world spiralling into decadence, excess, and all the weakness that riches brought.

Rome was left consumed with admiration at her opponents, but to maintain her pre-eminence had no choice but to suppress revolt. In the process of revolt, Rome and her rebels fed off one another. The key is that rebels are forever condemned to be remembered as the ones who lost the chance to shape the future. Ironically, the rebels provided a dynamic path to Rome's self-examination and in some senses her own renewal. This is not a phenomenon entirely confined to the Roman Empire. England's Lord Protector, Oliver Cromwell, appeared on new coinage issued shortly before his death in 1658, labelled and illustrated as a monarch in all but name. Like the king he had helped execute in 1649, his position as Protector too was now *Dei Gratia*, 'by the Grace of God'. Even the revolutionary use of English on Commonwealth coinage had been abandoned in favour of a return to Latin, despite its 'popish' associations that had tarred the monarchy of Charles I. Like Rome's rebels in Britain, Cromwell had come to realise that the best way to market his own regime was to do so in the established protocol and symbols of the very system he had tried to topple. He was even buried with all the pomp of a monarch's funeral, 'lying in effigie in royal robes, and crown'd with a crown, scepter and mund, like a king' (John Evelyn, *Diary* 21 November 1658). The event further debased the credibility of the Protectorate as a 'new' way, and the restored monarchy of Charles II was, as a result, far stronger in terms of popular acceptance than his executed father's. The crown went on to survive the Glorious Revolution of 1688 and has endured without any sustained challenge to its existence ever since.

Tacitus used Caratacus, Boudica and Calgacus to illustrate Rome's moral and political decline, and as a reflection of the regeneration of the Roman state in his own time at the beginning of the second century. Men like Postumus and Carausius widened the concept of ruling in a Roman idiom, and if anything reinforced it. In the longer run this also helped create the imagery of the great days of the British Empire, which modelled itself on the Roman world and indulged in fantasies of freedom within munificent imperialism. Britannia herself re-emerged on Charles II's coinage and medals in the 1660s while the king himself was depicted in the manner of a Roman emperor. The personification of the military province of Britannia had now become a symbol of a nation on the brink of becoming a world power under kings who used some of the language and style of Rome. In return for being excluded from full participation in the British political system, the American colonies in 1776 rejected Britain's rule and went on to win freedom in the War of Independence. But in the end the United States supplanted Britain's imperial role and adopted some of the iconography of Rome to do so. In winning that war and eventually becoming the most powerful state in the world, America has come to define what 'Rome' in our own time is. In antiquity Rome and her rebels were really fighting over the same thing: the chance to define and control the meaning of power. But a combination of bad timing and circumstance brought most rebels to his or her ruin, and a strange kind of immortal glamour in defeat enshrined in the history that has brought them down to us.

> *His rash fierce blaze of riot cannot last,*
> *For violent fires soon burn out themselves;*
> *Small showers last long, but sudden storms are short;*
> *He tires betimes that spurs too fast betimes.*
>
> King Richard II (II.i)

PRINCIPAL DATES IN
ROMANO-BRITISH HISTORY

Names in CAPITALS are rulers of Roman Britain, official or otherwise.

The First Century BC

55 BC Julius Caesar makes his first limited foray into Britain.

54 BC Julius Caesar makes his second foray into Britain. The resistance is led by Cassivellaunus of the Catuvellauni, controlling a voluntary confederation of southern tribes, apart from the Trinovantes. Caesar does no more than fight a few skirmishes in southern Britain on these occasions but he introduced the Roman world to the Iron Age tribes that made up prehistoric Britain. In fact, there had been commercial and social contact with the Mediterranean nations for centuries.

The First Century AD

AD 43 Aulus Plautius leads the invasion of Roman Britain on the orders of CLAUDIUS (41-54), and serves as the first governor. He conquers southern Britain and arranges a triumphal march into Colchester for Claudius.

47-52 Publius Ostorius Scapula becomes governor. Colchester is made the first colony of veteran troops. During this time Caratacus leads the resistance in the West. Scapula marches against the tribes in south Wales, and defeats a rebellion by the Iceni in East Anglia. Caratacus flees to Cartimandua but is handed over by her in 51.

52-57 Aulus Didius Gallus becomes governor. He held the Welsh tribes in check and found the Brigantes of northern Britain, Rome's allies, were splitting between the feuding king Venutius and his queen Cartimandua. NERO (54-68) becomes emperor.

57/8 Quintus Veranius Nepos becomes governor but dies in post.

57/8-61 Gaius Suetonius Paullinus becomes governor. He sets out to destroy the Druid stronghold in Anglesey, headquarters of the resistance to Rome. In 60 the Iceni are led by Boudica revolt. They defeat part of the *IX* legion. The Iceni burn Colchester, London and St Albans. Suetonius Paullinus marches back with the *XIV*

216

and *XX* legions and defeats Boudica, wiping out the rebels. No tribe will ever threaten Roman Britain again this way. Suetonius Paullinus keeps the army mobile and garrisons the south.

61-63 Publius Petronius Turpilianus becomes governor. The Roman historian Tacitus accuses him of laziness, but he was probably repairing the damage in Britain and reforming Roman government.

63-69 Marcus Trebellius Maximus becomes governor. He, too, is accused of laziness but faced a mutiny by the *XX* legion. *XIV* withdrawn about this time, returning briefly in 69. In 68 Nero committed suicide and the Roman civil war breaks out. GALBA (68-9) rules briefly. Trebellius seems to have fled to side with VITELLIUS (69) in the Roman civil war.

69-71 VESPASIAN (69-79) wins the civil war and establishes the Flavian dynasty. Marcus Vettius Bolanus becomes governor. He rescued Cartimandua from the Brigantian feud. In 70 *XIV* is permanently withdrawn.

71-74 Quintus Petillius Cerealis becomes governor. He annexed much of what is now northern England, and may have founded the legionary fortress of the *IX* legion at York. The *II Adiutrix Pia Fidelis* arrives around this time to replace *XIV*, and is based at Lincoln, *IX*'s former fortress.

74-77/8 Sextus Julius Frontinus becomes governor. He conquered the Silures in Wales. This is almost the last Roman war in Wales.

77/8-83/4 Gnaeus Julius Agricola becomes governor. In his term he finished off the Welsh war, conquered northern Britain, reaching as far north as the north-east tip of Caledonia

(Scotland) and circumnavigated Britain. He encouraged the erection of public buildings, temples and houses as well as the Latin language. He is recorded on an inscription from the new forum at St Albans (Verulamium). The historical accounts of Tacitus end here and thereafter we have much less detail.

79 Accession of TITUS (79-81). Eruption of Vesuvius in Italy.

81 Accession of DOMITIAN (81-96).

84 Domitian recalls Agricola, abandons Caledonia and pulls back the Roman army to what is now northern England. Now or within a few years *II Adiutrix Pia Fidelis* leaves forever. Britain now has only three legions.

96 Accession of NERVA (96-8). Gloucester founded as a colony.

98 Accession of TRAJAN (98-117).

The Second Century

100s Around this time the *IX* legion disappears. It is last recorded for certain on an inscription from York dated to 107-8.

117 Accession of HADRIAN (117-38).

119 Hadrian visits Britain. He orders the building of his celebrated Wall by the governor Aulus Platorius Nepos (*c*.121-24). He also encouraged public building. The forum at Wroxeter (Salop) bears his name. The great basilica of London was built about this time. The south of Britain is now a settled world with towns, roads, markets, villages, industries (e.g. pottery), and rural farmsteads. The north and west is a military zone with three legionary fortresses: Caerleon

(*II Augusta*), Chester (*XX Valeria Victrix*), and York (*VI Victrix*, probably arriving with Nepos in 121).

138 Accession of ANTONINUS PIUS (138-61). He fought a war in Britain and ordered a new wall, made of turf, to be built further north – roughly between where Glasgow and Edinburgh are now – by his governor Quintus Lollius Urbicus (*c*.138-42).

161 Accession of MARCUS AURELIUS (161-80).

163 War breaks out in northern Britain again. The governor Sextus Calpurnius Agricola (*c*.161-5) is sent against 'the Britons'. Hadrian's Wall is reoccupied and the Antonine Wall abandoned.

180 Accession of COMMODUS (180-92).

184 Tribes cross Hadrian's Wall from Caledonia and defeated a legionary contingent.

192 Commodus murdered.

193-7 A new civil war breaks out. CLODIUS ALBINUS, governor of Britain, is one of the contenders. SEPTIMIUS SEVERUS (193-211), the eventual victor, makes Albinus his imperial associate but later marches on him and destroys him at Lyons in 197.

The Third Century

205-8 Much military rebuilding in northern Britain.

208 Septimius Severus arrives in Britain to lead the reconquest of Caledonia to toughen up his sons, Caracalla (211-17) and Geta (211-12). The campaign is a struggle and inconclusive. The martyrdom of Alban may have occurred at this time.

211 Septimius Severus dies of exhaustion at York. CARACALLA abandons the conquests, kills GETA the next year and embarks on a reign of terror. Britain is quiet now, and the years ahead are marked by a vast amount of new military building on the northern frontier. In this period, some of the villas of the southern lowlands start their slow climb to wealth and greatness. In the towns, the age of public building is all but over. The rich are beginning to spend the money on themselves.

259 Gallic Empire: POSTUMUS seizes control of Britain, Gaul and Germany to create the Gallic Empire.

268 Gallic Empire: murder of Postumus, accession of MARIUS followed by his almost immediate murder. Accession of VICTORINUS.

270 Accession of AURELIAN. Gallic Empire: murder of Victorinus, accession of TETRICUS I and his son TETRICUS II.

273 Suppression of the Gallic Empire by Aurelian.

275 Murder of Aurelian. Accession of TACITUS.

276 Death of Tacitus, accession of FLORIANUS, death of Florianus, accession of PROBUS.

282 Murder of Probus, accession of CARUS.

283 Elevation of Carus' sons CARINUS and NUMERIAN to the rank of Caesar. Death of Carus, accession of CARINUS (West), and NUMERIAN (East) who was murdered later this year.

285 Murder of Carinus. Accession of DIOCLETIAN, following the murder of Carinus.

286 Appointment of MAXIMIAN by Diocletian to rule the West. CARAUSIUS, commander of the British fleet, seizes control in Britain and part of northern Gaul.

293 Murder of Carausius and accession of ALLECTUS in Britain. Diocletian appoints junior partners (Caesars) to assist him and Maximian: Galerius (East) and CONSTANTIUS I (West). This system is known as the Tetrarchy.

296 Defeat and death of Allectus by the army of Constantius I. Britain passes back under control of Maximian (Augustus) and Constantius I (Caesar), rulers in the West.

The Fourth Century

During this time a few of the villas grow to a great size. This is the age of the fabulously wealthy, though by Empire standards Britain remains a backwater. No Roman Briton will ever have an Empire-wide reputation.

305 Abdication of Diocletian and Maximian and elevation of Constantine I to Augustus in the West, with SEVERUS (Caesar).

306 Proclamation of CONSTANTINE the Great at York following the death of his father, Constantius I, on campaign there. This disruption of the Tetrarchic system led to protracted feuds and wars involving Maximian and his son Maxentius.

308 Settlement at *Carnuntum* passes control of the West to LICINIUS (Augustus) and CONSTANTINE I (Caesar), while Galerius (Augustus) and Maximinus (Caesar) held the East. The feuds continued unabated because Maximian and Maxentius, and Maximinus, tried to recapture power.

312 Battle of the Milvian Bridge: Constantine defeats Maxentius, using troops partly raised in Britain. The West is now under the exclusive control of Constantine I, while Licinius controls the East.

313 Edict of Milan guarantees total religious toleration.

324 Constantine I defeats Licinius.

337 Death of Constantine I and accession of his sons: CONSTANTINE II (Britain, Gaul and Spain), Constantius II (the East), and Constans (Italy, Africa and Central Europe).

340 Murder of Constantine II by Constans. Britain passes under control of CONSTANS.

343 Constans visits Britain for unknown reasons.

350 Revolt of MAGNENTIUS in Autun and murder of Constans.

353 Suicide of Magnentius following defeats. CONSTANTIUS II becomes ruler of the whole Empire.

360 JULIAN, cousin of Constantius II, proclaimed emperor in Gaul Picts and Scotti attack Britain.

361 Death from fever of Constantius II.

363 Death of Julian. Accession of JOVIAN, formerly commander of the imperial guard.

364 Death of Jovian. Accession of VALENTINIAN I (West) and his brother Valens (East).

367 Barbarian conspiracy overruns Britain. GRATIAN appointed joint Augustus in the West with Valentinian I. Arrival of Count Theodosius in Britain to repair defences.

375 Death of Valentinian I. Gratian now rules jointly in the West with his brother VALENTINIAN II.

378 Death of Valens. Gratian and Valentinian II rule the whole Empire.

379 Appointment of THEODO-SIUS, son of Count Theodosius, to rule the East.

383 Death of Gratian. MAGNUS MAXIMUS, senior officer in the British garrison, proclaimed emperor in Britain and straightaway invades Gaul. Theodosius' son, Arcadius, is made joint emperor in the East.

387 Valentinian II flees to the East to escape Maximus.

388 Magnus Maximus defeated and executed in Italy by Theodosius, who now controls the whole Empire. Picts and Scotti attack Britain again.

392 Murder of Valentinian II.

393 Theodosius' son, HONORIUS, is made joint emperor.

395 Death of Theodosius. The Empire is divided between his sons: Honorius (West) and Arcadius (East).

The Fifth Century

402 The last official bronze Roman coinage enters Britain. Stilicho withdraws a 'legion' from Britain.

405/6 Invasion of Gaul by Vandals, Alans and Sueves.

407 Proclamation of CONSTAN-TINE III in Britain. He moves to Gaul.

408 Constantine III takes Spain.

409 The revolt of Constantine's general Gerontius in Spain. Britain throws out imperial administrators. The Vandals enter Spain.

410 Honorius instructs Britain to look after its own defences.

411 Constantine III defeated and killed.

429 St Germanus arrives to suppress the Pelagian heresy in Britain.

From now on Britain continues to sustain its Romanised existence, but that had been gradually fading for decades. The towns become ruinous, the villas are slowly abandoned – natural disasters or normal crises like house fires were no longer followed by repair. We know very little about what went on but it is plain the end was slow. There was no abrupt disaster. The Christian church in Britain remained in contact with the continent, especially during the great crisis of the Pelagian heresy.

FURTHER READING

The literature concerning Roman Britain is extensive, but inevitably most of it is concerned with aspects of archaeology rather than history. Much of the information in this book was drawn from literary and epigraphic sources for the obvious reason that almost none of the individuals in this book subsist in the archaeological record in any shape or form. The simplest way of accessing the sources is through Stanley Ireland's *Roman Britain. A Sourcebook* (Croom Helm, London 1986 and later reprints). This is an outstanding and comprehensive anthology, and is an essential desk companion. The Penguin Classics series includes some of the material in translation, especially Tacitus and Bede, but later historians like Dio and Ammianus Marcellinus are only available as selections. However, these lack any of the Latin or Greek (for obvious reasons) and the more demanding reader will have to turn to the expensive and hard-to-find Loeb Classical Library (Harvard) for the original languages, laid out on facing pages with a translation. Occasional articles in the journal *Britannia* (Society for the Promotion of Roman Studies) discuss the merits and demerits of the various sources, usually in connection with a specific episode.

For inscriptions R.G. Collingwood and R.P. Wright's *The Roman Inscriptions of Britain* (Oxford 1955) has been updated by R.S.O. Tomlin in his new edition for Alan Sutton (Stroud 1995), to be followed soon by a new volume detailing all the inscriptions on stone found since the mid-1950s. The *Lactor* series of booklets provides an excellent summary of epigraphic sources in Volume 4, *Inscriptions of Roman Britain*, and historical sources in Volume 11, *Literary Sources for Roman Britain*. They can be obtained from LACT Publications Secretary, 5 Normington Close, Leigham Court Road, London SW16 2QS. My own *Companion to Roman Britain* (Tempus 1999) is a catalogue of the literary and epigraphic evidence for the history of Roman Britain. Antony Birley's *The People of Roman Britain* (Batsford 1979) is a rare book now but it is the only published discussion of the origins and nature of named individuals who lived and worked in Roman Britain.

There are a number of modern books that cover the general history of Roman Britain, for example Sheppard Frere's *Britannia* (1987), and Peter Salway's *Roman Britain* (1981). The latter has now been reissued in an abridged and illustrated form as *The Oxford Illustrated History of Roman Britain* (1993). Catherine Johns and the late Tim Potter of the British Museum co-wrote *Roman Britain* (British Museum Press, second edition 2002), a book that benefits from two lifetime experiences of dealing with Britain's premier Romano-British collections. Michael E. Jones, *The End of Roman Britain* (Cornell 1996) is a particularly interesting and scholarly (as well as readable) account of the transition from Roman to post-Roman Britain.

For the Iron Age background, Barry Cunliffe's *Iron Age Communities in Britain* (London 1990) is the standard work. Philip de Jersey' *Celtic Coinage in Britain* (Shire 2001) is an excellent, and well-illustrated, introduction to the subject. Those with an interest in more detail will find Richard Hobbs' *British Iron Age Coins in the British Museum* (British Museum 1996) provides an abundance of information, with every coin illustrated.

Few of the personalities tackled in this book have been the subject of modern individual books, not least because the paucity of data would stretch most of the subjects way beyond their limits. Paul R. Sealey's *The Boudican Revolt against Rome* (Aylesbury 1997) is a departure from Shire's tradition of archaeology books, and admirably covers the story of the Revolt from an historical and archaeological perspective. P.J. Casey's *Carausius and Allectus* (Batsford, London 1994) is the most up-to-date discussion of that extraordinary experiment in a British-based Roman Empire though it preceded the present author's identification of the Virgilian legends on Carausian coinage.

For an excellent survey of Roman Britain and how it functioned in terms of the landscape, the reader will find *An Atlas of Roman Britain* (1990) by Barri Jones and David Mattingly of great value. The present author's *Buildings of Roman Britain* (second edition, Tempus 2001) contains many reconstruction drawings of buildings in Roman towns. The aesthetics of Romano-British life are covered by Martin Henig in his *Art in Roman Britain* (Batsford 1995). Ken and Petra Dark's *The Landscape of Roman Britain* (Sutton 1997) seeks to explain how Roman Britain was defined by the physical background. Hugh Davies deals with the engineering logistics of roads in his *Roman Roads in Britain* (Tempus 2002). Andrew Pearson's *The Roman Shore Forts* (Tempus 2002) is an invaluable discussion of the evidence for the enigmatic coastal fortifications that characterised the age of Postumus and Carausius.

Tempus has been responsible for providing today's archaeological readership with an exceptional range of choice. Those interested in how Roman Britain's towns functioned in the latter days of the province will find my *Golden Age of Roman Britain* (Tempus 1999) and Neil Faulkner's *The Decline and Fall of Roman Britain* (Tempus 2000) offer completely different approaches to this difficult period. My *Eagles over Britannia* (Tempus 2001) is a history of the Roman army in Britain and its exceptional contribution to the development of towns, and *Gods with Thunderbolts* (Tempus 2002) is a narrative history of religion in Roman Britain.

INDEX

This is a select index of the most prominent individuals and places mentioned.